AF559896

The Dark-Coloured Waters

Praise for the book

'Danesh Rana has given us a most fascinating book on the Chenab, one of our great rivers arising from the glacial heights of Himachal Pradesh and flowing hundreds of kilometres to join the Indus in Pakistan. On one hand this long journey is a lyrical meditation as the author highlights syncretic faiths propounded by poets, bards and saints, and on the other hand it speaks of the immortal love stories nurtured by the river. The book, full of anecdotes about people and places, provides an excellent introduction to one of our lesser known but most important rivers. In fact, with the Indus Water Treaty having been suspended by India, the Chenab takes on increased importance. The book is both extensively researched and well-written, like the flow of the river herself.' – **Dr Karan Singh**

'Danesh Rana's journey along the Chenab becomes a journey through the heart of Kashmir's modern history. Vivid, unsettling, and profoundly humane, *The Dark-Coloured Waters* is essential reading for anyone who wants to understand the complexities of the region, and the river that threads through them all.' – **General V.K. Singh**

The Dark-Coloured Waters

A Journey Along River Chenab

Danesh Rana

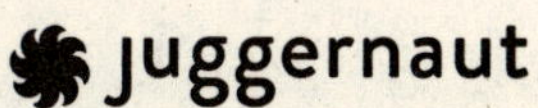
juggernaut

JUGGERNAUT BOOKS
C-I-128, First Floor, Sangam Vihar, Near Holi Chowk,
New Delhi 110080, India

First published by Juggernaut Books 2025

10 9 8 7 6 5 4 3 2 1

P-ISBN: 9789353457082
E-ISBN: 9789353454593

The views and opinions expressed in this book are the author's own. The facts contained herein were reported to be true as on the date of publication by the authors to the publishers of the book, and the publishers are not in any way liable for their accuracy or veracity.

Typeset in Adobe Caslon Pro by R. Ajith Kumar, Noida

Printed at Replika Press Pvt. Ltd.

For Agastya and Asavarie,
so that they know where they come from!

इमं मे गङ्गे यमुने सरस्वति शुतुद्रि स्तेमं सचता परुष्ण्या।
असिक्न्या मरुद्वृधे वितस्तयार्जीकीये शृणुह्यासुषोमया॥

Imaṃ me Ghaṅghe Yamune Sarasvati Sutudri
stemaṃ sacatā Paruṣṇyā
Asiknyā marudvṛdhe Vitastayārjīkīye
śṛṇuhyāsuṣomayā

Through this verse I praise you, O Ganga, Yamuna, O Sutudri, Parusni and Sarasvati:
With Asikni, Vitasta, O Marudvrdha, O Arjikiya with Susoma hear my call.

('Hymn 75: Nadi Stuti, X Mandala, Rig Veda)

And then there is the river, the most beautiful river, a river whose soul is love, a river which is the lover and the beloved, the devotee and the divine. A river which is the poetry of Gorakhnath, Fareed Shakarganj and Guru Nanak, the heart of Punjab, the body of Sohni, the tear of Sahiban. It is the lament of Sassi, the face of Shirin, the necklace of Laila. It is the devotion of Zulekha, the piety of Sita, the sensuality of Radha. The Chenab is the laughter of Heer.

(Haroon Khalid, *From Waris to Heer*)

Contents

Author's Note

My earliest memory of the Chenab River is from the early 1980s, and since then, oceans' worth of water must have flowed in it. By the virtue of belonging to a family with transferable jobs, I could explore places of abundant beauty that the erstwhile state of Jammu and Kashmir offered. This also included two exhilarating months of summer holidays in Kashmir, running away from the hot and humid weather of the plains of Jammu. After packing our clothes, books, cricket bats and badminton racquets, we siblings huddled up in the Ambassador car headed for Kashmir. Halfway through the gruelling journey, after zigzagging the mountains and pine forests, we reached Peerah – a small roadside town – famous for its *dhaba*s or the local eateries. We would invariably break our journey here and relish the lunch of famous rajma and rice with spoonsful of ghee. Peerah is the place where one gets the first glimpse of the Chenab, gently flowing in a deep gorge behind the dhabas. From this height, the river looks frozen, silent and almost innocuous, as if masking her ferocity and wrath.

On our onward journey, the Chenab accompanied the National Highway – then called NH-1A and now NH-44 – for nearly 50 km. Our car would join the slow and interminable queue, trailing behind and leading other vehicles – the tourist taxis, load carriers, buses and army trucks. Amidst the wafting of Hindi songs – mostly from the hit films of Amitabh Bachchan – and periodic banter, our car would trundle along the riverside. Throughout this part of the journey, I would crane my neck and gaze at the river, breathing it in, savouring it. The water used to be dark and murky, splashing against the rocky sides of the gorge, surging ahead like a boisterous rhyme. During that time of the year, the Chenab would bring some wood along with its current; the water would carry a few deodar and fir logs – cylindrical, shorn of the barks, to be used for furniture and the construction of houses. These logs would ride the strong waves of the Chenab, swirling, tossing and almost flying in some kind of water dance. It was fascinating to see this timber trail in complete harmony with the water. Over the years, with the coming of many hydroelectricity projects on the Chenab, the practice became less prolific and eventually vanished completely. On many stretches, the river would play a mischievous game of hide and seek. She would suddenly disappear, screened by a spur, or take a turn away from the highway, only to appear again! I loved to play this game in my imagination: Chenab would hide and I would seek her out, only to reverse our roles in the next round.

After the descent from Peerah, just short of the Ramban town, the river opens her arms, showing us her true face and the boundless waters within. Now, Chenab roars in an aggressive march and is almost intimidating. This scared me as a kid when I would rest my arms on the car window and watch the water angrily rise over the black rocks, tossing up the logs, only to gather them again. Out of fear, I would pray as I passed by her noise and force. This fear was further compounded by a newspaper report I had read in the early 1980s. I had started reading newspapers at a very young age, as I followed the world of sports vigorously – cricket, football, tennis, athletics and hockey. The headline in a local newspaper read: 'A Taxi Carrying a Honeymoon Couple Plunges into the Chenab'. A perpetual fear crept in and remained inside my heart for a long time, saddening me each time I thought about the incident. I did not know then what 'honeymoon' meant, but it intrigued me and sounded teasingly romantic, tantalizing, almost titillating. I don't know if the dead bodies of the honeymooning couple or the remains of the taxi were ever traced. But the story haunted me for a long time while growing up. Ideally, I would have liked to research about the lives of the couple, but despite all my efforts, I could not trace any police record of the incident. Now I feel that couple was destined to assimilate, like an ode, into the river, which is also known as 'Ashiqan da Dariya' or the 'River of Lovers'.

In the late 1990s, militancy spilled over to the deep forests and higher reaches of Ramban. To tackle the ensuing bloodshed, the town, which was part of the Doda district, was made into a separate police district. In 2002, I was posted as superintendent of police (SP) of Ramban district. The SP residence was housed in an old forest guesthouse called by another name of the river, Chandrabhaga. It was situated right on the bank of the Chenab. The river flowed by, at a great speed, belting out a noisy song. In the initial days, it was difficult to sleep with the sound of the river nearby but gradually, one absorbed the ever-present sound, as if it were a part of breathing.

Day after day, the water gurgled and surged ahead, bedecked with eddies and whirls, a scene best savoured from the wide balcony at the back of the house. For the next year of my posting, I lived with the river – going about my job, planning the operations against militants, reading books – the song of the river perfectly gelling with Bob Dylan playing on loop.

Over the years, the water of the river was tamed at various sites as many hydroelectric projects, bridges and railroad construction altered its existence and that of the people living along it. I, too, wised up to the job, which, in 2018, took me to Kullu as an election observer for the Assembly of Himachal Pradesh. The observer duties entailed a lot of touring in the districts I was responsible for. On one such tour, at a place called Tandi – 8 km short of Keylong, the district headquarters of Lahaul and Spiti – my liaison officer pointed towards a confluence of two rivers and said, 'This is Chandrabhaga which later becomes the mighty Chenab.'

I was intrigued. '*Wait a minute. Is this the Chenab?*' I made the driver stop the car and walked across the highway to click some pictures with my phone camera. Is this the dreaded river of my childhood? Wasn't it angry all the time, pugnacious, troublesome, bellicose, unruly, a hooligan, almost echoing a dirge?

I had never seen the river so docile and serene. This was the precise moment when the idea for this book came to my mind. Do rivers have stories to tell? I wasn't sure. I was reminded of Bashir Badr's couplet: '*Agar fursat mile paani ki tahriron ko padh lena, har ek dariya hazaron saal ka afsana likhta hai*. [If you get the time, do read the writing of the water. Every river writes a tale of thousand years.]' Would people like to read about the river and the lands it passes through? I pondered on the idea for a long time and finally decided to write this book. I was impressed, bewildered and determined.

Danesh Rana
New Delhi, May 2025

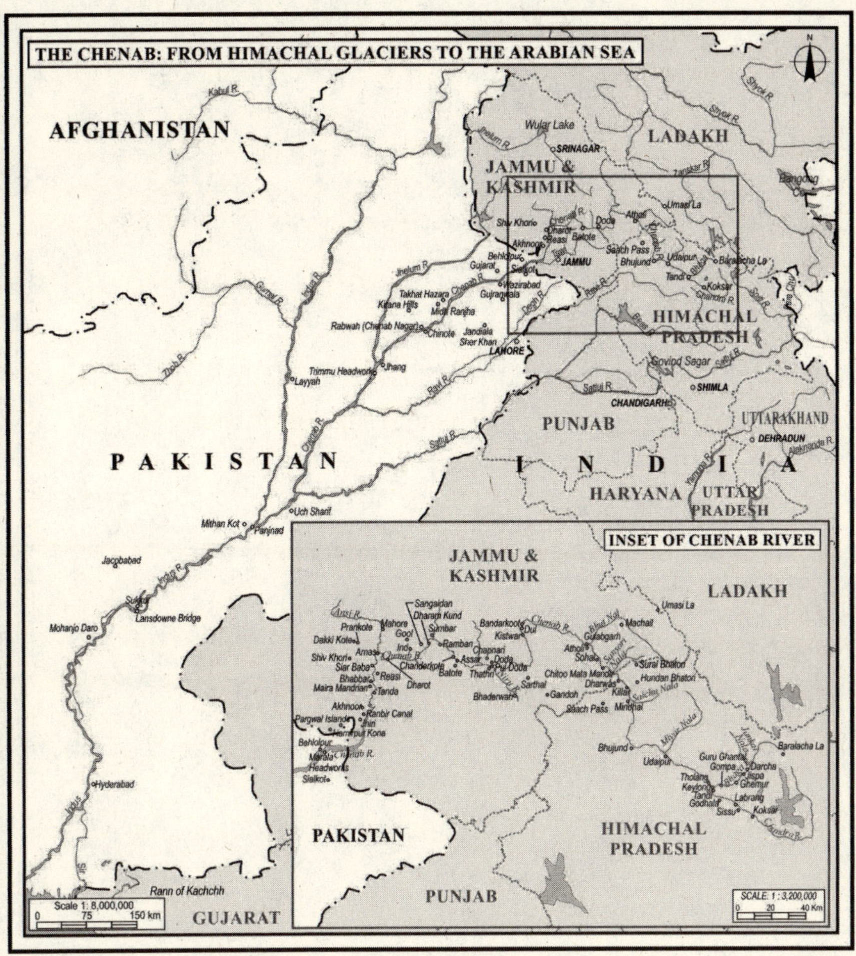

This map is not at scale and is for explanatory purposes only. It does not purport to reflect the official boundaries of India.

1

The Lovers

The 'Nadi Stuti Sukta' or the 'Hymn in the Praise of the Rivers' finds a mention in the tenth section of the Rig Veda. Overall, the hymn prominently speaks about ten rivers – from the Ganga in the east to the Kabul in the west, and the five rivers of Punjab in between. The cradle of early Vedic civilization flourished around a region referred to as Sapta Saidhav or the land of seven rivers. Taking a reference from the Avesta of the Zoroastrians, scholars believe that Sapta-Sindhu was referred to as Hapta-Hindu by the Persians, and that gave birth to the words 'Hindu', 'Hindustan' and, subsequently, 'India'.

The five rivers of Punjab include the Asikini, probably named after its dark-coloured waters, now identified as the Chenab. The name Asikini (the non-white one) could also be in reference to Lord Krishna, the Hindu god who is called the Dark-Coloured One. Interestingly, the river in the Atharva Veda is called Krishna. In some of the later Sanskrit texts, Asikini is also called Iskamati.

In Mahabharata, Asikini is referred to as Chandrabhaga – the confluence of two rivers, namely, Chandra and Bhaga – originating from each side of Baralacha La. The famous pass is situated in the snowbound western Himalayas of Lahaul-Spiti district in the state of Himachal Pradesh. On the east side of the pass, the Chandra originates from the crescent-shaped lake called Chandra Taal or Lake of the Moon. It is believed that the water of the lake contains mystical powers that can cure sickness and release humans from the cycle of birth and death, just like the Ganga.

Folklore abound that after defeating the Kauravas in the great battle of Kurukshetra, towards the end of their lives, the Pandavas and Draupadi undertook the *mahaprasthana*. It was the 'great journey' where they walked northwards, seeking salvation. The first to fall was Draupadi. Later, each brother died, and only Yudhishthira, the eldest brother survived. At the Chandra Taal, the king of gods, Indra, came to take Yudhishthira to the gates of heaven in his chariot.

Amidst the rugged terrain of the rocky mountain on one side and the striking landform shaped like a cowrie shell on the other, the Lake of the Moon is an enchanting destination for high-altitude campers and trekkers. In the summers, wild flowers bloom over the meadows, lushly enwrapping the edges of the lake. About one mile on the west of Baralacha La, Bhaga emerges from Surya Taal or Lake of the Sun. Smaller in size than the Chandra Taal, the Surya Taal is situated at a higher altitude of 16,000 ft.

According to a myth, Chandra and Bhaga were the daughter and son of Chandradev, the Moon God, and Suryadev, the Sun God, respectively. They were in love with each other and wanted to get married. However, their union was not accepted in Devlok or heaven. The Moon God wanted his daughter to light up the world at night and the Sun God wanted his son to bring light during the day. Heartbroken, the lovers descended on the Earth, took the forms of rivers and met at Baralacha La.

As a prelude to solemnizing their celestial wedding, they decided to circumambulate the sacred Himalayas. They parted in diametrically opposite directions, flowing southeast and southwest, encircling a large tract of the Himalayan valley. Chandra, being active and swift, easily negotiated the terrain, covering a distance of 115 km. On the other hand, Bhaga struggled through the narrow gorges, covering a distance of 61 km. They were destined to meet at a village called Tandi, to enter wedlock and turn into a large river called the Chandrabhaga.

The water of the Chandrabhaga is replenished by the melting snow, waterfalls and hill streams, turning it grey and dark, rendering it unsuitable for irrigation and drinking purposes.[1] A folk tale elucidates that in ancient times, the banks of the Chandra and Bhaga were thronged by sages who found the serenity of the place ideal for prayer and meditation. At that time, milk flowed in both streams instead of water. Soon, demons came to know about it and they decided to drive out the sages. To disrupt their meditation and pollute their dharma, one day, they killed a number of animals and threw the blood and carcasses into the two rivers. Unsuspectingly, the sages, deeply engrossed in their religious chores, drank the bloody water, mistaking it for their everyday milk. That day, the water tasted different, and in their horror, the sages cast a curse for the water to remain muddy and unfit for drinking and irrigation.[2]

On its desolate sojourn, the Chandra swirls down from the snow-covered mountains on a broken topography of cliffs created by glacial action. In the winters, the river completely freezes, halting its flow down the hill. However, in summers, with a copious amount of water, it is like an ebullient child, wildly frolicking over the rocks, singing a high-pitched song. When the snow melts at Rohtang La and Baralacha La, the two passes become motorable. The Rohtang Pass enables the entry into Lahaul from the Kullu Valley, whereas Baralacha La opens into Ladakh. Situated at a height of 13,000 feet, Rohtang La was one of the most important passes for ancient trade and cultural exchange. For the major part of the year, it remains inaccessible due to untimely snowstorms and avalanches. Perhaps that is why it is named 'Rohtang', which literally means 'pile of dead bodies' in the local Bhoti language.

On the southern side of the pass, a small water body forms the origin of river Beas that flows southwards. According to legend, it was created by Ved Vyasa, author of the Mahabharata, who meditated here for a long time. Another story says that a river had already existed here and Sage Vashishtha, the great-grandfather of Vyasa, after tying himself with several cords, attempted to drown himself by jumping into the river. However, it altered its form and transformed into a sandy bed. The cords or *pasa* broke off, and so, Vashishtha called the river Vipasa or 'the breaker of ropes'. Beas, belonging to the famous Sapta Sindhu sisterhood, is also hailed as *vipas* or unfettered – a possible allusion to the Vipasa story.

In Greek texts, Beas is referred to as Hyphasis. The river served as the easternmost limit of the Macedonian king Alexander the Great's military campaign. After completing the conquest of the Achaemenid Empire of Persia, Alexander started his Indian campaign in 327 BCE. He easily subjugated the north-western states in present-day Pakistan before facing his biggest challenge against King Porus of Paurava clan. In a hard-fought battle, he lost his favourite horse, Bucephaluas, and hundreds of trusted soldiers, sinking the morale of his army abysmally low. His army rose in a revolt on the banks of Hyphasis as they came to know about the might of their next opponent, the Nanda Empire, which boasted of a formidable infantry, cavalry and war elephants. The rebellion against Alexander was profound; his soldiers were homesick and longed to see their families whom they had not seen in years. Alexander had to relent, knowing that regicide was not uncommon among Macedonians. He was probably reminded of the killing of his father, Philip II, by his trusted bodyguards.[3]

The summers pave way for the meadows to emerge from under the cloak of snow. On her banks, Chandra gets carpeted with lush green grass. Now the yaks and dzos are seen freely grazing around the grasslands on either side of the river. Moving further up, the meadows are filled with goats and sheep, herded by the semi-pastoral tribe called Gaddis.

Clad in woollen tunics and Kullu caps, Gaddi shepherds carry wooden flutes tucked inside their cummerbunds. In summers, they set up their campsites all over Lahaul-Spiti. Though the exact origin of this tribe is unclear, they follow Hinduism and hail from assorted castes, tracing their ancestry to Delhi and Lahore. Some theories suggest that the Gaddis have descended from the persecuted escapees of the Mughals and other invaders. Additionally, they claim to be descendants of Lord Shiva. According to their beliefs, the *gaddi* or throne of Lord Shiva is located in Kailash, and their clan's name originated from that assertion.

For generations, the Gaddis have been able to preserve their unique culture expressed through language, dress, food and devout celebrations. Since their landholdings are meagre and yield little, they mostly depend on their animals and barter trade. During their migratory journeys, they interact with villages they pass by and exchange wool, goatskins and other products for grain and meat.

After all the exuberance and the haste to rush down the hills, Chandra becalms herself on meeting the Leh–Manali Highway.[4] Here, the river flows gently over the pebbles, running alongside a black, tarred road. Surrounded by high mountains, the picturesque Koksar village is the first habitation the river encounters. It is the coldest human habitation in Lahaul. At this juncture, Chandra freezes completely, and snow fills the narrow gorge, enabling the villagers and mules to cross over the river. The life of the locals, mostly of Tibetan and Indo-Aryan descent, comes to a complete standstill. They depend on the grain stored from summers and *chaang* – the local alcohol, brewed from barley. Most of the residents follow the Drukpa Kagyu branch, or the Red Hat Sect, of Tibetan Buddhism.

Since ancient times, the high mountains of Lahaul are rich with the stories of monks and spiritualism.[5] In modern times, the journey of Diane Perry, who was born in Hertfordshire, England, is the most celebrated. After losing her fishmonger father at the age of two, she, along with her brother, were raised by their mother in the Bethnal Green area of London. At the age of eighteen, Diane realized she was a Buddhist at heart while reading the book *Mind Unshaken* (1971) by John Walters. After leaving school, she worked as a librarian at the Hackney Public Library and later at the School of Oriental and African Studies (now SOAS) in London. After saving enough money, she sailed to India in 1964 to pursue her spiritual path.

In India, she taught English at the Young Lamas Home School in Dalhousie, to young reincarnated Lamas among the exiled Tibetan community. Here, she met His Eminence, the eighth Khamtrul Rinpoche, a great Drukpa Kagyu teacher, whom she recognized as her master. At the age of twenty-one, she became a nun and was renamed as Drubgyu Tenzin Palmo or the Glorious Lady Who Upholds the Doctrine of the Practice Successions. She had the honour of being one of the first Western women to be ordained as a Tibetan-Buddhist monastic. She continued to teach at the school and remained the secretary of Khamtrul Rinpoche for six years. Living at the monastery as the sole nun among hundreds of monks, she felt that some of the practices were misogynistic and discriminated against women. Tenzin Palmo was denied the higher monastic activities that were freely available to the men. Since the full ordination for nuns was not allowed in Tibetan tradition, she travelled to Hong Kong in 1973, and attained the *bhikshuni* ordination at the Miu Fat Temple.

In 1970, as directed by her master, Tenzin Palmo came to Lahaul in order to undertake more intensive practice and stayed in Tayul Gompa, a small monastery. Six years later, seeking more seclusion, she found a cave a few hours' hike from Tayul. The cave was enhanced by enclosing walls, creating a living space around 6 sq. ft. In the summers, supplies were delivered from Keylong, and she grew potatoes and turnips nearby. In the winters, when the cave was snowbound, Tenzin Palmo stockpiled rations. Amidst a lot of hardships, avalanches and snow leopards, she thrived in her solitary spiritual practices and meditation for the next twelve years. There were occasional visitors and trips to meet her master in the initial nine years, but the last three were spent in strict retreat.

After spending twenty-four years in India, Tenzin Palmo returned to Europe, where she started teaching spiritualism. During her association with Khamtrul Rinpoche, he had often asked her to start a nunnery. In order to fulfil her dream, Tenzin Palmo travelled worldwide and became an esteemed ambassador of equal rights for Buddhist nuns. She raised enough funds to establish the Dongyu Gatsai Ling nunnery or the Garden of the Authentic Lineage, near Tashi Jong in Palampur, Himachal Pradesh. In 2008, Tenzin Palmo was given the rare title of Jetsunma or the Venerable Master, in recognition of her spiritual achievements and her efforts in promoting the status of female practitioners in Tibetan Buddhism. Today, Tenzin Palmo spends most of her time in Dongyu Gatsai Ling, which houses about a hundred nuns, and occasionally tours the world to teach and raise funds.

Diane Perry's fascinating journey has been ably showcased in the book *Cave in the Snow* by the English writer Vickie Mackenzie.

Summer transforms Koksar village into a picture postcard of enchanting beauty. The place is resplendent with alpine flowers of variegated colours, terraced potato fields and water channels of silver froth. Hardy grass and shrubs line the banks of the Chandra, and sea buckthorns – a type of deciduous plant – are visible farther away. Fascinated by the beauty of the place, tourists troop in to witness the melange of water, snow, foliage and history. During this time the small bazaar of the town is redolent with the aromas of thukpa, dimsum and the snowtrout of the Chandra.

The real influx of visitors into Lahaul-Spiti started after the opening of the 9 km long tunnel beneath the Rohtang Pass, providing all-weather connectivity between the region and the rest of the country. The Rohtang tunnel has been aptly named after the late Atal Bihari Vajpayee, who was instrumental in its conception. Vajpayee had vigorously pushed for the construction of the tunnel during his second term as the prime minister in 1998. Though the efforts to build a tunnel under the pass had started during the British rule, it took more than six decades to finally drill the mighty mountain.[6]

It is said that Vajpayee's close friend from the area, namely, Arjun Gopal alias Tashi Dawa, convinced him to sanction the tunnel for the overall development of the remote valley of Lahaul-Spiti.[7] Dawa, a farmer by profession, had been good friends with Vajpayee since their days together at the Rashtriya Swayamsevak Sangh (RSS) training camp in Baroda back in 1942, when it was part of the Bombay Presidency. Life took the friends on different trajectories, and they seldom met. But whenever Vajpayee retreated to his summer home in Prini village on the outskirts of Manali, he always made it a point to call Dawa and have a heart-warming conversation.[8]

The villagers of Prini fondly remember the late prime minister and often state his love for poetry and trout fish. On his birthday, they organize functions, garland his photographs and pay glowing tributes. Vajpayee was also known for his concern for the environment and would educate the villagers about the importance of planting trees. A deodar tree planted by him in 2006 is eighteen years old now.

In 2000, during his third term as the prime minister, Vajpayee visited Keylong, the headquarters of the Lahaul-Spiti district. The visit was made possible due to the invitation of Tashi Dawa and amidst rapturous applause, Vajpayee announced the construction of the tunnel. Two years later, he laid the foundation stone of the approach road leading to the south portal of the tunnel on the Manali side. Unfortunately, both Vajpayee and Dawa had passed on to another world before the tunnel was formally inaugurated by Prime Minister Narendra Modi in October 2020.

During the inauguration of the horseshoe-shaped, single-tube tunnel, Modi did not fail to pay glowing tributes to both, terming the tunnel as an ode to a life-long friendship – a friendship that started during their teenage and was often referred to as one between Krishna, the king and Sudama, the pauper. When Modi flagged off a Himachal Roadways Transport Corporation bus from the north portal in Lahaul to pass through the tunnel towards the south portal in Manali, one of the first passengers in the bus was Ram Dev, a retired officer of the state information department, the youngest son of Tashi Dawa.

The opening of the tunnel was bound to transform the region, which had hitherto been cut off from the rest of the country for more than six months each year, perpetuating the backwardness of the area. During these six months, the people led a life of struggle in sub-zero temperatures. The annual isolation deprived the locals of better educational avenues, employment opportunities, trade and healthcare. Under these circumstances, the area remained underdeveloped, neglected, economically abysmal and politically irrelevant.

Chandra continues to gracefully traverse northwards, her waters glimmering in different shades of green and blue as day turns into night. Devoid of her initial vigour, the river is now shy and silent, tiptoeing to meet her lover, Bhaga. Running alongside the highway, the river passes by the foliage dotted with pre-fabricated dwellings and the camps of Border Road Organisation (BRO), with their yellow dozers and snow-clearing machines. Among other advisory boards on the road, the one that catches the eye is tongue-in-cheek: 'Don't be a Gama in the land of Lama'. The slogan exhorting safe driving can be seen on the roadsides throughout Lahaul-Spiti and Ladakh.

The adage draws inspiration from the story of Gama, a legendary wrestler known for his unparalleled strength and invincibility. Gama, whose real name was Ghulam Mohammad Baksh Butt, was born into a family of Kashmiri wrestlers in a village near Amritsar. He was honoured with the title of 'Rustom-e-Hind', conferred on those wrestlers who remain unvanquished. After the Partition, he shifted to Pakistan and died in Lahore in 1960. Despite Gama's remarkable wrestling skills, the axiom implies that one could be the world's great symbol of masculinity and strength but it would be prudent to be respectful towards nature. In other words, it is desirable to submit to the hilly roads and drive carefully to avoid accidents.[9]

At various spots along the highway, there are rows and clusters of *chortens* – hemispherical white mounds that are the burial places of Buddhist monks. Most of these structures commemorate the events in the lives of the Buddha and his disciples, symbolizing the aspects of Buddhist theology. The shape of the chorten represents the Buddha, crowned and sitting in a meditation posture on a lion throne. Similarly, there are *manye* or prayer wheels fixed under pagoda-shaped canopies. Other than the chortens, at regular intervals, strings of rectangular prayer flags can be seen fluttering in the breeze. Traditionally, these flags come in sets of five colours, representing the five elements: blue for sky, white for air and wind, red for fire, green for water, and yellow for earth. The flags have mantras inscribed on them, and each corner is adorned by four animals. These are the four dignities centric to Tibetan Buddhism – dragon, *garuda*, tiger and snow lion. These prayer flags are used to promote peace, compassion and wisdom. The Tibetans believe that the prayers and mantras will be blown by the wind to spread goodwill into the all-pervading space. Alongside, there are Hindu temples, enlivened by chiming bells, coexisting in complete harmony with the varied Buddhist insignia.

Amidst this syncretism, 14 km away from Koksar, the Chandra greets another picturesque village called Sissu. On the right flank of the river, the plantations of willows and poplars are so dense that they make it difficult for the sun's rays to penetrate through. An occasional beam of sunlight escapes to gleam over the placid waters of the Chandra. In late summers, the trees turn yellow and crimson, and their leaves strewn on the ground give a look of pristine beauty. In a breathtaking view, Palden Lhamo Dhar, a silvery waterfall, cascades down the mountain overlooking Sissu, which can be reached from a suspension bridge over the Chandra. The waterfall is named after Palden Lhamo, the glorious goddess of a Tibetan tantric order.

Outside the village, a lake of serene waters glistens amidst the foothill. The lake completely freezes in winters under sub-zero temperatures and it could become a good venue for ice hockey if the game were to be introduced in these areas. On their way back, the Siberian wild ducks and geese halt here, finding comfort on a swampy patch on the Chandra.

The ridge overlooking the Sissu village is towered by a jagged pyramid of the most propitiated Gyephang Peak. From the glaciers of the Gyephang Peak, Sissu Nullah flows through a narrow gorge to submerge in the Chandra. The peak is named after Lord Ghepan or Gyephang – the protector of the people and the presiding deity of Lahaul, housed in a temple in the adjacent village. Among much fanfare and religious festivity, the deity is taken out in a procession every three years. The occasion is revered as the most sacrosanct and attracts thousands of devotees drawn from various corners of Lahaul.

Above Sissu sits a small village called Labrang, from where the mesmerizing vistas of the valley are clearly visible, with the Chandra flowing through it. The river looks like a necklace fastened with the beads of whorls and eddies. Labrang houses one of the most revered Buddhist monasteries in the region. The monastery is a repository of wealth of Buddhist art and culture. The dim, cool interiors of the monastery glow with the brilliance of splendid murals, stuccos and magnificent silk thangkas.

Approximately 14 km further, the Chandra kisses a relatively larger village of Gondhla, surrounded by willows and poplars. Fed by the water of the Chandra, the land between Sissu and Gondhla is the most fertile in the region. Though neglected and dilapidated, the Gondhla Castle, which is the house of Thakur, the local chieftain, is the most important landmark of the village.[10] The fort was built in 1700 by Raja Man Singh of Kullu who had extended his influence beyond Baralacha La. The Raja also married a daughter of the Gondhla family to further strengthen his ties with the local Thakur.

Lahaul has, from time to time, been under the hegemony of Kullu, Ladakh and Chamba kingdoms, but the local chieftains called Thakurs have always remained prominent. These Thakurs were the local barons who held sway within their barony, residing in high and massively built castles and palaces, maintaining small armies. They also levied taxes and transit duties, and waged wars against each other.

Looking like a Swiss chalet, the seven-storey Gondhla edifice is a classic case of the local timber-stone architecture bound by clay. The fifth storey of the castle was exclusively reserved for the Thakur, consisting of a spacious veranda and a personal prayer chamber. From the veranda, the Thakur would hold court and listen to the grievances of his subjects and dispense justice.

Even today, about forty volumes of *Kangyur* (the 'Translation of the Word') and *Tengyur* (the 'Translation of Teachings') – the foundational Buddhist texts of the Tibetan Buddhist canon – can be seen haphazardly stacked on the wooden racks in the castle. Besides these, there are old utensils, decayed furniture, costumes, idols, and rusted weapons like arrows, quivers, bows, guns, canons and catapults. The most precious article a Thakur possesses is the *sharab raldi* or the sword of wisdom, which is made of thin wires hammered together, a style developed in Spain. It is believed that the sword was gifted to one of the forefathers of the Thakurs.

About 4 km uphill from Gondhla, the oldest and most revered monastery, Guru Ghantal Gompa, is located. The gompa, affiliated with the Drukpa sect, gives a clear view of the confluence of the Chandra and the Bhaga at Tandi. The monastery is said to have been founded by Padma Sambhava [born from a lotus] in eighth century CE. Revered as Guru Rinpoche, Padma Sambhava was one of the most prominent propagators of Vajrayana Buddhism and was instrumental in spreading the religion in Tibet and much of

Lahaul-Spiti. In 1857, a chased copper goblet dated to the first century BCE was found at Guru Ghantal by a British officer, evidencing that Buddhist monks stayed here long before Padma Sambhava. Popularly known as the Kullu Vase, it now finds a place in a British museum. Every year in July, a two-day fair is held in the monastery. Chham or the 'devil dance' enacted on the first day of the fair is a major attraction, and thousands congregate to witness it. Wearing elaborate costumes and masks, the dancers depict the life of Padma Sambhava and rituals associated with him.

Surya Taal lies just below the Baralacha La. In the summers, the pristine waters of the lake look like the reflection of the azure sky above, whereas in winters, it is one giant cauldron of frozen milk. From here, Bhaga starts to trickle down the hill, smoothening over rocks, keen to meet his beloved.

The first village the Bhaga passes by is Darcha, which is the northernmost inhabitation in the Lahaul Valley. Here, the Yotche Nullah and the Zanskar Chuu meet the Bhaga, widening it in braids. Being on a slightly lower altitude, the village becomes an ideal base for acclimatization for the expeditions to Baralacha La and other peaks of the Chandrabhaga range. It is the last village where one can see the sparse growth of trees. Beyond Darcha, the landscape suddenly turns desolate and barren, towered by bronze mountains that often change shades with the position of the Sun.

A few miles downstream, Bhaga encounters the sparsely populated village of Jispa. The river gets quite shallow here, rich with plentiful trout, making it an angler's delight. Apparently, the locals here do reasonably well in education and they attribute it to the trout – they believe it helps in sharpening their brains.

A few miles down, Bhaga passes by Ghemur – a village of few households, which has, in recent times, lost its splendour. Once upon a time, the village used to have the grandest building in the whole of

Lahaul-Spiti – a five-storey manor house with large stables, known as Ghemur Khar or the Ghemur Palace. The estate belonged to Thakur Mangal Chand, who was the ex-wazir of Lahaul, an explorer, painter, linguist and a progressive farmer.

The Thakurs of Lahaul are an old family, with a lineage going back twenty-four generations. The founder, Rana Nil Pal, was driven out of the Mandi kingdom by the then ruler and banished into the wilderness of the Lahaul Valley. Here, he fell in love with the daughter of a local chief and married her. The Thakurs continued to rule Lahaul through generations till the British took over the country. Since Lahaul was crucial to the British, being enroute to Leh and the Silk Route, it was administered directly through the wazir. For hundreds of years, in the summers, Ghemur Khar would hum with traders, officials, European explorers and scholars enjoying the hospitality of the Thakurs. The family has been mentioned in various accounts of important travellers like Moorcroft, who met the grandfather of Thakur Mangal Chand in 1823. Many prominent personalities like the Russian painter Nicholas Reorich, the American politician and writer Theodore Roosevelt Jr, the English officer and ornithologist Hugh Whistler and the writer Rudyard Kipling, among others, enjoyed the hospitality of Ghemur Khar. In 1975, Mrs Indira Gandhi, the then prime minister of the country, also visited the Khar.

After the Partition of the country, the Thakur family played a crucial role in saving Ladakh when raiders from Pakistan set out to annex the territory. Major Thakur Khushal Chand, the elder son of Thakur Mangal Chand, along with his elder cousin Major Thakur Prithi Chand and their maternal uncle Subedar Thakur Bhim Chand, were sent to Ladakh to defend it. The Thakurs had a strong bond with the place as they had married into its royal family and shared a common language and culture.

Khushal Chand was the first graduate of the Lahaul-Spiti Valley. Right from his youth he resolved to stand against injustice and unfairness. Once, as a teenager, he famously handed out a sound thrashing to a venal tax collector who would bully the villagers. He joined the East Punjab Militia in 1941 and served in Rawalpindi before Partition. Upon Independence, he became a part of the 2 Dogra Regiment.[11]

In February 1948, led by Thakur Prithi Chand, a small group of soldiers, including his cousin, uncle and a few other Lahaulis, crossed the snow-covered Zojila and entered Ladakh. At Leh, they lowered the Union Jack and hoisted the Indian tricolour shouting, '*Ki ki so so lha gyalo* [Victory to the Gods]' and 'Hindustan Zindabad'. They also raised a force of local volunteers (which became 'National Guards' and later became Ladakh Scouts) and trained them in handling arms and combat. Through guerrilla tactics, this militia kept the Pakistani raiders at bay till the reinforcements of the Indian army reached Ladakh.[12] However, Major Khushal Chand's legendary feat happened at a small town called Khalatse, about 90 km away from Leh and towards Kargil. Accompanied by a lone sepoy, he stood on one side of the Indus. On the other bank were hundreds of enemy soldiers baying for Indian blood, waiting to advance towards Leh. Severely outnumbered, Thakur Khushal Chand took the daring call of running across the wooden bridge under intense enemy fire, throwing kerosene oil on it and burning it down.[13]

Due to the valour of the Thakurs of Lahaul and the local militia, the advance of enemy was halted, allowing the reinforcements to arrive. Finally, the enemy was pushed back. For their acts of bravery, the cousins were decorated with the Mahavir Chakra, the second highest wartime gallantry award in the country, and Bhim Chand was awarded the Vir Chakra.

With the formation of 9 Dogra in 1949, Khushal Chand went on to command the unit for three years. He was handpicked to serve with the United Nations Peacekeepers in erstwhile French Indo-China (modern-day Laos) in the mid-1950s. Here, he was tragically killed in an air crash, at the young age of 38.

Meanwhile, Ghemur Khar was severely damaged due to an

earthquake and seepage from the hillside, and had to be dismantled in 1986. Ashok Thakur, the younger son of Lt Col Khushal Chand, got the Khar repaired in 2003. A retired Indian Administrative Service (IAS) officer, Ashok Thakur presently owns the estate and continues with the tradition of hospitality and warmth shown to the visitors. He has also constructed a chorten at Khalatse in remembrance of his father.

Having witnessed the grandeur, valour and hospitality of the residents of Ghemur Khar, the Bhaga streams down to flow by Keylong, the most populated town of Lahaul-Spiti. Being the district headquarters, most of the government offices are situated in this town, which includes the most important office of the district collector.

One of the most famous employees in the collector's office was Tsering Dorje. After receiving his education in an Urdu-medium school in Keylong, he followed the family tradition and went to Tibet to train as a Lama. However, he had to abandon his education midway and returned to Lahaul after the Chinese annexed Tibet. After the creation of the Lahaul-Spiti district in 1960, he got a job as a teacher of Bhoti language at the office of the district collector. With a salaried job, Dorje followed his heart and became the solitary authority on Western and trans-Himalayan regions. He was widely referred to as the Encyclopaedia of the Himalayas. In the mid-1970s, he got in touch with Tenzin Palmo and would trek to the 'cave in the snow' to fetch her supplies. He also became a good friend of M.S. Gill, the young collector of Lahaul-Spiti who rose to become the chief election commissioner of India, a Rajya Sabha member and a union minister. Gill acknowledged his friendship with Dorje in his book *Himalayan Wonder: Travels in Lahaul and Spiti* (2010).

Apart from his erudition, the people of Lahaul-Spiti also remember Dorje for playing a key role in the construction of the Atal Tunnel. He would often prompt his friend Tashi Dawa to impress upon the then Prime Minister Vajpayee the need of the tunnel. He accompanied Dawa to Delhi frequently to push the proposal, which ultimately culminated in 2020. After serving for many years in the collector's office, Dorje retired as a public relations officer. He passed away due to COVID-19 in 2020. Almost a year later, M.S. Gill followed him, with decades of friendship to be presumably renewed in the next world.

Keylong hosts numerous festivals, and is graced with many famous temples and monasteries. Renowned author Rudyard Kipling once said about the town: 'It is surely the God lives here; it is not a place for men.' The enchanting green landscape along the river Bhaga, flaunting white chortens, prayer wheels and Tibetan prayer flags at high points, make it a tourist's delight. For a long time, Keylong has been the pitstop for tourists, explorers, adventurists, photographers and religious scholars headed for Ladakh.

Till the late 1990s, a large number of foreigners used to visit Ladakh. However, with the advent of militancy in Jammu and Kashmir, many countries issued advisories to their nationals against travelling to these areas. Till recent times, hundreds of Israelis used to motor down the Manali–Leh axis, mostly on hired Royal Enfield motorcycles. After their compulsory army stints back home, their bank accounts stacked with enough cash, the Israelis found India an attractive destination because of the low currency exchange and availability of high-quality cannabis in Himachal Pradesh. Hordes of bikers would camp in Keylong, some pitching their tents by the banks of the Bhaga, singing and dancing with the clouds of *charas* smoke wafting over their exalted revelry. The songs of Bob Dylan, Nusrat Fateh Ali Khan, Jimmy Hendrix, Steppenwolf, The Doors, Credence Clearwater Revival and others would resonate over the waters of the river.

At Tandi, Chandra and Bhaga silently embrace and get consumed in each other. In this divine reunion, there are no wedding songs, music bands, confetti, marigolds or sacred fire. It appears that both were thirsty, and they quenched their thirst from each other as illustrated by a Pakistani Urdu poet, Farigh Bukhari: '*Do dariya bhi jab aapas mein milte hain, dono apni-apni payas bujhate hain*' [When two rivers meet, they quench their thirst.]

Tandi is a small village nestled in the Pattan Valley, overlooking the convergence of two rivers, about 8 kms southwest of Keylong. The sleepy village of Tandi has about fifty households and a few hotels. It is said that the village, originally called Chandi, was founded by Raja Rana Chand Ram of the Jubbal dynasty of Shimla. There are views that the place was called Chandi, meaning silver, due to the abundance of silver deposits. As the time passed, the name transfigured into Tandi.[14]

Two myths associated with the place allude to the concept of *tan dehi* or the giving up of the body in its mortal form. The first is attributed to Draupadi, giving up her body at this spot during the mahaprasthana. The locals believe that the *deva*s or heavenly beings arrive at night to bless the people of Lahaul for performing the last rites of the deceased queen and immersing her ashes in the Chandrabhaga. The myth goes that the villagers had abstained from touching the body for two days until the identity of the deceased was discovered. On the third day, the mortal body of the Pandava queen was cremated reverentially.

The second myth is attributed to Sage Vashishtha, who meditated near the hot springs of Manali and was supposedly burnt in a pyre in the village. Much like Haridwar, the place is sacred to the Hindu beliefs and a dip at the confluence is considered holy. Even Buddhists, after the cremation of their dead, immerse the bones and ashes in the Chandrabhaga at Tandi, in a ceremony supervised by monks.

At Tandi, the lovers lose their individuality in the divine union. Today, the paparazzi, the mainstream television channels and social media are obsessed with coining amalgamations of celebrity unions from film, glamour and sports world. Much earlier, Rishi Vyasa started it in the Mahabharata creating the portmanteau 'Chandrabhaga'. Hence on, the destinies of the two rivers get entwined, through sun and rain and snow, triumphs and trails, as they embark on a journey together, passing through Himachal Pradesh, Jammu and Kashmir, Pakistan and finally getting lost in an estuary of the Indus to be submerged in the Arabian Sea, taking with it all the stories the rivers had been writing from times immemorial.

2
The Secret Valley

After the confluence, the Chandrabhaga flows past Tholang, a small village, circuited by willow trees. The village has the highest per capita income in the state and is hundred percent literate. Tholang has given the state, the highest number of civil servants, doctors, engineers and other professionals. The success story of this village can be traced to the advent of Moravian missionaries, who opened their Keylong chapter in 1856.[15] Affiliated with ancient Bohemia and Moravia provinces in the present-day Czech Republic, the mission focuses on the social and economic upliftment of the people.

In the early fifteenth century, a priest from Prague named John Hus fulminated against the corruption of the church hierarchy. He was eventually arrested, given a show trial and was burnt alive. However, his ideas survived and his followers formed the Protestant Moravian church with the motto: *Unitas Fratrum* [the unity of brethren]. Soon, the church had thousands of followers in Bohemia, Moravia and Poland. The Moravians sent their first missionaries to the West Indies in 1732, followed by Greenland, Surinam (now Suriname) and South Africa. In the next century, the Moravian activity had spread to Africa, North and South America, Europe, Central Asia and even Bhutan. Wherever they went, the Moravians brought a strong sense of religious discipline. For an ordinary follower, this would be expressed in the observance of regular Bible readings and church attendance. Apart from religion, the mission also diversified into medical care, education, commerce and proselytization.

The Himalayan chapter of the mission was entrusted to two young missionaries: August Wilhelm Heyde and Eduard Pagell. They stayed near Shimla with a German priest in service of Anglican Church, and brushed up their Tibetan and Hindustani. Finally, in 1856, they got the permission to set up the mission's chapter in Keylong. They were also given fifty pine trees by the government. Next year, Heinrich August Joeschke, a German missionary and linguist, arrived in Shimla. He would go on to be associated with the Keylong mission for the next decade. When Heyde and Pagell went to meet Joeschke on horseback, the latter was dismayed and suggested that they sell off their horses. Quoting the prophet Isaiah, 'How beautiful upon the mountains are the feet of Him that bringeth good tidings,' he exhorted how it was better for the missionaries to walk.[16]

Once the building at Keylong was completed, the missionaries decided to marry. Three young women were selected by the Moravian elders in Germany and dispatched to Calcutta. Pagell went to welcome the three women and ended up marrying one of them. The other two were wedded to Heyde and Joeschke, amidst the boisterous crowd of local enthusiasts.

The Keylong station started to grow rapidly. In 1858, Joeschke obtained a lithographic printing press from Shimla, and the first of many mission publications, *Barth's Bible Stories*, translated into Tibetan, came out soon afterwards. Meanwhile, Heyde and Pagell actively preached all over Lahaul. Soon, the mission acquired a tract of land and opened a farm. The farm demonstrated more rational techniques of farming and introduced new crops like turnips, lettuce and potatoes. Meanwhile, the missionary wives organized classes for the local women to learn knitting and Bible verses. The mission also engaged in trading. They made an arrangement with the nomads of Rupshu (a land between Lahaul and Leh), who would drive 200 sheep to Keylong each year. The sheep were sheared and the fleece was bartered with vegetables. This arrangement provided plenty of wool for the mission's cottage knitting industry. Woollen socks, knitted in German style, are still one of the characteristic cultural features of Lahaul.

The Moravians have always placed great emphasis on education, and the first of many schools was opened in Keylong in 1860. Joeschke and Heyde wrote and printed a series of text books covering diverse subjects like mathematics, geography, astronomy and church history. In the beginning, the school had very few students. Since the children helped their parents with the herding of livestock and worked in the fields most of the summer months, the school was forced to open up for a few weeks in winter.

The Buddhist monks also opposed the school because they feared that a better educated laity might encroach on their own traditional preserves. Their fears were not altogether unfounded. The locals had started to employ school children rather than monks, since reciting the scriptures by the latter entailed higher expenses.

After the monks, the local Thakurs also came in conflict with the missionaries, fearing the undermining of their clout and authority. The mission had meagre local support owing to their failure in large scale conversions. The only converts associated with the mission were the Ladakhis, who were seen as outsiders. Derga Sherdol, who studied in the mission school, became a Christian in 1874. He was serving as a government official in Spiti, when he became a victim of poisoning because of his acquired religion.

In 1935, the relations between missionaries and Thakurs deteriorated further because of a murder case. Three members of the ruling family had killed a local man in broad daylight. A complaint was lodged against the Thakurs by the mission head in Dharmshala. When a government official came to investigate the matter, no witness came forward, and the case was dropped. In 1938, the Keylong community imposed a boycott on the Christians, refusing to sell them any goods and threatening to impose a fine on anyone who even talked to them. The boycott was lifted after the intervention of the deputy commissioner (DC), but the relations remained strained.

Despite continued local resentment, many missionaries came to serve in Keylong. Heyde, fondly called Papa, served till 1898, before moving to Darjeeling. He got back home after spending fifty years in India. Pagell, who had left the mission after a few years, never got to go back home and died in India in 1883. Joeschke left the mission in 1868 and shifted to western Tibet where he did extensive work as a linguist and translator. He, too, passed away in 1883.

A missionary named Peter and his sister were the last to serve in Keylong. Though they were Swiss citizens, they were forced to leave the mission in 1940, soon after the outbreak of World War II. There were rumours of the duo being Nazi sympathizers. Before Peter left, he was assigned the dismal task of closing down the Keylong station and selling off the farm land. Today, there are no Christians in Keylong. The only trace left by the Moravians is a dilapidated chapel and the cemetery with its dead sleeping in unkempt graves. However, the crops introduced by the missionaries still flourish. Potatoes in particular have become the main cash crop of the Lahaulis. The hosiery shops in the Keylong market are still flush with German-style woollen socks.

Decades after the Moravians left, every house in Tholang boasts of a government officer. It is owed to a mission school, which opened in the village in 1920. S.S. Kapur, a resident of the village and former chief secretary of Jammu and Kashmir, reminisces that most of the youth wished to join the civil services or enrol for professional courses like medicine and engineering. Today, this has changed, with the younger generation diversifying into many other professions.

The river Chandrabhaga takes a northwest turn to meander through barren mountains and reaches Udaipur, the second largest town in Lahaul after Keylong. Here, Mayar Nullah, rising from high hills, merges with the Chandrabhaga. Verdant with pine trees, the town was earlier known as Margul or Markul, named after Markula Devi, an incarnation of Goddess Durga whose temple is situated here. In the seventeenth century, the place was renamed Udaipur in honour of Udai Singh, the king of Chamba.

Markula Devi temple witnesses a sea of pilgrims from all over Kullu, Chamba, Lahaul and the Doda district of Jammu and Kashmir. The temple, built of stone and wood, has a strong influence of Kashmiri and Tibetan style. According to the legends, the temple was built by the Pandavas of the Mahabharata from a singular block of wood. However, historians date the temple to the tenth or eleventh century CE. The exterior of the temple looks unimpressive with the wood-tiled conical roof and simple walls exposed to inclemency of extreme climate. There is a stone in the courtyard weighing several hundreds of kilograms. It is believed that twelve persons can lift the stone employing one finger each, while chanting 'Hail Mother Bhagwati'. Purportedly, the stone cannot be lifted by going against either stricture: The chant and the single finger are imperative! The interior of the temple is gilded with beautiful wood carvings depicting the ten incarnations of Lord Vishnu and a few scenes from the Hindu epics. The sanctum sanctorum houses an idol of an eight-armed Durga made from alloys of eight metals. The idol was stolen in 1972 and was eventually recovered from Manali. It was hidden beneath a rock near Beas River.

There is a belief among the people that when visiting this temple, one must not say 'let us go' – it is considered inauspicious. That is why people do not speak but gesticulate to their companions to retreat from the temple premises.

Short of Udaipur, a road climbs up the left bank of the Chandrabhaga and reaches another ancient temple – that of Trilokinath, the lord of three worlds. This temple, shimmering in white hue, stands at the cliff-top, showcasing the eclectic mix of Hindu and Buddhist mythologies. Tibetan prayer flags decorate the entrance, and inside the premises, Buddhist prayer wheels, along with Nandi the bull and a granite phallus, make it a unique amalgamation of faiths.

The origin of the temple is frequently told in a story of a cowherd and an angel. According to the legend, the Thakur of Tundeh had hired a cowherd who would take his *choori*s (cross-breed of a cow and a yak) to graze in a nearby pasture that had seven water springs. One day, the cowherd saw angels appearing from the springs and they walked to the glade to play. Startled at the happening, the cowherd decided to narrate the story to the Thakur. However, on his return, he forgot all about it. This carried on for several days – he would secretly watch the angels frolic and dance and then the memory would vanish from his mind. One day, he thought of a plan and tied a little stone to the horns of one of the chooris, thinking that the stone would remind him to tell the Thakur about the angels. Nevertheless, he again forgot to tell the story to anyone. That evening, when the Thakur's wife was milking the choori, the stone fell into the milking pot, breaking it. Infuriated, she complained to the Thakur, who summoned the cowherd and reprimanded him. The cowherd remembered the angels and he narrated the episode to the Thakur, who refused to believe him. 'If it is true, bring an angel here as proof,' Thakur told the cowherd. Next day, when the angels appeared from the springs, the cowherd jumped from his hiding place and caught hold of the youngest angel. Grabbing her hand, he ran towards the village. The other angels chased them, pleading with him to look back to see what they wanted to offer him in exchange for their youngest companion. The little angel warned him and dissuaded him from looking back lest they freeze into stone images. The cowherd ran as fast as he could, and as soon as he was in sight of the village, the temptation got the better of him. No sooner had he looked back than he and the angel both turned into stone statues. Overawed by the miracle, on that very site, the Thakur built a small temple for the beautiful idol of the angel.

The main deity in the Trilokinath temple is worshipped by the Buddhists as Arya Avalokiteshwar, a form of the Buddha, and by the Hindus as Lord Shiva. It is believed that the deity shows a frowning countenance to sinners and a beaming one to the good souls. The divinity of the temple was also proved in 1863 when an avalanche almost swept away the whole village, but the temple remained unscathed. And again, in a severe avalanche in 1979, though the temple was razed to the ground, the sanctum sanctorum remained intact.

Every year, in August, a festival named 'Pauri' is held in Udaipur for three days. It begins with an enchanting prayer ceremony inside the premises of the Trilokinath temple. The following day, there is an extravagant procession, full of glitter and colour, accompanied by music and dancing. The striking feature of this ritual is the horse that leads the procession. Caparisoned with an embroidered drape, gilded with flowers and other accoutrements at its reins and stirrups, the horse enjoys all the attention it gets. No rider mounts the horse, as the local belief goes that it is being ridden by the Lord himself. The procession terminates at the house of the local ruler or the Thakur, where the horse is extended a warm welcome and showered with sweets. This is followed by a grand feast for the pilgrims. Later, the Thakur mounts the horse and leads the procession back to inaugurate the fair.

The Chandrabhaga moves northwest, lapping against sandy banks, taking the large rocks head-on, never stopping and getting stronger and ferocious. It is wide with a strong current and runs along the Udaipur–Pangi road, flanked by stretches of greenery and farmlands. Most of the river course is straight, but it also takes a series of bends and loops, small and large, at various stretches, curvaceous like the sensuous gait of a courtesan. Alongside, the black, tarred road climbs up the gradient, only to slant down sharply before ascending yet again.

One of the villages the river passes is Mindhal, situated on its left bank. A link road branches out from the Udaipur–Pangi road and heads for Mindhal, passing over a single-lane iron bridge over the Chandrabhaga. The village is famous for its revered temple of Chamunda Devi, commonly referred to as Mindhal Mata. According to the legend, the spot where the temple stands once had a double-storeyed house. The house belonged to an old woman who had seven sons. One day, while cooking, she noticed a black stone protruding out of the hearth. Without taking much interest, she pushed the stone back. Strangely, the appearance of the stone became a daily affair. One day, it did not budge despite the old woman's best efforts.

Knowing that the Devi had visited her house, the old woman rushed out and hailed her sons who were working in the fields. She urged them to come home and seek the blessings of the Devi. Her sons made light of the whole affair and quipped, 'The Devi is neither going to complete the ploughing for us with only one bullock nor grant us a revenue free land to cultivate.' Disappointed with her sons, the woman invited the villagers to visit her home and witness the miracle for themselves. But the villagers scoffed at her too.

Infuriated, the Devi froze all the villagers into stone statues. Since the old woman was the only one who had paid her obeisance, she was spared and the Devi even granted her a boon. Having lost her sons, the old woman was not desirous of anything. Instead, she pleaded to the Devi to turn her into a stone statue as well. The Devi was taken by surprise but bound by her word; she decreed that her devotees would first worship the old lady's image before worshipping her. It is interesting to note the place is still strewn with stones all around, and to this day, the people yoke only one bullock to the plough.

From Mindhal, the main road winds uphill and gets narrower. The river, too, is now at a deep fall, flowing silently along the narrow non-metalled road without crash barriers and parapets. Several nullahs stream down from the mountain, the bigger ones with iron bridges and the smaller ones passing through cement pipes to channel water into the Chandrabhaga

Finally, the Chandrabhaga enters the Pangi Valley – a tehsil of the Chamba district – at a place called Bhujind. Chamba is a district in northwest Himachal Pradesh, with its headquarters in Chamba town. Nestled at the crossroads of the Zanskar range in Ladakh and the Dhauladhar range, Chamba Valley is gifted with breathtaking slopes, forests, lakes, streams, meadows and wildlife. From its hills, fast-flowing streams drain into the river Ravi on the northern side and into the Chandrabhaga on the northern fringes.

Known as Parushini in Rig Veda, Ravi is one of the rivers of the 'Nadi Stuti Sukta'. In other Vedas, the river is also referred to as Irawat, and the ancient Greeks called it Hydraotes. Rising at Bara Bhangal in Kangra district, Himachal Pradesh, Ravi follows a north-westerly course through the states of Himachal Pradesh, Punjab, and Jammu and Kashmir to enter Pakistan, and finally merges into the Indus River.

Perched on terraced flats, Chamba is an idyllic town, overlooking river Ravi and its confluence at Balu Bridge with a small river, gliding down from the Sal Valley. The people of Chamba are vibrant and energetic; their lives exemplify the interdependence of man and nature. A popular Himachali song exemplifies this:

Mere hikudye gadbad hoi bhalo, Chambay takiyan chadti jo
Mere hathan che chalay pay bhalo, main Chambay dana kutdi jo

[My stomach is churning, as I climb the cliffs of Chamba
I have blisters on my hands, as I grind the grain in Chamba.]

The township of Chamba was founded by Raja Sahil Varman in 920 CE. It was at the insistence of his daughter Champawat, locally worshipped as a goddess, that the Raja shifted the capital of his kingdom from Bharmour to Chamba. The town is so exquisitely beautiful that another local folksong opens with the enchanting lyrics:

Shimla ni basna, Kasauli ni basna, Chamba jana zaroor.

[Settle not in Shimla, nor in Kasauli, visit Chamba for sure.]

The old town of Chamba has a cluster of tin-sloped and flat-roofed houses, asymmetrically located on the terraces of a hillock. The quaint bazaars are congested with jewellery shops, hotels, groceries and rows of shops selling the famous Chamba *jutis* [footwear] and Chamba *rumaal* [handkerchiefs]. At the foot of the town, next to the Deputy Development Commissioner's (DDC) office, there is the Chaugan ground – *chaugan* is a term used for plains in the local language – covered with a carpet of lush green grass and circled by trees. The ground is brought to many uses but has been mostly famous for some cricket matches. In 1940, an English team played a cricket match with the Chamba state team, which had been groomed by the local king. Thousands of locals had gathered around the ground to cheer for the local cricketers. The English team scored 180-odd runs that were easily chased by the local team, thanks to the sheer brilliance of a local lad named Mahant. He wore no pads and shoes but scored a swashbuckling century, studded by some glorious hits. Earlier, he had taken four wickets and single-handedly ensured the easy victory of his team. That time the Raja had boasted, 'With my team, I can defeat any team of the world.'[17]

Chamba had a thriving cricket culture and regular matches were played among the provinces of Chamba, Kullu, Suket and Mandi. Some people also said that Aamir Khan's famous movie *Lagaan* (2001), which has a cricket match between the ragtag local team and a much superior English team, was inspired by this cricket match. However, the makers of the film have refuted the claim.

With its high altitude and vagaries of the weather, Chamba is one of the most backward districts of the country. Within Chamba, the far-flung Pangi Valley is even more backward. The remoteness of Pangi has been legendary, and it is often referred to as the 'secret valley' because of the difficulty in accessing it. Due to heavy snowfall, the valley remains closed to the outside world for about eight months a year.

The first motorable approach road to the Pangi Valley was built from Chamba in the 1980s. After passing through small towns and summer inhabitations, the road reaches the Saach Pass, situated at a height of more than 14,000 ft in the Pir Panjal Range. After being buried under the snow for seven months of the year, Border Roads Organisation (BRO) clears the snow and the pass is opened in late June. A few kilometres ahead of the Saach Pass, there is a white expanse, which is actually a frozen lake. The lake is called Bhoot Maidan [Ghost Ground]. Though the etymology of the name remains unknown, it is believed that in 1998, ghosts of different kind haunted the place.

In August 1998, suspected Pakistan-sponsored militants, operating in the Doda district of neighbouring Jammu and Kashmir, crossed over to the Chamba district through thick forests.[18] They massacred thirty-five Hindu and Buddhist construction labourers and injured eleven others, at two places of Tissa region. The labourers were working on the Saach Pass road and were woken up by about a dozen long-haired terrorists – some believed to be from Pakistan and Afghanistan – while they were sleeping in their temporary shelters. The news became public when two of the injured, trudged 8 km through the dense forests and reported the massacre to the nearest police post.[19]

The 1998 massacre had, for the first time, flared communal tensions in the alpine forests of the Chamba district, comprising vast grassy meadows used for pastoral activity.[20] The local Gaddis, who were Hindus, deeply resented the summer migration of the Muslim Gujjars and Bakerwals. These Gujjars trod hundreds of miles in summers with their livestock, from the plains of Gurdaspur and Pathankot in Punjab and the Kathua district of Jammu and Kashmir. They have been doing this for ages, and permits are issued to them for particular grazing pastures, up in the hills.

That year, fearing a backlash after the massacre, the Gujjars started to move back to the plains earlier than usual. The Himachal police, apprehensive of more killings, issued orders asking the Gaddis to move down from the pastures. In Tissa, the relatives of the victims of the massacres carried out vigorous protests and made attempts to attack the Gujjars who had already started to leave. They blamed the Gujjars for harbouring the terrorists and providing them food, transport and shelter. However, the Gujjars refuted this claim and alleged that it was a well-thought ploy by the Gaddis to encroach into their pasture lands. The problem was further compounded by the killing of three Gaddi nomads in the same region. Battle lines now appeared to be clearly drawn between two communities that had been living in harmony for ages. Hitherto, the tension between Gujjars and Gaddis had been only on sheep thefts and money deals.

From the Saach Pass, the road curves down to enter the Pangi Valley. After crossing an iron bridge, the first glimpse of the Chandrabhaga is found at a village named Karyuni. The river flows through a gorge bounded with hazelnut trees, locally called *thangi*.

Even when the curse of terrorism permeated into the Chamba district, the Pangi Valley largely remained unaffected by it. The Chandrabhaga played a major role by creating a natural barricade against transgressions, since it cannot be forded due to its depth and intimidating currents. However, antique methods of crossing the river have existed. The *jhulla puls* [swing bridges] are still common. They are usually made of flexible willow twigs, whose slender branches can be entwined to make a strong rope. Three cables are made and spread across the river. The lowest cable was to walk on and the other two, at a slightly higher level, one on each side, were for hands to grasp. These cables were tied to strong beams on the two banks of the river. In another common method called *trangari*, two wooden beams are laid from bank to bank, parallel to each other, about two feet apart. On these are placed wooden planks, which may or may not be latched to the beams.

The road from Udaipur was hewn from the sandstone mountain alongside the Chandrabhaga. The first major village the river meets in the Pangi Valley is Purthi, perched on a hill with a scattered population of about fifty-odd households. The village is known for its local son, the late Deena Nath Thakur.

Appointed as a sub-inspector in the Border Security Force (BSF) in 1990, he rose to the rank of inspector. On 9 April 2000, while being on internal security duty in Kashmir, he led his team of ten personnel and stormed a house in Saar village, Pulwama. In the ensuing encounter, he faced a volley of fire from hiding terrorists and was martyred. For his bravery, he was posthumously awarded the President's Police Medal for Gallantry, the highest-ranking honour for valour in police and paramilitary forces. Like other places in Himachal, the Pangi Valley also has a great tradition of the local boys joining the Indian army and other paramilitary forces, to serve the country.

In Purthi, the Forest Rest House was constructed by a British range officer named Todd. Situated in a thick-wooded grove, it is surrounded by flat, green lawns, and the Chandrabhaga flows below. Originally, it was the range officer's residence and is referred to as Todd's Bungalow. It is said that when taking time off from his stressful schedule, Todd was fond of walking his dog on a narrow footrail above the river. On one such stroll, the dog unexpectedly darted back and inadvertently wrapped the leash around his owner's legs. Todd lost his balance, toppled into the Chandrabhaga along with his dog and drowned. However, it is also said that he never left his beloved bungalow, and that he is sighted often. People believe that he comes down the chimney of one of the bedrooms. The whole apparition is rarely seen, and usually only two sturdy legs are visible in the fireplace. It seems that the spectre has never harmed anyone or created a ruckus; it is contented to visit a property that was once its own.[21]

In a large area in the hills, about 20,000 souls live in the Pangi Valley, which includes sub-valleys of Sural, Saichu, Hundan and Kumar-Parmar. Every sub-valley has a series of villages leading up to the top of the mountain. Interestingly, lower villages are inhabited by Hindus, and the ones higher up are Buddhist villages called Bhatoris.

The advent of the Pangwal tribe in this area is shrouded in mystery and there are different theories propagated by anthropologists and historians. Some say the first inhabitants were originally from the Lahaul and Kullu Valleys and low-lying areas of the Chandrabhaga valley. They came here in search of cultivable land and pasturage.[22] Another version is that the valley straddling an insurmountable high mountain range was colonized by political offenders and convicts who were exiled to these areas by the king of Chamba.[23] Lending credence to the above theory is the remarkable resemblance of the traditional cap worn by men to the ones that state prisoners once used to wear.

In certain folk songs, Pangwals claim to be descendants of Macedonian Greeks, who were part of Alexander's army. When the soldiers rebelled against their king on the banks of the river Beas, many of them escaped to faraway lands, including the Pangi Valley.

Certain historians espouse the hypothesis that in order to escape persecution by the Mughals, especially during the reign of Aurangzeb, some Rajputs exiled their women and children to these areas, with instructions never to return unless called for. Since the men got killed in various battles, these women and children could never go back. The men who remained with them were the soldiers and helpers who had accompanied them.

Then the stories abound about other men who went to Pangi and never returned. Most were government officials assigned tasks in the area by the raja of Chamba. Folklore says the raja used to pay funeral expenses in advance to the officials deputed for duties in the Pangi Valley. Apparently, these men were not expected to return alive![24] So treacherous was the snowy valley that the postman who carried the mail from Chamba was given one gold coin to undertake the hazardous journey.

Since the women of Pangi were enchantingly beautiful, the visiting officials often got smitten by their charm. Some women married these men solely on the condition that they would not move out of Pangi. The women from other parts of Chamba always resented their men going to Pangi for the fear of losing them to the 'witches' there.

Natives of Pangi are hardy, combating the hostile nature, which has moulded their social life, religion and customs. They drown the drudgery and monotony of their existence by indulging in songs, dance, theatre and art. Every housewife paints one corner of a wall in her house and decorates it with traditional motifs during different festivals. Typically, the villagers let out their pent-up emotions through songs covering every aspect of their lives. These soulful renditions encompass a medley of emotions ranging from passionate romance, love and valour, and also eulogize legendary traditions. Though there are ballads about kings and local chieftains, the bulk of the songs revolve around the common man and his joys and sorrows. These are songs of love, religion, heroism, festivity, seasons and ceremonies.

For example, a major theme of local songs is the way the women of Pangi are lured by their admirers. In a popular song, a lover, Madho, a forest guard, tries to entice away his beloved Bhotle from her home:

> Madho: My beloved Bhotle, on the pass I will
> construct a beautiful house for you
> Bhotle: Madho dear, in this bungalow there be many windows
> Madho: My beloved Bhotle, in the windows

There would be glass panes
Bhotle: Madho dear, please put them
On all four sides of the house
Bhotle: Madho dear, to cut grass. I would
Go to reserved forests
Madho: My beloved Bhotle, beware,
The forest people would catch you
Bhotle: Madho dear, there are enemies
Standing betwixt us;
Madho: My beloved Bhotle, I will
Crush the heads of our enemies
Bhotle: Madho dear, the evil people
Would not let us meet;
Madho: My beloved Bhotle then let us meet
Go to a far off place
Bhotle: Madho dear, how would I cross the pass
Madho: For you, me beloved Bhotle
I will bring a palanquin

The Pangi women, simple and docile, were vulnerable to exploitation by outsiders. The problem had become so grave that in 1924, the then raja of Chamba had to intervene. He issued a royal notification proscribing the marriage of non-resident men with the native women of Pangi. All exceptions had to seek his personal permission.

~

The lower ranges of the mountains in the Pangi Valley are swathed with cedar, oak and pine forests. And at their feet, the Chandrabhaga flows angrily, lashing against the adamantine geography that shackles it. As the river surges forward in summers, it gathers more water from the waterfalls and small streams slithering down the slopes. Every few miles, the river passes by open nooks, which may have been small lakes of the bygone age formed by the river cutting its way through a rocky barrier. Most of the Pangwali villages are located in these patches: small, sparse and aloof.[25]

The most prominent town of the Pangi Valley is Killar. It is the administrative headquarters and all the government offices, including that of the resident commissioner – a middle-rung officer and head of the administration – are located here. The construction of a tunnel from Pangi to Tissa has been the main demand of the people, persisting for decades now.

During the visit of former Prime Minister Indira Gandhi in 1984, the demand for the tunnel was immortalized in a song:

The first tour, the very first tour,
To Pangi Killar of Indira Gandhi,
Garlanded ceremoniously with thangi garlands.
She looked majestic wearing thangi garlands.
She wore the *joji** and the pulley,
Joji and pulley looked nice on her.
First demand, their first demand,
The people voiced for a tunnel under Cheni.
She granted, she granted the first demand,
A tunnel under the Cheni pass.

Three months later, when Indira Gandhi was assassinated by her bodyguards, the people of Pangi mourned her:

Treacherously killed, treacherously killed
Indira Gandhi was treacherously killed.
The people wept, the public wept,
The people wept and the public wept.
Curse be on the murderers, curse on the killers,
Curse on the traitors of the land,
Curse on the traitors.

---

* The typical head-dress of Pangwali women, made of cotton or silk.

The struggle for the tunnel continues till date, spearheaded by a committee of locals: Pangi Surang Sangrash Samiti. The tunnel, when it comes to Pangi, could really be a game changer, much like the Atal Tunnel.

Piled up with matchbox-shaped houses of stone masonry, Killar is the only place in Pangi that shows some signs of urbanization. Most of these houses are double-storeyed with flat roofs. In the lower storey, animals are penned, and in the upper, the family lives. However, during winters, the family shares the ground floor with the livestock to keep themselves warm and cosy. The town is straddled by Chowki Bazaar – the main market – and is lined with new hotels and homestays. In the upper part of the town, there is a helipad that is used in winters. The helicopter services are provided by the government in cases of extreme medical exigencies. In summers, Killar buzzes with groups of nature lovers, off-roaders, trekkers and pilgrims.

The place has many small temples devoted to Lord Shiva and ancient Buddhist monasteries. Like Lahaul, the people here are very religious by nature. Perhaps because of extreme conditions and adverse weather, they attempt to propitiate nature by worshipping her. This phenomenon has been observed from the earliest-known civilizations on the Indus in the Indian subcontinent, the Huang Ho in China, the Nile in Egypt and the Euphrates and the Tigris in Mesopotamia. The worship of nature along with animistic religion gave rise to many myths and superstitions, which the local folk wholeheartedly embrace.

In Killar, the pilgrims mostly come to pay obeisance at the historical Nag Devta temple, also known as Dehatnag. Surrounded by cedar trees that accentuate the spirituality of the place, the temple houses a black stone idol symbolizing the Nag or the serpent.[26]

The legend is that there was a nag originally located in the village Jhalma in Lahaul, and human sacrifice used to be offered to him. In the village lived a widow whose six sons had already been sacrificed. It was now the turn of her last surviving son. The poor woman was wailing while preparing delicacies for the nag. A Gaddi named Kittu, who was passing by, heard her wails. When the woman narrated her tale of woe, Kittu offered to exchange places with her son. Next day, when he was led to the nag to be beheaded, he urged the people to let the nag devour him instead. For this purpose, in succession, he offered different limbs of his body to the nag, but no harm came to him. Enraged, Kittu declared the nag fake; he picked up its idol and tossed it in the Chandrabhaga. The swift currents of the river carried the idol to Killar. Here, a local woman noticed that one of her chooris was not yielding any milk. When it happened for the next two days, she decided to keep a vigil on this particular choori. Next day, she saw the stone idol coming out of the river and sucking the teats of the choori. Caught in the act, the nag had to disclose his identity. On being assured that no Gaddi named Kittu lived in the vicinity, the nag decided to come out of the river and make the place his permanent abode. The woman carried the idol on her back, and as per folklore, the idol tumbled from her back at the present site of the temple, falling flat on its face. The idol was enshrined in a small temple, facing inwards. As per the legend, no sooner was the consecration done then the cedars appeared, surrounding the temple! At the onset of winter, the temple hosts a four-day flower festival called Phulaich. Along with dance, music and feasting, the devotees pray to the idol for his benediction during the harsh winter ahead.[27]

The Chandrabhaga hums forward, and 9 km from Killar, the river passes by Dharwas, the largest village in the valley. It is known for a natural spring called Tilmili, which is rich with minerals. Purportedly, the king of Chamba would drink the water from this spring for medicinal purposes. Gallons of water were carried to his palace from the spring situated by the groves of hazelnut trees.

A little ahead, a rest house called Cherry Bungalow is located on the right bank of the Chandrabhaga. From here, several exciting treks commence, the most famous leading to the Saichu Twan Wildlife Sanctuary. The sanctuary, spread over an area of 390 sq. km, is home to a variety of fauna like the Himalayan brown beer, snow leopard, musk deer, long-tailed marmot, red fox and ibex. The sanctuary also has a variety of butterflies and about fifty-four species of birds, including the Himalayan monal and koklass pheasant.[28] About 10 km later, a road climbs up to the Hundan Bhatori village as the Chandrabhaga goes further down, looking like a grey serpent hissing its way through the high mountains. An old gompa in Hundan Bhatori follows traditions of animism and Shaivism. In August, the village hosts a festival that is attended by both Hindus and Buddhists drawn from various villages of the valley.

Further east, the most picturesque sub-valley of Sural is nestled in the majestic mountains. The valley is rich with the Himalayan birch, the deciduous tree of high altitude. Birch is locally called 'betula' and is also referred to as 'bhojpatra'. In ancient times, the white parchment like the bark of the tree was used for writing. The four Vedas, passed on from generation to generation of Brahmin families by word of mouth, were finally scribbled on bhojpatras.

Sural Bhatori is the largest village, verily the outermost inhabitation of the Pangi Valley. It borders the Kishtwar district of Jammu and Kashmir and Zanskar subdivision of Ladakh. The most loved trek from here leads to the silver waterfall at Chabi. The waterfall then shapes into a downstream and flows into the Chandrabhaga. Sural also houses one of the oldest monasteries in the Pangi Valley. The gompa is a veritable treasure house of paintings, a few, almost 300 years old.

From Sural Bhatori, the river roars forward in a deep gorge, smashing against rocks and intermittently turning languorous. Overlooked by what is considered one of the world's most dangerous road, the river is about to enter the new land of Jammu and Kashmir.

The road, with blind curves and hairpin bends, gets so narrow that, at times, it is barely wide enough to fit in a car or a jeep. With no guardrails or secure edging, the unpaved road chiselled out from the rock is nothing but a worn-out pathway at a steep gradient. The overhanging rocky contours of the mountain often scrape against the vehicle roofs.

On the other side of the road is the jaw-dropping, almost perpendicular dive into the Chandrabhaga, which looks like a narrow drain from such height. The verticality of this geography is the reason that there are hardly any inhabited areas in this arc, till the road descends and the valley opens up. From a distance, the vehicles that cling to this road look like ants climbing up a hill. The unpredictable weather, accentuated by speedy winds and unexpected drizzles, can trigger mudslides. Despite all these impediments, the heady concoction of spine-thrilling challenges and exhilaration allures many adventures.

3

The Old Snow Lady

The Chandrabhaga enters Jammu and Kashmir and meets up with the Sansari Nullah, about 35 km short of Gulabgarh, the headquarters of Paddar subdivision of the Kishtwar district.[29] Paddar is an expansive valley, whose name is derived from an old crop called *paddaru* that has now vanished from the diet of the locals. Another perspective is that the name comes from *padhar*, which means a vast meadow. Yet others propound that the name is a derivative of the word *panwdar*, which is a combination of two Hindi words, *panwa*, which means feet, and *dar*, implying fear. Buddhists propagate another theory – that the word had evolved from *padam*, which is part of the Buddhist chant: *Om Mani Padme Om*. Padam means a lotus. Therefore, the valley is evocative of a lotus flower, with the encircling hills being the petals.

Paddar, endowed with a great wealth of natural beauty, is bound by Zanskar in the north, Pangi in the east, Bhalesa of Doda district in the south and Nagsena in the west. A scattered population of about 30,000 resides on this vast area. In the summer, this number swells due to the influx of nomads. But from where did the first people come to this inhospitable terrain? It is said that the shepherds from the neighbouring areas of Bhaderwah, Himachal and Zanskar were the first to access the valley, attracted to its extensive grazing lands. Gradually, these people started settling down in the Paddar region. After the Hindus, the Buddhists began inhabiting the upper regions of Machail, Kaban and Gandhari Valleys.

The Sansari Nullah is considered the border between Himachal Pradesh and Jammu and Kashmir. Once the nullah meets the Chandrabhaga, the river gets a new name – Chenab, which is perhaps the Persianized version of Chandrabhaga. The name finds mention in the works of Iranian scholar, Al-Biruni, who travelled in the Indian subcontinent in 1017 CE.

Some say that name emerged because people thought it flows from China, thus, the word 'Chin-ab', 'Chin' for China and 'ab' meaning water. The confusion probably arises from the Mongoloid features of the Lahaulis. The most accepted view expatiates that it is a derivative of 'Chen-Ab', 'chen' meaning 'Moon' and 'ab' meaning 'Water'. Therefore, it is also known as the Moon River. Whatever the genesis of the name, this is the mighty Chenab, the angry Chenab, Ashiqan da Dariya, the dark-coloured waters, the river of destruction and the river of folktales.

After crossing the bridge over the Sansari Nullah, the road takes a steep incline and the Chenab flows past Ishtayari, a beautiful, vast region consisting of five Hindu villages scattered on the hillock. The road ahead of Ishtayari – a stretch of 4 km – gets steeper and narrower and is considered the most dangerous part of the journey. It is called a 'cliffhanger' because of the way the road hugs the mountain and has a perpendicular drop down in the Chenab. The road is so dangerous that the wheels of the vehicles can cause the edges to crumble. After surviving the cliffhanger, the road leads to Tayari, another Hindu area comprising five villages.

The people of villages in Ishtayari and Tayari have lives full of hardships, struggling against the extreme forms of nature. In the summer, the herders move to the upper hills for grazing. In early 1990s, when militancy gained a foothold in the upper reaches of Paddar, the Chenab acted as a natural barrier, and these areas largely remained untouched. However, in 1998, terrorists came down from the opposite spur and crossed the Chenab over a wooden bridge connecting to Tayari. They targeted a General Reserve Engineering Force (GREF) camp, roughed up the labourers and decamped with explosives used for road construction.

Three years later, the militant presence reached the ridge of Chitoo Dhar, which faces the Tayari cliff on the left bank of the Chenab.

In the summer, the Hindus take their livestock up the ridge endowed with large pastures. One day, the herders encountered few gun-wielding terrorists who kidnapped some of them, dragging the hapless villagers deep inside the jungle on the adjoining ridge. The kidnapped men turned lucky to have been released unhurt after a few days. However, they were robbed of their sheep and other belongings.

From Tayari, the Chenab surges forward and passes by a large village called Sohal, located on its right bank. A few Nepalese also reside in this predominantly Hindu village. They came here a long time back, looking for Morchella mushrooms, hazelnuts and pine seeds. Some of them adopted the professions of masons, labourers and stone breakers. Most of them left or were driven out, but some married the local girls and settled here permanently.

From Sohal, a wooden bridge over the Chenab leads to Chitoo village after a steep trek through the pine forests. Chitoo is famous for the temple of Singhasan Mata. It is said that the Mata appeared in a stone manifestation or a *pindi* for the first time in the house of a local lady called Zyus Dai. Fearing losing her home, Dai was not too keen to host the unwanted guest. That night, the Mata revisited her in a dream and empathized with her concerns. Then she asked Dai to follow the dense plumes of sacred smoke the next day and ensure the Mata's abode at the place where the smoke originated. Zyus Dai accepted the command and, the next day, consecrated the place where smoke emanated.

Today, a temple carved out of wood stands at the place on four concrete columns. Inside the sanctum sanctorum, the goddess is present as a *niraakar* or formlessly, hiding behind seven curtains. No one, not even the caretakers and priests of the temple, is allowed to glance behind the curtain. It is said that the glow of the pindi is so glaring that it causes blindness.

Once, a revenue official of Chamba administration came to the village for official work. After praying at the temple, he was adamant to look behind the drape, despite being fervently advised against the adventure. As soon as the official parted the curtains and peeked behind, a bright light struck his eyes, and took his vision.

Like St Valentine, the Chitoo goddess is a great propagator of love. She is said to come to the aid of lovers whose liaison is not accepted by their parents and society. The believers say that the families who do not accept the eloped couples are driven to misery because of Chitoo Mata's curse. Even today, the lovers seek divine intervention of the goddess for blessing their union.

The people continue to believe in the miracles Chitoo Mata bestows on her devotees. In 1991, when the wife of a local police officer fell seriously ill, the best of treatment turned futile. Then Chitoo Mata appeared in his dream and asked him to bring his wife to her abode. The police officer complied and his wife recovered fully. The officer resigned from his job and became a full-time devotee of Chitoo Mata. In 1994, he started an impressive yatra from his native village of Chishoti, which culminated at the temple of Chitoo Mata.

Apart from having unflinching faith in Chitoo Mata, the people of Sohal believe in many other myths that have been handed over to them from generations. In the village crematorium, situated on the banks of the Chenab, seven monolithic pillars have been standing for ages. According to the local legend, these pillars are in memory of seven villagers, who were swept away in a cloudburst and their bodies were never recovered. Their widows committed sati at the place where the pillars are erected.

Once, the village saw an acute draught, bringing severe misery to the people. This is also evident from the etymology of the village's name. The name 'Sohal' emerged from the word *shoo*, which means *sookha* or dry. As the draught persisted, the people beseeched Chitoo Mata and the myth of the guiding rainbow of Paddar emerged. Bringing rains, the Mata appeared as a rainbow and instructed the villagers to construct a canal along the path of the guiding rainbow. The villagers acquiesced, and their water woes were over.

However, another story says that during the drought, the village was suddenly hit by a massive avalanche. This altered the course of the Shandheeri Nullah and it started to flow close to Sohal, making the land cultivable. The nullah travels 20 km downstream from the Kaban Valley and debouches on the right bank of the Chenab.

Sohal has left a huge footprint on history. On the upper part of the village, a dilapidated structure of a water fountain has been facing neglect. Four more such fountains existed in the village but they gradually vanished. The villagers extracted their slabs to use in house constructions. The people of Sohal believe that the fountains were constructed by the wandering Pandavas, who had visited these places during their exile. However, the historians have attributed the fountains to Raja Chattar Singh of Chamba. Moreover, the fountain slabs have been unique to the Chamba kingdom and they lie scattered all over Pangi and parts of Paddar. These epigraphical records were erected at springs and fountains and were dedicated to Varuna – the god of water. The inscriptions covered with quaint figures and ornamental carvings, mostly commemorated important events including deaths. The fountain slabs also helped to geographically mark the water sites.

Chattar Singh was a progressive king, but he also believed in expansionist policies. After conquering the Pangi Valley in the middle of eighteenth century, he subjugated the local Thakurs of Paddar who were perpetually at war with each other. He stationed a small garrison of troops in Sohal. For the convenience of his troops, he got a 15 ft well dug out from the hard rock. The jar shaped well – narrow at the top and wide at the bottom – was used to store water.

The soldiers of Chattar Singh were devotees of Kali Mata and since there was no temple of the goddess in Sohal, they constructed one, near the well. Therefore, the well came to be known as Kaal Khappar: *Kaal* for Goddess Kali and *Khappar* means a hole or a pit. The temple is associated with a popular festival called Paryali ki Zaat, which is celebrated once in three years in the month of February.

The festival, resplendent with dancing and singing, is held in memory of seven girls of the village who belonged to seven different families. Popularly called 'seven sisters', the girls once crossed the Chenab and went uphill to fetch some alluring flowers from the forest. During their hunt, a huge boulder rolled down the hill, crushing six of them to death. The seventh girl, who was injured grievously, somehow managed to reach the village and inform the villagers about the calamity before succumbing to her wounds. Struck by this colossal tragedy, the villagers decided that a sacrificial rite was mandatory for ensuring salvation for the maidens. Therefore, a rite was performed in the courtyard of the Kali Mata temple, where a concoction of walnuts, dry aubergine, rice and the meat of a one-eyed black sheep was offered to the goddess. This was the beginning of Paryali ki Zaat, which begins with fasting and the traditional sacrifice. It is followed by devotional songs, dancing and feasting.

The Kali Mata temple is also the transit point of the annual yatra to Chitoo Mata, which starts from Jammu in June and culminates after five days. A flame in a brass lamp, known as 'Jyot of Chitoo Mata', is brought from Jammu encased in a glass shade. A convoy of buses and cars accompany the Jyot and halts for a night at the Kali Mata temple. Next day, the pilgrimage continues on foot to reach Chitoo Mata.

On its forward journey, the Chenab widens considerably. The water smoothens in quietude; its waves tousle the surface of the river, hiding the rage in its undercurrent. Only when the river meets the Bhot Nullah in Gulabgarh does it regain its fury. Bhot Nullah or the

Buddhist River rises high in the Paddar hills and flows downstream, majestically cresting over the large boulders and rocky ledges. The nullah travels about 25 km southwest and comingles with the Chenab at the right bank.

The Paddar Valley opens up like a bowl, with the twin towns of Gulabgarh and Atholi, located on plateaus, flanking the river. The high mountains surrounding the valley overlook the local dwellings sitting amidst terraced patches of cultivated land, government buildings and religious places.

After consolidating his rule over Paddar, Chattar Singh constructed an imposing fort on an elevated piece of land, on the right bank of the Chenab. Soon, a small inhabitation called Chattragarh sprouted around the fort. At the behest of the Chamba kingdom, Ratnu Thakur was installed as the first governor of Paddar. Chattar Singh would visit the place in the summer with his entourage of palanquins and horses, treading through the Pangi Valley on a track alongside the Chenab.

Ratnu Thakur ruled with an iron fist and would ruthlessly quell any internecine strife. He had earmarked a deodar tree not far from his fort, which was used for hanging the conspirators against Chamba rule. With each hanging, a branch of the tree was cut and tossed into the Chenab. The record of the executed was kept by carving a line on a rock near the tree.

As the Dogra rule consolidated in Jammu, Zorawar Singh wrested Paddar from Chamba. He destroyed Chattragarh and built his own fort on the ruins of the earlier fort and named it after his master, Gulab Singh, the raja of Jammu – Gulabgarh. Some ruins of the fort are still found in Gulabgarh. At a distance from the ruins, a deodar tree stands stoically, bearing witness to history. There are eleven lines engraved on the rock next to the tree.

Gulabgarh has a predominantly Buddhist population, peacefully coexisting with Hindus and Muslims. A majestic gompa sits on a tableland amongst the Buddhist houses with prayer flags fluttering on their roofs. The gompa was inaugurated by His Holiness the

Dalai Lama in 2012, becoming the only monastery in Paddar visited by the spiritual head of the Buddhists. On one side of the gompa, the Chenab gushes by, its roar finding a perfect sync with the chants from the gompa. On the other side, the lofty deodars embellish the idyllic surroundings. Inside the complex, there are three prayer wheels shaded by a canopy. One of the attractions of the gompa is a tree that was planted by Dalai Lama during the inauguration.

Apart from an occasional aberration, the three communities have always lived in peace. In 2012, an unfortunate incident of unrequited love marred this harmonious existence. Apparently, a local Muslim youth had been smitten by a Buddhist girl and had been constantly pursuing her. The girl did not respond to his advances and always ignored him. That fateful day, on the bridge over the Chenab, the boy waylaid the girl and proposed marriage to her. As always, the girl walked away haughtily. He followed her, asked the question thrice and warned the girl that he would jump into the river if she didn't concede. Not getting any response, he climbed up the railing of the bridge and jumped into the river to embrace his watery grave. The incident has been long forgotten, the girl being happily married now, yet it left an indelible scar behind.

As in Lahaul and Pangi, winter is a curse for the people of Paddar. The folklore of 'Old Snow Lady' or 'Hyuna Bwadhi' has been woven around this fact. In Paddari language, *hyun* is snow and *bwadhi* is an old woman. As per the story, at the onset of winter, an old crone descends from her perch in the glacier and appears on the bank of the Chenab. She takes a bath and vanishes into the river and does not emerge till the winter lasts. No one knows from where the snow lady comes and where she goes ... Some believe that she resides in a place below Luj, a small hamlet on the border of Pangi and Paddar. Since the villagers are wary about the snow lady, nobody ventures to those parts.[30]

The people of Paddar believe that Hyuna Bwadhi is an evil spirit that portents misfortune. They equate her with winter's timelessness.

On her dreaded arrival, they refrain from stepping out of their homes. Instead, they huddle around a fire of oak wood, locally called *hiru*, which burns in the master room.

Self-sufficiency has been a hallmark of the people of Paddar as they make their own homes, weave grass beds, knit their woollens – tunics, trousers and caps that cover heads and ears, locally called *kantop* – and make shoes of local grass called *polle*. However, after the arrival of Hyuna Bwadhi, a lingering lethargy creeps into them. They don't even go out to collect firewood and even stop bathing. In order to shake off this unhygienic existence, the families destroy all traces of shoes, dirty clothes, lice-infested material, rotten flour and wood ashes. The male members of the household step out to hurl away the accumulated filth, hoping to ward off the nefarious influence of the Old Snow Lady. While doing this, they recite the songs passed on for ages:

Ghe Hyuna, Ay Barshal,
Dhoon daben, fwal barge,
Lag-chag, ghar apan bag,
Ghe kuyo aze baithyo,
Ghe dhamio, aze kamio,
Ghe chaario aze dudhario.

[Go winters, come summers,
Smoke fades, flowers bloom,
Take to your fields all the rituals and traditions,
Go girls, come daughters-in-law,
Go invited ones, come active ones,
Go buttermilk, come milkmen.]

After the ritual of discarding the filth, the men go back to their houses and knock on the door of the master room. The rest of the family refuses to open the door, leading to another delightful, poetic conversation.

Khol darwaza.
Kon beer?
Mahaveer.
Kyun aaya, kahan se aaya?
Ghar Lanka se aaya.
Kya kya laya?
Heere, moti daal, jowhar, yeh sab laya,
Patya tlak tlak.

[Open the door.
Who is there?
Great man.
Why and from where have you come?
I have come from Lanka.
What have you come with?
Diamonds, pearls, pulses and grain – all this I have brought.
Sound of bird.]

At the end of the winter, the Old Snow Lady emerges from the Chenab. The men carry her in a palanquin towards the mountain summit. Enroute, she and the palanquin bearers feast on goat meat. The ritual has been passed on for generations and so has the lore of the Old Snow Lady. Some people also believe that she has mystical powers just like snow, which helps to nurture the fields and replenish the river. They also say the wrinkles on her face are the shrinking glaciers, hinting towards imminent climate change.

Along with the legends of despair, there are songs of vivacity and joy about a place endowed with abundant natural wealth, as showcased in the following Paddari song:

Mashore, Paddar purana ho goochi, kala zeera, and ganay jungle, lathy neelam khan ho!

[The famous Paddar Valley is old. Here you find the Morchella mushrooms, caraway, thick forests and sapphire.]

4

Napoleon of the East

The Chenab Valley has a chequered political history of ambition, valour and betrayal. In consonance with the roar of the river, numerous vignettes of bravery echo alongside. On the political battlefield, many valiant sons not only defended their motherland but also transcended physical and mental barriers to carry the victory flag to unimaginable territories, paving the way for the present map of Jammu and Kashmir and India.

Gulab Singh, the architect of the modern state of Jammu and Kashmir, was a strapping young man. He, along with his two brothers – Dhian Singh and Suchet Singh – who belonged to a junior line of the ruling family of Jammu, would go on to make history. The Jammu estate was on a decline after the death of Ranjit Dev, the most prominent king of Jammu. The younger brother of Ranjit Dev was the great grandfather of the Dogra brothers. Their grandfather and father had held small *jagir*s in the Jammu estate. This was the time when the Mughal Empire was crumbling and the Sikh *misl*s or sovereign states were at a constant war with one another. Their territorial ambition included the hilly principalities of Himachal and Jammu. In 1808, a sixteen-year-old Gulab Singh fought against Sikh invaders and earned a lot of fame for his bravery and military prowess.

As per the folklore, once on his way to Akhnoor – a small town about 20 miles east of Jammu, on the banks of the Chenab – Gulab

Singh was transporting jaggery and rice on a camel. Midway, he decided to stop over for the night at Sui, in the hut of a sage named Baba Prem Dev. The sage belonged to Rajasthan and, after a pilgrimage to the Amaranth shrine in Kashmir, had settled in Jammu. Initially, he stayed in Surinsar, about 30 miles from Jammu. This place is surrounded by low forested mountains and has a big lake in the middle. The Hindus believe that Arjun, one of the Pandava brothers, had shot an arrow in the ground in Mansar and the arrow had emerged 10 miles away. At both places, springs of water gushed out, becoming the sources of the sister lakes, Mansar and Surinsar.

Gulab Singh first met Baba Prem Dev at Surinsar. By reading the furrows on Gulab Singh's forehead, Baba predicted that he was destined for great things in life. At that point, he advised Gulab Singh to join some king's army to display his talent as a soldier.

That night in Sui, Gulab Singh had a dream that he narrated to Baba the next day. In the dream, he was leading a large army towards Pir Panjal to conquer the Kashmir Valley. Baba reminded him of his Surinsar prophecy and once again urged him to join some king's army. His command was, 'Don't show your face to me unless you achieve some dignified status in life.'

Gulab Singh accepted his calling and appeared in Maharaja Ranjit Singh's court in Lahore. He started as a trooper in the Sikh cavalry and was posted near Sialkot. He proved his mettle and rapidly ascended to higher military positions, becoming cavalry commander. By the early nineteenth century, the Lahore durbar had gained control over all principalities in the hills, including that of Chamba, Jammu and Rajouri. Gulab Singh played a significant role in these victories. By 1812, Jammu was completely annexed and Ranjit Singh bestowed the estate on his son Kharak Singh.

By this time, Gulab Singh's brothers had also joined the Lahore durbar. Dhian Singh, who had caught the eye of Ranjit Singh, was made officer of royal *deodhi* or the doorkeeper who got the power of extending or denying access to the Maharaja. Soon, he became the prime minister and wielded unlimited influence and power. The third Dogra brother, Suchet Singh, was appointed as a conveyer of petitions.

Impressed by the loyalty and competence of the Dogra brothers, the Maharaja kept bestowing jagirs on them, and by 1820 they, held considerable estate. In 1822, Gulab Singh was finally recognized as the raja of Jammu. By the same decree, Suchet Singh was conferred the estates of Samba and Ramnagar, whereas Dhian Singh was made the raja of Bhimber and Poonch. Dhian Singh would remain prime minister for twenty-five years, serving four more Sikh kings after Ranjit Singh.

Baba Prem Dev's prediction had come true. Ranjit Singh personally travelled to Akhnoor for the coronation of Gulab Singh at Jio Pota on the right bank of the Chenab. The place has been named after a tree, Jia Pota – whose botanical name is *Putranji varoxburghhi* – under whose shade Ranjit Singh, in a colourful ceremony, applied a saffron paste on the forehead of Gulab Singh to formally install him as the raja of Jammu. The event is important in history because it was the first step toward the foundation of the modern state of Jammu and Kashmir.

While the younger Dogra brothers continued to stay at Lahore court, paying constant attendance upon the Maharaja, Gulab Singh shifted to Jammu, from where he administered his estate and other jagirs of the family, extending from Ravi to Jhelum.

Ever since Kharak Singh was bestowed the estate of Jammu, the rule of indigenous dynasties came to an end, which was resented by the local people. Some rebellious groups rose in revolt, and the most prominent and long-lasting resistance came from a young Rajput named Mian Dido. Born in Jagti village on the outskirts of Jammu, Dido was trained in sword fighting and archery from childhood, excelling in both.

Mian Dido tried to unite Jammu against the hegemony of Lahore durbar. He left home and raised a private militia of locals, training them in guerrilla warfare. In order to equip and sustain his band of fighters, Dido started to indulge in highway robberies. He continued to defy the Sikhs, and his action against the revenue officials frustrated Kharak Singh as the tax collection had dwindled abysmally. His lightning attacks on Sikh garrisons during the night hours instilled tremendous fear in the army.

The news of Dido's popular rebellion reached Lahore.

Ranjit Singh was further infuriated when he learnt about Mian Dido's falcon. It was identical to his own favourite raptor – a majestic white falcon. A falcon symbolized authority and liberty, which Maharaja thought was the sole prerogative of the royalty. He decided to reach out to Dido and dispatched a team to bring his falcon. Mian Dido welcomed the emissaries but unexpectedly launched an attack on them, killing ten members and injuring others. Dido became a major irritant in Lahore durbar, and despite earnest efforts to capture him, he remained elusive.

Mian Dido was hard to catch because of the support he got from the locals, who would never divulge the details of his whereabouts. His Robin Hood-like image gained credence when he started to act against moneylenders, feudal lords and dowry seekers. He would loot the caravans of the rich and feed the poor and needy. Mian Dido protected the local women who often fell victim to the prurient gaze of Sikh soldiers.

Jurah Langeh, who had fought alongside Mian Dido in his heyday, was living a retired life in Bhalwal, on the outskirts of Jammu. When the local Sikh commander Champa Singh came to know about the beauty of Langeh's daughter, he desired to marry her. Not only was there a huge age gap between the two, but the community also looked down upon inter-religion marriages. The anguished father, accompanied by community members sought help from Mian Dido. Enraged, Dido asked Jurah Langeh to accept the proposal; thus he hatched a plan. On the day of marriage, Champa Singh, along with the wedding procession, waited in the vicinity of Bhalwal, drinking and merrymaking. Meanwhile, Dido, along with a team of his daredevil warriors, reached the village playing drums and cymbals, masquerading as relatives of the bride. In no time, they attacked the unguarded Champa Singh and killed him, along with most of his entourage. Later, Jurah Langeh was summoned to Jammu durbar and an order for his execution was issued.

The aggression of the Sikhs kindled more fire in the rebellions of Mian Dido. Once, he intercepted baskets of flowers, pashmina, apples and dry fruits being sent to the Lahore durbar from Kashmir and replaced the gifts with cow dung and filth.

The antics of Mian Dido had become a major nuisance, and Ranjit Singh resolved to quell this rebellion. With great perspicacity, he contemplated that only a Dogra could liquidate Mian Dido. And as per some historians, this was how the Jammu estate was conferred on the Dogra brothers in 1820, which is also evident in the deed of grant:

> The taluka of Jammu is granted to Mians (Kishore Singh and his three sons), the devoted servants of Sarkar (Maharaja Ranjit Singh) on the condition that they owe four hundred cavalrymen to the Sarkar and hold themselves in readiness for rendering suitable services whenever called upon to do so. They must guard the route to Kashmir used by the caravans of pashmina traders. They must either arrest or handover Mian Dido, kill him or drive him beyond the Sutlej.

Gulab Singh pursued Mian Dido with a judicious mix of offensive campaign and diplomacy. He even tried to make him surrender with a promise of a high position in his durbar. Dido outrightly refused such incentives and chose to continue fighting for the freedom of his people. Gulab Singh won over some of his close confidants to isolate Dido in the Trikuta Hills.

A contingent led by Attar Singh was dispatched to Dido's house in Jagti, where his ninety-year-old father was present. Before the old man could draw his sword from the sheath, Attar Singh killed him and dismembered his corpse. He allegedly hanged the remains on the walls. When this pursuit reached Trikuta Hills, Mian Dido killed Attar Singh in a duel and took his revenge. After chopping his enemy into two pieces, Mian Dido haughtily trudged up the hill with his bloodied sword and squatted there to casually puff into his hookah. The enemy stood in his view, no one daring to move forward. Suddenly, a bullet from the matchlock of a Sikh soldier pierced the neck of Mian Dido, ending the most courageous rebellion against the mighty Sikh Empire.

Gulab Singh was anguished at the death of Mian Dido, whom he secretly admired for his valour. He adopted both sons of Mian Dido and raised them as his own children. Mian Dido, throughout his life, fought for the freedom of Jammu and deeply despised the Sikh dominance. In Dogra history, he is extolled as a hero, an intrepid warrior, a freedom fighter, a man of dignity and messiah of the poor. The tales of his courage and dare devilry have been extolled across generations in the form of ballads.

Hazara Singh Mian de kaar, Dido jamaya
Jamaya o bada e puyada
O pehli sattan Domana lootya, dooji baari jayi lootya Phillora
Teriyan khabran gayian takth Lahoray
Mian Dido diyan khabran gayian takth Lahoray.

[In the house of Hazara Singh Mian, Dido was born.
He was born naughty,
on the first occasion he looted Domana, and on the second, he looted Phillora.
His news reached the throne of Lahore,
Mian Dido's news reached the throne of Lahore.]

Such ballads eulogize the military campaign of Mian Dido and his love for freedom.

Samne khadoi Mian Dido lalkara je ditta
Beriya chodi de, sadi Kandi chodi de

Apne Manjhe da mulk sambhal
Apne Lahoray da mulk sambhal
Pagdi talwar Mian Dido halle je kitta
Badi badi mundiyan beri dian tange garne naal
Ladkan bal garne naal, hath nahin aunda nahi Dido Jamwal

[Mian Dido stands proud throwing the challenge,
Strangers leave, leave our Kandi* land
Go back and mind your country, Manjha
Go back and mind your country, Lahore
Mian Dido straightened his turban, attacked the enemy with a sword,
The heads of strangers dangled from garna† trees
Dido Jamwal was not easy to capture.]

With his administrative acumen and shrewdness, Gulab Singh was able to keep the British, Russians and Sikhs all in good humour. The ambitious king found his perfect soldier in General Zorawar Singh. Together, they made a formidable team that expanded the territories of Jammu to the inhospitable Himalayan highlands, where no Indian king had earlier dared to venture.

Zorawar Singh was born in 1786 in Ansar village of Bilaspur, presently located in the state of Himachal Pradesh. A brave and reckless boy, he was brought up in a traditional Rajput society of immense martial spirit. At the age of sixteen, he killed his uncle over a property dispute and escaped to Haridwar. Here, he came in contact with the raja of Galian and Marmati – a small estate in Doda of Jammu and Kashmir – who had abdicated the throne in favour of his son Fateh Singh. At the insistence of the erstwhile king, Zorawar enrolled in Fateh Singh's army and mastered the skills of swordsmanship, riding and archery.[31]

---

* Kandi is the non-cultivable, arid land of Jammu

† A local plant grown in the arid region of Jammu, which bears a wild fruit. It is locally called *karonda* and its scientific name is *Carissa carandas*.

Once, on pilgrimage to Sarthal Mata, Mian Dido camped in Khilani, a small village on the bank of the Chenab.[32] Offering his hospitality, Fateh Singh sent Zorawar Singh to the service of Dido. In a nearby village, a religious congregation was underway. In the night, the crescendo of prayers accompanied with drums and cymbals reached Dido's camp. Recalling his experience of killing Champa Singh, Dido thought it was a ploy by Fateh Singh to get him killed. He ordered his men to plunder and burn down the village. Fateh Singh got livid; he summoned Zorawar Singh and reprimanded him, calling him a coward to have done nothing to stop Dido's men. Being called a coward was an insult hard to swallow for Zorawar Singh. He quit his job and left Marmati.

After whiling away his time, he reached Lahore, where he enrolled in Ranjit Singh's army.

At Multan garrison, one day, he was caught smoking a chillum with his cronies. This was strongly objected to by the Sikh commander of his unit and he abused Zorawar with the filthiest of invectives. His pride wounded, Zorawar Singh, with one blow of his sword, killed the Sikh officer. After the murder, he fled the garrison with two companions. He stayed in obscurity for a few months before joining the army of the Kangra kingdom. At that time, Kangra was resisting the attempts of subjugation by the Sikhs. In one such battle, Zorawar Singh was captured and jailed in a fort near Kangra. But he was not the one who would be incarcerated for long. One night, he got rid of his chains and jumped into the Beas, which flowed below the fort wall. With the support of a log, he swam for many miles and made good his escape.

Intrepid and proud, Zorawar Singh had failed to adapt to the regimented life of garrisons. However, his moment in the sun was about to arrive – he would go on to make a formidable partnership with Gulab Singh.

Zorawar Singh had his first formal meeting with Gulab Singh on the bank of the river Tawi.[33] The story goes that Gulab Singh jocularly mentioned about a deserter, who had fled from the battle scene. He wished to know Zorawar's perspective on the situation.

'Time will reveal what I can do in the time of crisis,' Zorawar Singh humbly replied. A pleased Gulab Singh inducted him in his service and he was immediately dispatched to Reasi.

After the jagir of Reasi was bestowed on the Dogras, its dispossessed chief Mian Diwan started attacking the troops frequently. In order to take a strong hold on the town, Zorawar Singh decided to rebuild the Bhimgarh Fort, which was in dilapidated state. Mian Diwan continued to make attacks to scuttle the ongoing construction. Zorawar Singh was able to quell these rebellions and he rose to the rank of commandant.

Taking charge of the garrison, Zorawar Singh detected huge misappropriation in the rations being supplied to the troops. He was able to cut down the pilferage and saved at least 1 lakh in a year. Impressed, Gulab Singh made him the commissariat officer of all the forts lying to the north of Jammu. Zorawar Singh regulated the supplies in these forts, filling coffers of the Dogra treasury. Now Zorawar Singh's loyalty to the Dogras was so profound that he would claim that Kahlur was his birthplace only in name, and that his real home was Jammu.

In subsequent years, Zorawar Singh went on to subjugate the hilly principalities lying in the vicinity of Gulab Singh's fiefdom between the Chenab and the Jhelum, which were directly ruled by Muslim chieftains. In 1823, he was made the governor of Kishtwar, Reasi and Arnas, practically controlling the whole of Chenab Valley. He was given the power to levy taxes and carry out military campaigns. He undertook a number of revenue and judicial reforms and streamlined the administration. All the hill forts were repaired and reinforced with supplies. Many young, able-bodied men were enrolled in the army and were imparted training in higher reaches, specializing in mountain warfare. With Kishtwar as his springboard, Zorawar Singh set his eyes on Ladakh. In 1834, the Dogra army marched through the rugged highlands, scores of glaciers and frozen rivulets before entering the Zanskar Valley. Subjugating the timid resistance on their way, the

Dogras reached the Suru Valley, where they camped for months. Zorawar Singh established a fort in Suru and installed a garrison. He stopped the standard practice of destroying the standing crop, for which he earned appreciation from the local peasantry and landlords.

The Dogra army was now all set to march towards Leh – the capital of Ladakh – where its Gyalpo, or the ruler, Tsepal Namgyal, hoped to find help from the East India Company. By sheer coincidence, a Scottish traveller, Dr Henderson, happened to be visiting Leh at this crucial juncture. The Gyalpo detained Henderson and his fortuitous presence was used to create a smokescreen: that he was the British envoy of East India Company, who was to ensure military support to Ladakh. Unaware of the Gyalpo's ingenious bluff, Zorawar Singh halted his advance.[34]

Gulab Singh had a tacit understanding with the British through the Lahore durbar. Before the further advance of Dogra army, the political agent of the British in Ludhiana reaffirmed that they had no interest in Ladakh and Dr Henderson was an ordinary adventurer. After his sham was exposed, Tsepal Namgyal tried to negotiate a truce through his ministers. Initially, the Gyalpo agreed to pay Rs 15,000 annually to the Raja of Jammu, but later went back on the promise. In fact, when Zorawar Singh sent his team to collect the tribute, the collectors were brutally killed. The Gyalpo carried out fresh rounds of conscription and consolidated his army for the impending battle. The stalemate continued for the next few months, and Zorawar Singh had to retreat to Suru where he waited for the winters to pass.[35]

Finally, in the spring of 1836, Zorawar Singh started his advance towards Leh. The Gyalpo once again tried to buy peace. He met Zorawar Singh at Bazgo and agreed to pay an annual tribute of Rs 20,000. Zorawar Singh, along with a hundred of his troops, entered Leh, where he stayed as the Gyalpo's guest for four months. The whole of Ladakh kingdom was restored to the Gyalpo, but he was henceforth to be considered as a vassal of the Jammu durbar.

Zorawar Singh seated his representative in the Leh court and started to withdraw to Kishtwar. However, the rebellions began immediately after his retreat. The Suru Fort was captured by the rebels, and the whole Dogra garrison was put to sword. Zorawar Singh retaliated brutally, hanging or beheading hundreds of rebels. At this onslaught, the local landlords once again submitted to Dogra suzerainty.

After Zorawar Singh's return, insurrections broke out in Leh. Tsepal Namgyal imprisoned the Dogra representative and refused to pay the annual tribute. He also closed the pashmina trade with Kashmir, an action deeply resented by the Jammu durbar. Namgyal did not expect retaliation from Zorawar Singh any time soon. The cruel winter had set in and most of the passes were closed due to snow. But the Gyalpo did not know that Zorawar Singh was made of different mettle. In a swift reaction, the Dogra general reached Zanskar and intended to use the shortest route to Leh. But there was lack of reliable guides who could help the troops navigate through the treacherous route.

Finally, a local named Midphi Sata offered his services, and Zorawar Singh presented him with a pair of golden bracelets, besides the promise of a jagir in Zanskar. With 11 kg wheat and a bag of gram on each horse, in ten days, the Dogra army stood on the banks of the Indus with neighing horses and glittering swords. The Gyalpo was taken by surprise and as he was not in a position to defend his kingdom; he once again begged for forgiveness. Zorawar Singh was in no mood to relent this time, and imposed stringent conditions on the beleaguered opponent. He levied additional indemnities and also confiscated the personal belongings of the princesses along with tea, wool, and gold and silver utensils. He deposed Tsepal Namgyal, as he had not been trustworthy, and installed his minister Ngorub Stanzin as the new Gyalpo. Then he built a fort in Leh and stationed his troops there. On his return to Kishtwar, Zorawar Singh brought along some prominent Ladakhis, including the son of the new king, in order to ensure his loyalty.

Due to the distances and climate, these turned out to be unstable political arrangements with the Himalayan fiefdoms. The rebellions started to get afoot again, and by the end of 1838, the Dogra soldiers were massacred, and their garrisons uprooted in most of Ladakh. Encouraged by the uprising of Ladakhis another revolt erupted, this time much nearer to Kishtwar in Paddar. Ratnu Thakur, the caretaker of Paddar, instigated the people and seized the unsuspecting Dogra soldiers in Chattragarh. Some of them were taken prisoners and others were sent to Chamba.

On his return from the Ladakh campaign, Zorawar Singh led a strong army and reached Chattragarh. Anticipating a defeat, Ratnu Thakur halted the foe's advance by demolishing the bridge over the Chenab. The frustrated army had to wait on the banks of the swollen river for three months. Undeterred, Zorawar Singh, with the help of locals, constructed a ropeway bridge over Bhot Nullah and led a furious attack on Chattragarh. Ratnu Thakur was captured and sent to Jammu, where he was imprisoned for four years. Chattragarh was set on fire, and many rebels were executed or disfigured. The Gulabgarh Fort was constructed and Dogra troops were stationed there. Paddar became a part of the Dogra estate, overthrowing the Chamba rule.

After sorting out Paddar, Zorawar Singh made his third expedition to Ladakh in the spring of 1839. Once again, he took the direct route to Leh through Zanskar. Ngorub Stanzin, the Gyalpo, fled to Lahaul, from where he was captured and brought back. Tsepal Namgyal was once again enthroned in Leh, and the annual tribute was raised to Rs 23,000.

In 1840, Ngorub Stanzin, in collaboration with local chieftains, which included the Muslim ruler of Baltistan, conspired to oust Tsepal Namgyal. Zorawar Singh got a whiff of this conspiracy and rushed to Leh with a strong force. He got Ngorub Stanzin and few others arrested and shifted them to Jammu. He thrust a pension on Tsepal Namgyal and let him retain the Leh palace, while installing one of his own trusted men to manage the affairs of Ladakh. In this manner, Ladakh became part of the Jammu kingdom through the military brilliance and political manoeuvring of Zorawar Singh.

After consolidating his control over Ladakh, Zorawar Singh now turned his attention to Baltistan, a predominantly Muslim principality. He had chosen the right moment due to the fratricidal struggle in Baltistan, the engagement of the British in the Afghan wars and the death of Ranjit Singh in 1839. He strengthened his army by enrolling Ladakhi and Balti soldiers, and even included the deposed Tsepal Namgyal in his expedition. On seeing Dogra troops approach, the Baltis dismantled the only bridge over the Indus, leaving the troops stranded on the riverbank. After many days of fighting hunger during the day and frostbite at night, an ice bridge was made with the help of the local Dard tribe. Without much resistance by the Baltis, the Iskardu Fort was strategically overpowered by the Dogras.

Encouraged by his resounding victories, in the spring of 1841, Zorawar Singh decided to undertake his most ambitious task of conquering western Tibet, the highest plateau in the world. This conquest became necessary because, historically, western Tibet was part of Ladakh kingdom, and its occupation was necessary to defend Ladakh and Kashmir. Zorawar Singh raised a strong army of about 10,000 men, which included Baltis and Ladakhis. Most of the Dogra soldiers carried matchlocks, swords, shields and small artillery guns, whereas the locals were mostly used as porters.

In a three-pronged strategy, Zorawar Singh led the largest column from the south of Pangong Lake and, without encountering much resistance, entered Gartok, the district headquarters of western Tibet. Gartok had already been abandoned by its inhabitants on being alerted about the advance of the Dogras. Soon after, two other columns joined Zorawar Singh's army and marched on the old caravan route between Ladakh and Lhasa. After a mixed resistance, Zorawar Singh finally reached Taklakot or The Tiger Castle, where he stationed his troops.

From Taklakot, Zorawar Singh proceeded for a pilgrimage to Mansarovar Lake and Mount Kailash, considered the most sacred sites of Hindus, Bons, Buddhists and Jains. Hindus believe that

Kailash is the abode of Lord Shiva, who tamed the river Ganga at this spot, forcing her to flow below the Himalayas to nourish the Indian plains. At the foreground of Mount Kailash lies the crystal blue, freshwater lake of Mansarovar with a circumference of 54 miles and an identical saltwater lake of Rakshastal. These lakes are sources of the greatest rivers of the subcontinent: The Brahmaputra, Indus and Sutlej, as well as Karnali, a major tributary of the Ganga.

Zorawar Singh took a dip in the lake and performed the customary circumambulation. Some historians say that the main purpose of Zorawar Singh's western Tibet campaign was to annex these most sacrosanct Hindu sites and include them in the Jammu kingdom. Some others opine that western Tibet had gold mines and rich monasteries; therefore, this adventure was purely to acquire wealth. Tibet was also important to control the highly lucrative Pashmina trade via Ladakh to Kashmir. Notwithstanding the motive, the conquest of these Himalayan territories was a great military achievement of General Zorawar Singh who earned the title of Napoleon of the East. And much like the French conqueror, he was about to meet his Waterloo.

After the pilgrimage, Zorawar Singh remained engaged in consolidating his hold on the newly acquired territories and set his eyes on Lhasa. The Dogra army's plan alarmed China. To thwart its advance, a strong Sino-Tibetan army was raised. After getting the information of the arrival of a formidable Tibetan army, Zorawar Singh opened peace negotiations. He promised to withdraw on the condition of acceptance of Dogra suzerainty and annual tribute. However, Tibetans were in no mood to pay any indemnity. The two armies were on the anvil of a deadly battle at the icy heights.

In the following weeks, the Tibetan army moved forward with considerable gains, freeing the positions held by the Dogras, including Taklakot. The beleaguered Dogra army was increasingly facing the shortage of food and wood fuel. With the closure of the passes and intense cold, there was no scope of reinforcements. Much like Napoleon's failed Russian attack in 1812, the bitter winter played a role here too. The Dogra soldiers started perishing due to starvation, frostbite and freezing wind. Many lost their fingers and toes. Desperate, they started to burn the wooden parts of their machetes to keep themselves warm. Finally, the Tibetans seized Chi-Tang, where the Dogras had built a strong stone fort. Zorawar Singh tried to reach this fort, but the Tibetans blocked all the approach routes. The Tibetans and the Chinese regrouped and met the Dogra army in the battle of To-Yo. On 12 December 1841, a gunshot in the right shoulder severely wounded Zorawar Singh. He kept fighting with a sword till a Tibetan horseman thrust a lance in his chest, ending one of the greatest sagas in military history. After Zorawar Singh was killed, his army fell into disarray. Most of the fleeing soldiers were pursued, killed or captured. A large number of Baltis and Ladakhis surrendered and were taken to Lhasa.

The valiant Dogra general, till his last breath, faithfully served his master and achieved eternity. In the Dogra history, Zorawar Singh has become an epitome of ambition, bravery and loyalty. He is credited with the expansion of the estate of Jammu and Kashmir to touch the boundaries of China and Central Asia, paving way for the present map of India. However, in political history, one land's hero can be a villain for the people he vanquished. From the perspective of the Ladakhis, Zorawar Singh's conquest was seen as a tragic chapter in the history of Ladakh. Their anguish festers till date. In winter, a day is earmarked to remember their tormentor in an attempt to rekindle the memories of his alleged atrocities. Men, women and children in identical tunics and hats assemble in the polo ground Leh to witness an absurd ritual. In a rather macabre tradition, a series of hollow horns filled with animal blood are suspended on wooden poles. The ritual, known as 'Apo Garam Singh', indirectly hints at hot-blooded Zorawar Singh. A party of Indo-Tibetan Border Police shoots at the dangling horns and blood oozes out. Amidst great exhilaration, the people rise in joy for having symbolically vanquished the general, exulting over his end at the hands of the Tibetans in the battle of To-Yo.

5

The Land of Sapphire

The high mountains of the Zanskar range north of Paddar are rich with sapphire reserves. *Sapphire* is a Greek word for 'blue', and is locally known as *neelam*. Sapphires are cherished gemstones and are found in green, yellow, pink, black and blue colours. The intense cornflower blue is the most coveted hue of the mineral corundum.

From time immemorial, sapphire has been attributed virtues beneficial to mankind. This stone has been used for healing purposes, magic, astrological prognostication and occult powers. Arabian kings were known to wear sapphires to protect themselves from envy and physical injury. The early sailors, who navigated the oceans, believed that sapphires would protect them from perishing at the sea. In medieval times, crusaders, travellers and other peripatetic men used sapphires for the test of fidelity on their partners – it was thought to change colour if worn by promiscuous and unfaithful women.[36]

Sapphires have held a significant place in religion. In ancient times, it was decreed that every cardinal must wear a sapphire ring, since it suppressed libido and promoted chastity. Moses wrote the Ten Commandments on tablets of sapphire so strong that a hammer swung against them would be smashed to smithereens. According to ancient Persians, the Earth was balanced on a giant sapphire, and its reflection shimmered in the colour of the heavens, along with the shining light of rubies and emeralds. Buddhists consider sapphires as stones of wisdom and serenity. They believe that the gem facilitates devotion to prayer and meditation.

In India, sapphire has been venerated since ancient times. The earliest Sanskrit texts ranked sapphires, along with rubies and diamonds, in the category of maharatni, or the great gems. The blue sapphire was referred to in the Sanskrit texts as Neelmani, and was further classified into Indranila and Mahanila – the former being rarer and more precious than the latter, including within it, the impurity of darker hues.[37]

For ages, India has been famous for various gemstones. The story of the world's largest cut diamond, Kohinoor, or 'The Mountain of Light', is legendary. Exchanging numerous hands, from the Mughals to Nadir Shah, Maharaja Ranjit Singh and Gulab Singh, it finally became a part of the crown jewels of the British. Sieved through alluvial sands, the diamond has a long saga of blood, romance and intrigue associated with it. In their book *Koh-I-Noor: The History of the World's Most Infamous Diamond* (2017), Anita Anand and William Dalrymple work their way through more than four centuries of Indian history to trace the truth about the diamond. Today, the diamond is safely embedded in the crown of the King of England, but it doesn't deter India, Pakistan and even the Taliban of Afghanistan from laying claim to the precious stone.

The Indian royalty's obsession with the gemstones has gripped many maharajas, nawabs, aristocracy and kingdoms. According to Rudyard Kipling, providence created the maharajas simply to offer mankind a spectacle. And what a spectacle it was! Sport and sex were their preferred pastimes, but jewels were their passion.[38] The Maharaja of Baroda had his court tunic spun of gold, with only one family in his state allowed to weave its threads. The family's fingernails were grown long and then notched like the teeth of a comb, all the better to caress the golden threads to perfection. Among his most precious treasures were a collection of tapestries made entirely of pearls, woven with ornate designs of rubies and emeralds.[39]

Somewhere in the Jaigarh Fort, the private treasure of Jaipur royalty lay buried.[40] Once in a lifetime, each maharaja was allowed to visit the treasury and select a single item. Man Singh chose from the treasury a bird of solid gold, studded with rubies of extraordinary fire, so heavy that a woman could hardly lift it. Jai Singh, the last king of the Jaipur House, did not get a chance to visit the treasury. Despite his exclusion, his jewels included a triple-stringed necklace of red spinels – the stones having been contributed by various Mughal emperors, each bigger than a pigeon's egg – along with three huge emeralds.

In his large kingdom, the Nizam of Hyderabad lorded over Golconda, famous for its diamond mines. The pearl collection of the seventh Nizam, Osman Ali, was said to be so vast that it alone could cover the sidewalks of Piccadilly Circus, London. His wealth included two lemon sized diamonds of over 180 carats each, of which one was used as a paperweight. Despite his riches, it is said that the Nizam was considered as the world's biggest miser. Visitors to his palace would be presented with only one cup of tea, one biscuit and one cigarette. After they left, the Nizam would drink any remaining tea, eat the crumbs of the biscuit and smoke the cigarette butts to the end.

There was also a prince of Mysore who was told by a Chinese sage that the finest aphrodisiacs contained crushed diamonds. The prince went on to deplete the state treasury in the quest for potency.

The Maharaja of Patiala, who was known for his love for sexual orgies, cricket and polo, possessed a breastplate containing 1,001 diamonds.[41] Until the twentieth century, it was the custom for him to appear once a year before his subjects, wearing nothing but the diamond-encrusted breastplate, complemented by his sexual sceptre, in regal erection.

India not only had a rich deposit of minerals but also developed the techniques to extract them. The export of precious and semi-precious gemstones like pearls, beryl, diamonds and carnelians to other civilizations has been well documented over the period of history. While the land of subcontinent bears many a mineral and pearl, one gemstone – widely considered as the epitome of love, trust and fidelity – is of particular interest. The belief was further validated when it was gifted to Princess Diana by Prince Charles on their wedding. Worshipped across many civilizations and a prized possession for all, the blue sapphire is not only a treasure to behold but also has much cultural and historical significance. Also referred to as the Himalayan Motherlode, this rich, pristine and beautiful stone is peerless.[42]

In Indian culture, gemstones are said to influence the cosmos and, therefore, are central to astrology. Indian astrology is primarily concerned with the Sun, Moon, five visible planets, two lunar nodes of Rahu and Ketu, and their positions in one's horoscope. It is believed that these 'planets', as they are collectively called, impact our lives on many levels and contribute to our mental, physical, material and spiritual well-being. Each of these planets emits coloured rays of light – Saturn emits blue light, and sapphire is associated with it.

The stone and the planet need to be in consonance so that the right energy is transmitted to the wearer of the stone. Because gemstones have the ability to absorb, reflect and radiate different frequencies of light, they can be used to correct or amplify planetary influences. Consequently, as per Vedic astrology, wearing blue sapphire is seen to remove hurdles from one's life. It is widely believed that the sapphire doesn't suit everyone and thus, should be used only after careful study and deliberation.

The trail to the sapphire mines in Paddar is an arduous journey that zigzags up the hills, crossing over the Chenab and Bhot Nullah. One has to negotiate a precarious rope bridge over the Bhot Nullah flowing in a narrow canyon underneath, to access the other side of the valley. Zorawar Singh had followed the same route for his excursions into Ladakh. Today, this beaten track turns vibrant during the annual yatra to the temple of Chandi Mata situated in the upstream village of Machail.

One of the holy trinity, Maa Chandi, locally known as Machail, Mata is the most revered in the region. The origin of the shrine is shrouded in obscurity, there being no recorded history about the structure. According to a popular myth, the Goddess is *swayambhu* or self-manifested. She first appeared in Mindhal village of Lahaul in the form of a flame, and later in the form of Singhasan Mata in Chitoo village. The actual shrine has one *pindi* or stone form, and three idols of Mahakali (Mindhal), Mahalakshmi (Machail) and Mahasaraswati (Chitoo).

Though the locals have been worshipping the goddess for ages, it was in 1980s when the pilgrimage was formalized. Every year in August, the yatra starts from Chinote in Bhaderwah with great gaiety and merriment. The holy mace leads the yatra, followed by thousands of believers, drowned in devotion. It is held that the mace provides strength and courage to the devotees and enables them to finish the arduous yatra with Her blessings. The locals erect colourful gates on the route of the procession and decorate the side paths with flowers, buntings and tinsel. Some onlookers weep, the whole ambience evocative of a bedecked bride leaving for her in-laws' house. The procession is seen off with sad songs:

Sun bhakta meri maiya se kehna, Chandi maiya se kehna
Thakur yaad kare, Thakur yaad kare
Baag Chinote main ho gaya khali.
Ud gayi bulbul, rota hai maali;

[Listen, believers, do tell my mother, tell my Chandi mother,
Thakur remembers her all the time,
The garden in Chinote is empty,
The bulbul has flown away and the keeper is crying.]

The yatra, with rows of vehicles having flags aflutter on their roofs, trundles past the upstream Chenab. The river passes by the towns of Bhala, Premnagar, Thathri and Kishtwar, and finally reaches the base camp of Atholi.

A few years back, a two-way helicopter service for the yatra was made available from Atholi. However, majority of the devotees prefer to undertake the yatra on foot, moving in groups, aided by drums and tongs. They rejoice in devotional songs:

Paddrey di rani ho, gal dil di sunani ho;
As tere bachde, te tu assa di maa.

[Hey Queen of Paddar, from my heart I say,
We are your children and you are our mother.]

The holy mace is welcomed in Machail by the priests and office bearers of the temple committee. The local Buddhists, clad in their traditional dresses, also line up to greet the procession. The Hindus believe that Machail Mata has the unique distinction of the simultaneous appearance of Shiva and Shakti. Goddess Chandi is housed in the temple, and her consort, Mahadev, is manifested through a shivling, perpendicularly perched on a hard bed in the opposite mountain. The mountain is called the Shiv Pahad or the Shiva Mountain, which often remains shrouded in black clouds.

It is well known that Zorawar Singh was a great devotee of Maa Chandi. On his expeditions to Ladakh, he never failed to visit the temple and seek blessings from the Goddess.

Suncham, the last village of Paddar, is at a trek of 7 miles from Machail. The twenty-odd households here belong to Buddhists of Tibetan descent. A steep climb of 3 miles from Suncham leads to the lower end of a small triangular valley, formed by a bifurcation of one of the spurs that run down from the lofty peaks to the north. It is here that the sapphire mines originate. When the sapphire was first discovered, the residents of Suncham were the first to lay their hands on it. They would collect the stones and sell them to the merchants of Lahaul at abysmally low prices. Then the gems would exchange a few more hands, the price soaring, till they reached the jewellery markets of Shimla and Delhi. Among others, one of the prominent traders of sapphire in Lahaul was Thakur Hari Chand, father of Thakur Mangal Chand, the ex-wazir of Lahaul, who made a fortune from the trade. Inside Ghemur Khar, the blue gems glittered many a times.

The Paddar sapphire – with its tinge of cornflower blue and velvety touch, resembling the neck of a peacock – is considered the best in the world, and is also referred to as Kashmir sapphire. Dubbed as the king of the sapphires, there is exquisite refinement in the Paddar gems, something mysterious and ineffable. The brand value of these sapphires is so high that jewellers compulsorily tend to attach the appellation 'Kashmir' to any fine sapphire regardless of its geographical origin.

Various stories are told about the discovery of sapphire mines in Paddar. Somewhere in 1880 or thereabouts, a hunter, while roaming in the wilderness of the northwestern Himalayas bordering Zanskar, started looking around for a fragment of hard rock to kindle a light for his smoking pipe. During his search, he discovered a series of bare rocks beneath the soil, emitting adularescence. He picked up a piece of sapphire buried under the debris of a landslip.

Geologists assert that the area, not long ago, had been covered by glaciers, which started receding due to climate change. The giant ice-shields gave way to open expanse of bare land prone to weather and gravitational forces. This, in turn, led to landslides, which exposed the valuable geological formation hidden in the belly of the Earth.

Perhaps fascinated by the sparkle of the gemstones, the hunter collected many pieces and pebbles. Back in Lahaul, he sold the stones to a trader for a paltry sum, who further sold them to a merchant in Shimla, making a reasonable profit.

According to another story, one summer in the Shimla market, traders from Rupshu were depositing their wares in a local merchant's shop. One of the traders, while emptying a bag of borax, noticed a blue stone rolling out. He casually picked up the stone and tossed it into the street. Mr Jacobs, a famous jeweller, happened to be passing by. He picked up the stone. As he beheld it, was awestruck by its beauty. The jeweller purchased the stone after paying a small sum to the trader and struck a deal for more. He also promised to double the price for each stone.

In another story, Maharaja Hari Singh, the last Dogra ruler, told Albert Ramsay about its discovery in person: In 1834, a group of red-bearded Afghans, part of a mule caravan, was headed towards Delhi. They passed by a landslide in the hills of Kashmir and discovered blue stones scattered in the rubble. Out of curiosity, they stuffed their saddlebags with the stones. In Delhi, they traded the stones for salt. Thereafter, someone who recognized the corundum as rough sapphires bought them. After a chain of buying and selling, the stones reached Calcutta (now Kolkata) where they fetched a whopping price equivalent to $400,000.

Albert Ramsay wrote:

> In India my eyes have been dazzled by such jewels as never have been seen in the Western world. When I was last in the Srinagar palace of the Maharaja of Jammu and Kashmir thirty trays were brought before me, and if I were to say that any one tray, sent to market, would fetch a million dollars, I would be giving only a faint impression of the astonishing wealth and beauty of those treasures of an Indian gentleman. He further writes: Today, I should think, those Kashmir sapphires are worth $3,000,000. One of them is as large as an eggplant. For one of the smaller fragments I offered His Highness $25,000. He just laughed at me; he does not want to part with any object in his beloved collection, but, oh, how I should like to buy some of those treasures!

The discovery of the precious mineral led to many speculations about the location of its origin. The confusion was further compounded by the similarity in the names 'Padam' in Zanskar and 'Paddar' in the Chenab Valley. Finally, the spot was traced to the Buddhist village in Suncham, bringing gangs of gem hunters to Paddar. The exact location of the mines was further authenticated in Volume 22 of the series Memoir of the Geological Survey of Kashmir by Richard Lydekker. He quoted the locality, correctly given in a letter by Reverend A.W Heyde, the Moravian missionary at Keylong – 2 or 3 *kos* the east of Machel village in Paddar.

In the beginning, most of the sapphire hunters came from Zanskar through the Umasi La. When they crossed the pass and entered Paddar, a ritual of offering prayer flags at the pass developed. Illegal miners continue to undertake this dangerous journey even today, mostly in winters. This is a perilous adventure, involving many glaciers hiding fatal crevices. The locals shrug off any death as 'due to karma' and the hunt for alluring sapphires continues unabated.

The discovery of the Paddar sapphire looked much like the American Gold Rush of 1848. When gold was discovered in the mountains north of present-day Los Angeles, thousands of gold hunters descended on California. They came from all over America and other parts of the world.

In the first years of discovery of sapphire, primitive methods like manual search were applied for hunting. The early hunters, without digging deep, would scour the debris and find the shining pieces of blue easily. Qualitatively, too, the extraction in these years was the best and was termed as the 'glory period' as some of the stones mined were the size of eggplants.

The news about the discovery of sapphire reached Jammu durbar. When Maharaja Ranbir Singh – who had succeeded to the throne after his father Gulab Singh abdicated in 1856 due to ill health – held a high-carat blue gemstone in his hand for the first time, he was totally mesmerized. Truly besotted by its sparkle and colour, he stood gazing at the stone for a long time. After hearing about the unabated plunder of the mines, he immediately dispatched his troops to safeguard the area. The Maharaja made all possible efforts to undo the illegal sapphire deals happening in what he thought was his property.

Valentine Ball, in 1885, wrote:

> The Maharaja of Cashmere, then intervened by sending a regiment of sepoys, with their officers, to take possession of the mines; and, it would appear, with *carte blanche* to harry the inhabitants who had, or who were suspected to be having, any of the stones in their possession. Indeed, so thoroughly did they fulfil their mission, that any one they laid hands upon who was found to have money, was suspected of either having sold or being about to purchase sapphires, was thereupon despoiled, and if not arrested and confined, was placed under observation.[43]

The Maharaja was able to trace some of the earlier transactions and negotiated for the return of the traded gems. He had also received the news of the transaction by Afghan traders, which eventually landed in Calcutta. Every single transaction in the long chain had to be undone. The man who had sold the sapphires gave back $400,000, and so the chain reaction continued through many towns until a merchant received a few bags of salt.

Maharaja Ranbir Singh undertook a number of administrative reforms to regulate the mines. In 1882, a few specimens of the gems were sent down to the Indian museum in Shimla, where they were examined by F.R. Mallet, who published a full account of their chemical and mineralogical properties, concluding that they were true sapphires.

After the takeover of the mine by the Maharaja, its access was restricted to only the government authorities. An officer was appointed to look after the affairs of the mines exclusively. By 1907, the full-fledged department of mining was established.

What happened to the rest of the sapphire extractions during the glory period? It is believed that many of the finest stones were obtained by the Maharaja and stored in the *toshakhana*, or the State Treasury. There are a number of accounts stating that a large number of sacks and chests containing literally a king's ransom worth of rough and cut sapphires lay hidden away in the Kashmir State Treasury Chambers.

In 1931, C.S. Middlemiss described this hoard:

> We are aware that one of these outcrops, namely that of the Old Mine, continued yielding gemstone [sic] for an appreciable time, and gave an extremely good output of very large stones from about the year 1881 to about 1887. This is a historical fact and is well known to many living people. A few specimens of sapphire then collected are still preserved, jealously guarded by the State, in the toshakhana, and have been seen by the writer. Of these there is at least one large piece, bigger than a polo or croquet ball, and others smaller all of a rich blue colour. There are also many cases of cut gems of pendant size which are superficially as large as florins.[44]

Within five years of the discovery of the mines, the yield started to rapidly wane. Profits were now steadily diminishing. Therefore, in 1887, the Maharaja decided to seek expert help from the British to revive the mines, which entailed geological survey and mapping.

Finally, the British government offered the services of Tom D. LaTouche, deputy superintendent of the Geological Survey of India. After negotiations, LaTouche was hired for one year at a monthly salary of Rs 640 excluding travel expenses. He reached Srinagar in August 1888, and after gathering the preliminary information about the mines, set out for Paddar.

His report, *The Sapphire Mines of Kashmir*, published in 1889, details his journey to Paddar:

> Crossing the Marbal pass at the head of Kashmir valley, I reached Kishtwar, near the junction of Wadwan and Chenab

> rivers, both of which had to be crossed by rope bridges in six days. Thence a somewhat difficult path led up the left bank of the Chenab to Gulabgarh. The river runs through an exceedingly deep and narrow gorge, and the path generally keeps at a considerable height above it, but the numerous side streams, which also run in deep gorges, necessitate a descent and ascent of two or three thousand feet in several places, so that the marches are very trying: the path is, however, practicable for unladen ponies. At Gulabgarh the valley opens out considerably and is well cultivated: here the Chenab is again crossed by a long and somewhat shaky jhulla bridge close to an old fort which stands at the junction of the Bhutna with a larger river. Soomjam, the highest village on the southern side of the lofty range dividing Zanskar from Chenab valley, this was formerly occupied by an extension of glaciers which now descend only as far as its upper end from the passes leading into Zanskar, a large moraine stretching from side to side of the valley immediately above Soomjam, and the polished surfaces of the cliffs on either side, indicating their former extent.

On his arrival in the area, LaTouche discerned that material was from two different sites. The first of these sites, now termed as 'Old Mine', was a group of shallow pits sunk into an actinolite-tremolite rock containing small pegmatite lenses.

LaTouche further writes that when he visited the mines in July 1888, there were still patches of snow scattered around the landslip. During his next twenty-five days of exploration, he discovered that the Old Mine was at the verge of exhaustion. Therefore, for future mining, new avenues had to be explored. On this pursuit, towards the northern side of the ridge, on the placers of the valley floor, he discovered large blocks of granite crowded with crystals of corundum with a bluish tint. This was the 'New Mine', but it yielded mediocre results. During that working season, LaTouche made several excursions into the nearby valleys and also engaged natives in a hope to discover new localities for sapphires. These endeavours did not find success except on one occasion when he found a large block of granite, which contained numerous pinheads of blue hexagonal crystals of sapphire.

The work done initially was basic and included digging the pits to explore for the gems or simply collecting the debris and washing it in a specially designed washing apparatus assembled by the deputy superintendent of the Geological Survey of India. During that season in 1888, with a hundred workers engaged for digging, LaTouche could extract only 1,630 *tola*s of conundrum, of which only one-fourth had commercial value. The average weight of the stones discovered was not more than ten grains. According to him, this was not a profitable proposition considering the inaccessibility of the locality, short working season and difficulty in obtaining labourers. LaTouche's contract was not extended, and the mining activity came to a halt.

For the next sixteen years, mining remained officially halted. However, poachers continued to mine illegally. In order to garner some revenue and discourage the poachers, the Maharaja decided to lease the mines once again. In 1905, R.A. Prideaux, on behalf of a British company, initiated correspondence with the Maharaja's government for a prospective license. On the grounds of not having enough capital, the company sought concessions, which were denied. Similarly, John Taylor and Sons, London, impressed upon the Maharaja the need for granting a license. In their correspondence, the company flaunted their apparent success in mining gold in the state of Mysore.[45]

Finally, in 1906, C.M.P. Wright was granted a license after hard bargaining. The company was asked to submit a map and plan of the area they intended to mine. It submitted an area of 320 acres, which was curtailed to 100 sq. miles. Then the finances were worked out: The company was to pay 70,000 rupees in advance and monthly sum of Rs. 3,500 for the upkeep of the garrison at the mines. It also had to pay the nominal ground rent of one rupee per acre of land under exploration. The royalty was worked out at 30 percent to be paid for the gross produce of sapphires. It was also decided that the company would be called Kashmir Mineral Company and an accredited agent based in India would spearhead the mining operations. Major General (Retired) A.D. Anderson was appointed as the accredited agent of Kashmir Mineral Company.[46]

While going through the correspondence between the company and the Maharaja's administration, the trust deficit becomes quite apparent. Unlike modern-day capitalist ethos, it seems that the employee and the employer saw each other with suspicion – perhaps accentuated by the high stakes. Pilferage was a realistic danger. One little stone in a secret pocket could mean a fortune.[47] Therefore, the administration ensured to send a trusted man to keep a watch on the mining activities of the British. He was designated as Mohtmid, or a reliable person, an advisor who would work as eyes and ears of the Maharaja. The Mohtmid had to ensure that the mining was fair and conformed to the conditions of the lease. The Maharaja's men exercised tremendous power over the miners. Way back in 1887, when LaTouche had visited the mines, he had complained about an official of the garrison who would frisk him and his men before and after the exploration of mines.

Wright lavishly explored the mines for two years and extracted some of the finest stones from the region. In 1907, the company also discovered another mine, some hundred metres southeast of the erstwhile Old Mine, but this again proved to be an uneconomical venture.

The company licence was not extended as the Maharaja wanted to mine indigenously. With the British backing away, the Maharaja roped in a few prominent jewellers of Jammu and gave them prospective licenses. In 1911, Lala Jyoti Parshad became the first native to mine the area southwest of the New Mine. However, his exploration did not produce fruitful results. Subsequent attempts by the native miners also remained dismal. However, in 1924, Pandit Labhu Ram, an assistant superintendent of Mineral Survey, mapped the entire area and collected useful information on the locations where sapphire could be mined. In 1926, Lala Jagan Nath of Jammu obtained a prospecting license. He restarted the mining activity in the New Mine that had been discovered by Wright and found 60 kg of corundum. However, within a year, the Maharaja's government cancelled his license due to some financial irregularities. The Kashmir government then took over the exploration, and within two weeks, extracted 450 kg of sapphire from the mines dug by Lala Jagan Nath.[48]

Since 1963, the mines have been managed by Jammu and Kashmir's Geology and Mining Department. Every year, around the month of June, a team from the department visits Paddar and undertakes exploration and mining activities. On an average, the company extracts a dismal amount of 5,000 gms of the mineral annually. With the onset of militancy around these heights, the mines became a no-go area for the mining authorities. The result of no inspections from the government's side was rampant poaching. In 1998, when a government team visited the mines, they found that crude methods, including detonations, were being used for the hunt for sapphires.

In 2004, Discovery Channel, in their popular series *Game of Stones*, aired an episode titled 'Himalayan Motherlode' on Paddar sapphire. The programme showed how a team met a band of smugglers with whom they made a deal of 12 million rupees for a 4.22-carat piece of sapphire. It was a trail straight from the movies, from Jammu and Kashmir to Jaipur, then to Mumbai, Bangkok, London and finally at Geneva, Switzerland, where the stone was sold for a whopping $1.5 million. In May 2013, a 19.88-carat sapphire was sold for an exorbitant amount of 24 crore rupees. In July 2011, three Sri Lankan nationals, along with a local accomplice, were held in Paddar for attempting to smuggle sapphire in a car.[49]

Apart from sapphire, the people of the Chenab Valley are also obsessed with the mythical 'Trathgola' or the 'Ball of Fire'. Actually, these hilly areas are prone to frequent cases of lightning during rains and cloudbursts. The people believe that when the lightning strikes any solid object, it gets transformed into a paranormal object to possess supernatural powers. Many hunt for these 'heavenly objects', just like they do for sapphire. Sometimes, when they manage to amass some burnt residual, they try to sell it to gullible buyers. In demonstrations, the seller tries to showcase the 'rice puller': the material's unique feature of attracting grains of rice.

Trathgola is marketed as an essential component for space research, cryogenic engines and nuclear programmes, and is much sought after by organizations like National Aeronautics and Space Administration (NASA), Indian Space Research Organisation (ISRO) and Bhabha Atomic Research Centre (BARC). Despite many rebuttals by these organizations, many people continue to pedal the belief that the material can fetch millions of dollars.

There have been sensational and funny cases of people falling into the trap of Trathgola. In 2015, the crime branch registered a case against a gang of inter-state criminals for duping a buyer by selling him Trathgola. One of the gang members was arrested from Telangana, who posed as a scientist exclusively hired by NASA and Defence Research and Development Organisation (DRDO) to certify the quality of precious Trathgola. He was able to extract 3 crores from the buyer before a complaint was lodged. His arrest led to a resident of Doda, who was the initial deal maker and supplier of Trathgola.

After the discovery of sapphire mines in Paddar, geologists have speculated about other hidden wealth in the regions around. The miners have already excavated deposits of bauxite, granite, gypsum, dolomite, quartz, borax, etc. However, in 2023, the geologists hit upon a motherlode in the Reasi district when they found inexhaustible reserves of lithium.

The Reasi district, nestled in the high and middle mountains, is bisected by the Chenab. In the mid-1990s, the geologists had surveyed the area around Salal and spotted a high quantity of lithium deposits, suggesting further exploration. In 2018, a team from the Geological Survey of India camped at Salal. They performed reconnaissance surveys as well as preliminary and general exploration, and collected samples for research. The outcome of this exercise was made public in February 2023, when the Ministry of Mines announced the presence of 5.9 million tonnes of lithium in the Salal–Haimana belt.

Over the years, the shiny-grey light metal has evolved in the global market as 'white gold'. A few months after the discovery, Elon Musk tweeted: 'Price of lithium has gone to insane levels! Tesla might actually have to get into the mining and refining directly at scale, unless costs improve.'[50] 'Lithium batteries are the new oil,' Elon Musk asserted.[51] He invests largely in future technology, and lithium batteries are his main source of power. Apart from being used in batteries to power smart phones, laptops and almost all other gadgets, lithium is a vital component in the rechargeable batteries that run electric vehicles, including the ones produced by Tesla. Lithium also has a range of other uses including lubricants in ceramics and glasses, for medical purposes and even in power grids and nuclear plants. The discovery of large lithium reserves is expected to make India one of the major producers in the world ending our dependence on imports. It will not only give a boost to electric vehicle industry but also help India to tackle the climate change crisis and lead her to green transition and achieving the goal of becoming carbon neutral by 2070.[52]

In hindsight, the initial euphoria about the find has not been followed by actual work on the ground. Environmentalists have also raised their concerns about the impact it will have on the surroundings as the exploration would involve air, soil and water pollution. Moreover, the Salal belt houses about 8,000 people, whose proper rehabilitation poses a major challenge. The human resettlement is bound to evoke emotions as these people have faced the brunt of militancy, and most of them fall below poverty line. Therefore, the rehabilitation plans of the government have to adequately compensate the displaced people.

6

The Doda Files

The midnight between 14 and 15 August 1947 marked the end of the British rule in India. Based on religious lines, the country was divided into the dominions of India and Pakistan. All the princely states had not been a part of British India were given the choice of joining either of the dominions by signing an instrument of accession. The Maharaja of Jammu and Kashmir, the Hindu king of a Muslim-majority state, dilly-dallied because, deep in his heart, he wanted to remain independent. He envisaged his state to be a kind of Switzerland, a hotspot for international tourism. Cradled between two newly created countries, this was not going to be easy.

In the North-West Frontier Province of newly created Pakistan, the 'jihad' fever, instigated mainly by the local clerics – Peer of Manki Sharif and Wana – was burning in the streets. Each fighter recruited was sent to the nearby police station, given a rifle and asked to report for training near Abbottabad and Muree, two prominent towns east of Rawalpindi. The training camps were set in secret locations so that the British officers controlling the Pakistan Army remained ignorant of the mobilization.[53]

Historians Larry Collins and Dominique Lapierre recounted this mobilization in their bestseller, *Freedom at Midnight* (1975):

> Within hours, in the mud-walled morkhas, or compounds, their villages, in encampments, in Landi Kotal, along the Khyber …

the Pathans passed the ancient call of Islam for holy war, jihad. From bazaar to bazaar, secret emissaries began to buy up stocks of hard tack and gur, a mixture of corn meal, ground chickpeas and sugar. A few mouthfuls of that mixture taken two or three times a day could sustain a Pathan for days.

Soon, Pathan militias, mainly comprising the Mahsud, Afridi, Swati and Wazir tribes, were ready for an armed aggression into Jammu and Kashmir. Codenamed Operation Gulmarg, the militia was fully armed, funded and equipped by the Pakistan Army.

Dr Andrew Whitehead, editor of BBC World Service News, a journalist and a social historian, in his book *A Mission in Kashmir* (2014), has given detailed account of the buildup of the tribal invasion and its terrible aftermath. He quotes a British Army officer, Frank Leeson who was a witness to this mobilization:

> The tribesmen of North-West Frontier had been waiting for some such call and here at last was the chance of a lifetime. For some it was a crusade; for others a chance for a scrap; for many, it must be admitted, an opportunity to pillage and loot with a clear conscience. They streamed down in busloads; Mohmands and Mahsuds, Afridis and Afghans; from Buner and Bajaur, Swat and South Waziristan, Khyber and Khost; the light of battle in their eyes, half-forgotten war cries on their lips. From Bannu the lorries streamed north and east to Abbottabad and Rawalpindi loaded with the tribesmen.

Joined by a few Punjabi Muslims and regulars of the Pakistan Army, the tribesmen or the Kabalis had gathered at Garhi Habibullah on the Pakistani side of Kashmir border. Around midnight of 21 October 1947, they waited for a pre-decided signal from across. The signal came from members of the Maharaja's army guarding the bridge at Domel that marks the confluence of the Jhelum and Kishanganga rivers. The Muslim guards first killed their Hindu supervisors and overpowered other Dogra soldiers, and then opened the bridge for raiders. By the early morning of 22 October, the marauding tribesmen in lorries, buses and wagons were on the streets of Muzaffarabad, overrunning the town. Muzaffarabad had a considerable Hindu and Sikh population: many of them had fled, few put up a little resistance, while most got killed.

The Maharaja's army was decimated as many of its Muslim troops had deserted. Krishna Mehta, the wife of the newly appointed DC of Muzaffarabad, wrote a powerful personal memoir, titled *Kashmir 1947: A Survivor's Story* (2006), about the travails of her escape with her children from the beleaguered town. She recorded that several Hindus and Sikhs were killed and women were raped; many others jumped into the Jhelum along with their children to escape the assault. Mehta's husband, who had decided to stay back and defend the town, was killed instantly.

From Muzaffarabad, the Kabalis advanced eastwards along the Jhelum Valley Cart Road, burning and looting many villages enroute and ravaging the town of Uri. Though the Dogra army, under the command of Brigadier Rajinder Singh, gave a tough fight to the invaders, it was outnumbered and could only delay the advance of the tribesmen. On their further march, the Kabalis seized the hydroelectricity project of Mohra. They snapped the electricity, plunging the whole city of Srinagar into darkness. Brigadier Rajinder Singh was killed in the outskirts of Baramulla, thus ending the resistance of the Dogra troops.

Baramulla, the second biggest town in the Kashmir Valley, was an important trading centre, with its fruit and timber businesses. The town is bisected by the Jhelum, which is one of the seven rivers of the Sapta Sindhu region mentioned in the Nadi Stuti hymn as Vitasta. The river originates from a spring in Verinag, situated in the foothills of the Kapran Mountain, and flows through the Kashmir Valley. Surging past Srinagar, Baramulla and Muzaffarabad, it assimilates into the Chenab near Trimmu in present-day Pakistan and later merges with the Indus.

Sensing the looming threat, many non-Muslims in Baramulla had started to flee to the adjoining hills and further south towards Srinagar. These families collected their meagre belongings and found whatever transport was available to them. The fare for a 34-mile journey to Srinagar cost fifty times higher. As these carriages clip-clopped over the roads and overloaded transport trundled past St. Joseph's Hospital and the Convent, situated on the Baramulla–Srinagar road, the tension seeped into the hospital as well, prompting many patients to leave in a hurry.

The Christian missionaries had set their foot in Kashmir in the 1860s. A number of Protestant medical missionaries from Britain brought allopathic medicine to Srinagar, and established dispensaries and hospitals. The Mill Hill Missionaries of North London, popularly known as St Joseph's Missionary Society, was given the task of evangelizing Kashmir. In 1891, a Catholic mission school was opened in Baramulla by male missionaries, which later became St. Joseph's Higher Secondary School. These missionaries then sought help from the Franciscan Missionaries of Mary to reach out to the women of Kashmir who were in dire need of health services. Five years later, the nuns came to the mission and established a small convent and a chapel. The initial task of the nuns was to visit women in their villages on horsebacks or shikaras to provide them medical care. Soon, a small dispensary was opened, which in 1929 became a fifteen-bedded maternity hospital.

Whitehead writes in his book:

> The rumblings of the tribal march from Uri towards Baramulla had reached the mission, so had its rapacious excesses. Deep in their hearts the missionaries did not see any harm coming their way; after all they were there for the good of the local Kashmiris.[54]

However, everyone was not convinced. The hospital had started to empty en masse. Some of the patients had left within a few days of their confinement. They mostly comprised of women half-dead with tuberculosis or cancer, young mothers with their new born, and children with their stomachs burnt by *kangri*s or the little wicker-covered fire pots. These patients were hurried off their sickbeds, mostly forced by fearful husbands, taken away on horse-drawn *tonga*s, on beds, or painfully made to walk. Hindu, Sikh and Muslim women fled from the advancing shadow of the bogeyman from Waziristan, the menacing demon of rape at their heels.

Whitehead has liberally quoted from the unfinished desk diary of Father George Shanks, the chief priest at the mission, preserved in the archives of Mill Hill Missionaries. In 1952, Father Shanks recorded an incomplete yet a vivid detail of the happenings of October 1947 and possibly the only true eyewitness account. He wrote:

> The hostel kitchen appeared unusually deserted as most of the Hindu and Sikh boarding students had left a day earlier, to the comparatively safe environs of Srinagar.

Mohammad Yousaf, one of the students had warned Father Shanks gravely:[55]

> 'You have heard, Father, that the Pathans may enter Baramulla this evening?'
>
> 'I do seem to have heard such rumour, Yousaf. What about it? I hope you are not losing your nerve. Aren't you glad they are coming to liberate you from the Hindus? And haven't you got a big feast ready for them in the Wazir's compound? I believe you are a member of the students' section of the "Committee of Welcome"?'
>
> 'That is true, Father, but all the same, these are wild people. It may be that some of them might get out of hand, do some mischief.'

Mohammad Yousaf Saraf was a prominent resident of Baramulla, who later became the chief justice of Pakistan-Occupied Kashmir (POK). He studied at St Joseph's College, Baramulla, where he was the president of the student's union. He dabbled in local politics, first aligning with the National Conference and later joining its rival the Muslim Conference.

On 26 October 1947, the fifth day of the invasion, the Kabalis entered Baramulla. They were an assortment of men, from aged ones to teenagers, sporting ragged beards, Pathani suits, pakol caps and black turbans. These mercenaries brandished Lee Enfield rifles, Bren guns, double-barrelled shotguns, pistols, axes, swords, daggers and machetes. For the next few days, a macabre dance of horror visited the streets of Baramulla. Smoke billowed from many places and as the non-Muslims scampered for safety; the women were abducted and raped. The Kabalis took over Nishat Talkies, the sole theatre in the town. They brought the abducted women and passed them from one man to another. Many Sikh and Hindu women jumped into the Jhelum to avoid this fate. The Kabalis ransacked every house and shop that came their way and looted everything – carpets, blankets, crockery, valuables, money, utensils, furniture, even hair oil and alum – whatever they could lay their hands on. The brass samovars were the most coveted, the gullible raiders assuming them to be crafted from silver. The loot was piled up in trucks and, along with some abducted women, was sent back to Pakistan. These trucks returned with more tribesmen.

The next morning, on 27 October, a posse of tribesmen swarmed down from the fir tree–rich mountain, on whose steps sprawled the St. Joseph's Hospital and the Convent. They scaled the walls of the complex and, making their way through orchards of apple and walnut trees, reached the hospital. From the hospital, they moved to the convent, hostel, quarters and presbytery, forcing open the doors with their axes and looting whatever they could. The place and its Christian symbols were desecrated – the altar, statuettes, crucifixes, reredos, hymn books and rosaries.

That day, the roll call listed sixteen nuns in the mission, including the Belgian superior, Mother Aldetrude. There were nuns from Spain, Portugal, Italy, Scotland, Germany, Ireland, England, the Netherlands and a solitary nun from India. The hospital also had Malayali nurses and pharmacists as well as a few other helpers. In the blitzkrieg that followed, six people lost their lives.

The invaders had entered the patient's ward, and they started to rob the ailing. Motia Devi Kapoor from Almora, a North Indian hill town, perhaps resisted; she was stabbed through her heart. A South Indian nurse called Philomena was shot dead when she tried to protect the patients. Outside the ward, some invaders molested Sister Belan from Spain and tried to drag her away. Jose Barretto, the husband of the hospital surgeon, tried to intervene. He was pinned to a tree and shot through the head. Hearing the commotion, the mother superior, along with her newly arrived Spanish Assistant Sister Teresalina, rushed out and came under the arc of the bullets. Sister Teresalina leaped in front of the mother superior. She took the bullets in her chest and was grievously hurt. Before dying she uttered in Spanish: '*Ya termino frezco mi vida por la conversion de Cachemira* [I'm already finished, I offer my life for the conversion of Kashmir].' Father Shanks gave her a last absolution and suggested some invocations in her familiar Spanish.

During this mayhem, Lt Col Tom Dykes had arrived at the mission to take his family back to Srinagar. His wife Biddy Dykes had given birth to their third son a fortnight earlier and was still recuperating from the childbirth. Lt Col Dykes was trained at the Royal Military College in Sandhurst and was commissioned into the British Army. Here he was a contemporary of Sam Manekshaw and both became good friends. In 1940, Dykes married Biddy, a vivacious military nurse in Agra. He fought the Japanese in Burma (now Myanmar) in World War II and rose to the rank of lieutenant colonel. After India's independence, he was ordered to stay on for a few months as an officer in the Indian army's Sikh regiment to help the transition. A true soldier, he came to the rescue of hapless nuns but was immediately shot dead. His wife, who ran after him, ended up getting killed too. Biddy Dyke's body in her undergarments was later found inside the campus well. Their sons, aged five and two, along with the newborn, were orphaned overnight. The Dykes family's cocker spaniel, too, was shot by the bloodthirsty killers.

While the Kabalis laid siege to the mission, Saurab Hyat Khan reached the site on a motorcycle, wearing civilian clothes. A major in Pakistan Army, he had been commanding the Kabalis. Since he had studied in a convent in Peshawar run by the Presentation Sisters, he empathized with the nuns of the mission and came to their rescue.

The next day, a large grave was dug in the orchard at the far side of the campus, and the five Christians were interred. These graves, flanked by crosses and graced with befitting epitaphs, continue to exist today, shaded by the walnut trees.

On 24 October, Maharaja Hari Singh sat on his golden throne, conducting his Dussehra durbar. All his ministers and bureaucrats were in attendance to pay him homage. Suddenly, the lights went off. This was the time when the Kabalis had seized the Mohra hydroelectricity project that provided power to Srinagar city. When the palace plunged into darkness, the impending arrival of the tribesmen became more profound, triggering panic in the Dogra durbar. The following day was spent in hectic packing of the valuable, movable items including a lot of precious jewels, presumably the Paddar sapphires as well. The next day, well before sunrise, a long convoy of Rolls-Royce cars rolled out of the palace for the arduous journey to Jammu. The convoy included the Maharaja's customized hunting wagon with a high roof at its back. The crown prince, Karan Singh, was convalescing from a fractured leg and was on a wheelchair. Since he was not in a position to be seated in any of the cars, he had to travel in the hunting wagon, seated on his wheelchair.

The Maharaja drove one of the cars himself with a co-passenger and two guards with loaded revolvers sitting in the backseat. For the major part of the journey, he looked sullen and did not say a word. By the time the convoy crossed the Banihal Pass, the first light had bathed the Pir Panjal mountains. Apparently, the Maharaja looked back one last time before solemnly proclaiming, 'We have lost Kashmir.' Incidentally, he could not set foot in his beloved valley again.

The Maharaja's sudden departure was not taken kindly by the Kashmiris, who dubbed it an unforgivable betrayal. Srinagar was in the hands of the volunteers of Sheikh Abdullah's National Conference, most of whom wielded nothing but sticks. These volunteers, including some women, were imparted basic training in weapon handling and were all set to defend Srinagar city.

The day of 27 October 1947 was a turning point in the history of Jammu and Kashmir. While the Kabalis were vandalizing and bloodying the Christian mission, the first Indian Dakotas were landing on a rudimentary airstrip on the outskirts of Srinagar. Incidentally, it lacked a tarmac and did not even have basic fuelling facilities. Records state that the previous day, the Maharaja had signed the instrument of accession, formalizing Jammu and Kashmir's accession with the Union of India. Some of the first troops to land, from the Sikh regiment, headed towards Baramulla, but finding themselves outnumbered, took positions a few miles to the east of the town, waiting for reinforcements. They were oblivious to the fact that their acting commandant, Lt Col Dykes, had already become a victim of the invasion.

Meanwhile, the Kabalis had taken nearly eighty people hostage inside the baby ward, including the surviving nuns, Father Shanks, few townsmen and the patients. The indefatigable Dr Greta Barretto, who had lost her husband, continued to treat both the victims of the tribal violence and the injured tribesmen alike. The nurses continued to attend to the babies, including the two-week-old Dykes' baby, feeding them, changing diapers and administering medicines.

There are multiple versions about the ordeal in the hospital in the ensuing ten days. Though Whitehead recounts in his book that the alleged sexual assault of the nuns lacks conclusive proof, other sources and journalistic investigations point to the opposite.

In 1950, Herbert Ernest Bates wrote a novel, *The Scarlet Sword*, loosely based on the siege of the St. Joseph's Mission. Many historians believe that the rape and pillage unleashed by the Kabalis in Baramulla, especially in the Mission, was responsible for their inordinate delay in reaching Srinagar. This defeated their resolve of celebrating Eid on 26 October in Srinagar.

While narrating the days of turmoil, it is worthwhile to mention the little-known story of a local Kashmiri called Maqbool Sherwani.

Sherwani, then in his late twenties, a National Conference[56] worker, turned out to be an apostle of secularism. He came to limelight in 1944, when he had disrupted Jinnah's visit to Baramulla, since he perceived him as a non-secularist. Sherwani, who was working as an undercover operative of the National Conference militia in 1947, usually moved from village to village on his motorcycle, propagating religious unity. He has been credited with single-handedly stalling the advance of the tribal invaders to Srinagar by misleading them. Apparently, he had informed the tribesmen that the Indian Army was camping outside Baramulla and that a move towards Srinagar would be catastrophic for them. The enemy froze in its tracks and wasted crucial time in Baramulla, halting its violent advance. This pre-emption, provoked by Maqbool Sherwani, granted the much-needed time for the Maharaja to sign the historic instrument of accession, and the Indian army landed in Kashmir the very next day.

However, Sherwani had to pay with his life after his bluff was caught by the Kabalis. He suffered horrendous torture in the following days and finally ended up nailed on a wooden plank not far from St. Joseph's Mission – almost a crucifixion. The following words were scratched on his forehead: *The punishment of a traitor is death.*[57]

Despite the insufferable agonies, Sherwani kept sloganeering in favour of his leader, Sheikh Mohammad Abdullah: 'Sher-e-Kashmir Zindabad' [Long live the Lion of Kashmir]. He was shot at fourteen times, his body riddled with bullets. The day of Sherwani's execution proved to be the last day of tribal invasion; many of them were killed and the rest retreated.

Sheikh Mohammad Abdullah, Jammu and Kashmir's first prime minister, ensured that Srinagar's iconic civil line street, Residency Road, was named after Maqbool Sherwani. A municipal hall in Baramulla still exists with Sherwani's name. Besides, there is Maqbool Sherwani Ward at Sher-e-Kashmir Institute of Medical Sciences in Soura, Srinagar.

The heroics of Sherwani have more or less remained unsung, but from time to time, his contribution as a true patriot gets revived. In 1964, Mulk Raj Anand, the pioneer of Indo-Anglian fiction wrote a book on the sacrifice of Sherwani called *The Death of a Hero: Epitaph for Maqbool Sherwani* (1993). The tribal invasion is best illustrated in the Kashmiri language in a chapter of *Kuliyat-e-Mehjoor* [The Collection of Mehjoor's Poems]. Ghulam Ahmad Mehjoor has been one of the greatest modern poets of Kashmir, with a body of work highlighting the cultural and literary opulence of Kashmir. In his poem, 'Nalla-e-Sherwani' [The Story of Sherwani], Mehjoor sums Sherwani's sufferings, when he was in captivity of the raiders, and echoes his message to the people of Kashmir on the last night of his life. Mehjoor, through Sherwani, calls the raiders 'cannibals' and 'scoundrels'.

Sherwani's message was:

The cannibals have descended from the mountains,
They have the blood of a multitude of innocents on their hands,
They have made my country a veritable hell.
It was a garden of flowers and they have laid it waste,
They trained their arrows on the nightingales,
They threw stones at crystal shops.
Had you been armed, they wouldn't have dared to attack.

Interestingly, Sherwani has been forgotten in Kashmir's cultural and historical milieu. Seventy-five years later, there is no signboard to show the direction of Sherwani Road, still known by its British colonial name of Residency Road. The Sherwani Hall at Baramulla was gutted in a mysterious fire around 1989 and was later reconstructed. Even *Kuliyat-e-Mehjoor* is not available in bookstores, reading rooms and public libraries of Jammu and Kashmir. Its first and last edition appeared in 1985.

~

The inconclusive war of 1947 divided the state of Jammu and Kashmir into two parts, each controlled by India and Pakistan, thus germinating a problem that has lingered till date. The first Indian troops that landed in October 1947 triggered the beginning of the militarization of the region – a phenomenon that continues. So do the nefarious designs of Pakistan over Kashmir.

For the next four decades, India and Pakistan were caught in a political and diplomatic stalemate over Kashmir, interspersed with innumerable skirmishes, aggressive posturing and two wars. After the infamous elections of the state assembly in 1987, an armed uprising erupted in the Kashmir Valley. Sponsored by Pakistan, hordes of local youth went across the border, got trained and came back with Kalashnikovs swinging on their shoulders. The militancy did not remain indigenous for long, as the foreign mercenaries from other Islamic countries referred to as 'guest militants' joined the conflict.

In the initial years, militancy remained confined to the Kashmir Valley, and the Chenab Valley largely remained unaffected. This was not to stay for long since Doda is strategically placed, neighbouring the militancy affected Anantnag district in its north. Spread over a vast area, Doda has a sparse population of only forty-five people per sq. km. The mountainous terrain with towering slopes, dense coniferous forests, deep gorges and the river Chenab flowing through it made Doda a safe haven for the terrorists to thrive.

When the military pressure increased in Anantnag, the militants operating there would escape to the adjoining hills of Doda. Since the deployment of security forces in the Chenab Valley was minimal, the terrorists survived without being noticed. In the 1990s, when infiltration of armed militants increased in the Rajouri and Poonch districts, the Chenab Valley became a transit point for their entry into the Kashmir Valley. The initial sightings and intelligence about the presence of these terrorists could not be meaningfully responded to because of a lack of road network and communications. The few existing link roads were prone to landslides and remained closed for long periods due to snow. Besides, the colossal river Chenab and its numerous tributaries were natural impediments for the movement of security forces.

It was just a matter of time before the Chenab Valley started to have its share of resident militants. Right from the beginning, there had been fringe elements – especially in Kishtwar and Bhaderwah regions – sympathetic to the cause of separatism. With their roots in Jamat-e-Islami, some of these activists would later have a smooth transition towards the cause of the All Parties Hurriyat Conference, a conglomerate of separatist parties of Kashmir that came into existence in 1993. This trend was mainly fuelled by the existence of a wide network of masjids and madrasas of Deobandi and Ahele Hadees schools, turning the Chenab Valley into a tinderbox about to be ignited. Another factor that would go on to fan the flames of militancy was the demography of Doda, which was seen as a 'cultural bridge' between Jammu and Kashmir. It was a melting pot of culture, traditions and languages. There are about a dozen languages and dialects spoken in the district, which keep changing after every 10 km. With 57 per cent Muslim population and the rest Hindus (apart from small fragments of Buddhists and Sikhs), none of the communities got intimidated easily and continued to stay precariously perched on the communal faultline. This situation was on the threshold of a massive tectonic shift due to militancy.

Initially, the armed terrorists came from the Anantnag district of south Kashmir, slowly trickling into the wilderness of the Marwah, Dachan and Wadwan Valleys, lying along the Marsudar River which is a major tributary of the Chenab. Most of these were foreigners accompanied by a handful of Kashmiris. These militants sported long beards and hair, spoke varied accents and wore Pathan suits with camouflage jackets strapped with bandoliers. They carried Kalashnikovs and Pika guns, and sometimes had rocket launchers mounted on their shoulders. With their latest wireless communication devices, they directly took orders from their handlers sitting in Pakistan. Remaining unchecked, they mostly lived in natural caves and even pitched their tents in the meadows. In the summers, the militants would seek shelter and food from the clans of transhumant Gujjars and Bakerwals who swarmed these heights. Some of the nomads started to run errands for the militants as guides, couriers and informers. The terrorists elicited both fear and respect and were called *mujahedeen* or the holy warriors. Those who extensively quoted from the Quran and the Hadith were referred to as *maulvi*s or Islamic scholars.

This spillover from south Kashmir gradually engulfed the whole of Chenab Valley. Systematically, the militants spread their network and put in place a circle of close confidants who became the overground workers and harbourers. Then the first locals were recruited – the radicalized youth who went missing from their homes, one by one. Vowing their allegiance to the jihad, they were helped to cross the border from Kashmir or Rajouri–Poonch. On their return, these fully trained boys became heroes overnight, venerated for their mission.

Aided by the foreign mercenaries, training camps were set up in the jungles, and the distinction of locally trained militant (LTM) and Pakistan-trained militant (PTM) became part of the local parlance. When there are guns, the temptations to use them becomes real. Soon, the minorities started facing the brunt of the terror unleashed in the region.

The first militant act in the Chenab Valley happened in Bhaderwah in 1989, when a crude bomb exploded under a bridge. It was a reaction to the death of Shabir Shah's father, allegedly in police custody. Shabir Shah is the founder-president of the Jammu and Kashmir Democratic Freedom Party – one of the main organizations seeking the 'right to self-determination'. A prominent secessionist voice in Kashmir for more than fifty years, Shabir Shah was arrested for the first time in 1968, aged fourteen, for organizing a student demonstration against India. After spending three months in jail, he formed the Young Men's League. His tryst with imprisonment had started back then and continues till date. Since then, he has spent many years in jail and was dubbed by sympathizers as the Nelson Mandela of Kashmir and a Prisoner of Conscience. Later, it was learnt that the blast under the bridge was the handiwork of a local youth, Firdous Ahmed Baba. It was not difficult for Baba to procure gelatin to assemble a bomb since his father was involved in road construction.

Baba was born in 1967 in an affluent Kashmiri family of Bhaderwah. Later, the family shifted to Jammu, where he was enrolled in a prestigious school. In 1983, he, along with an elderly cousin, happened to visit Amritsar. After paying obeisance at the Golden Temple, when they emerged, Baba saw truckloads of Khalistani supporters brandishing swords and shouting slogans in favour of Sant Jarnail Singh Bhindranwale, who was spearheading the Khalistan movement. The spectacle had a great impact on young Baba and his imagination was fuelled by the rapturous support for the Khalistani leader. Back in Jammu, he narrated this incident to his friends, who were equally overwhelmed. The restless minds of Baba and his friends were also influenced by the Iranian revolution and the resistance rendered to the Soviet Union's invasion of Afghanistan.

Though possessing a bright mind, Baba failed his matriculation examination and quit school. It shattered the dream of his father who wished to see him as a lawyer someday. Being at crossroads for some time, Baba decided to learn about Islam and joined a forty-day course by Tablighqi Jamat at the Deoband seminary. However, few days into the course, he felt that the conservatism being preached there was contradictory to the liberal tenets of Kashmiri beliefs. As a result, he quit the course and returned to Jammu. Despite quitting the seminary, Baba had become religious in his own way, and with his like-minded friends, he formed a small organization called Young Muslims.

In 1986, a petition was moved in the court for removing the restriction on Hindu worship in the Babri Masjid premises. Babri Masjid, or the Mosque of Babar, was built in the sixteenth century in Ayodhya, at a site believed by many Hindus to be the birthplace of Lord Rama. In 1949, some Hindu activists surreptitiously placed idols of the Hindu deity inside the mosque, after which the government locked the building to avoid communal dispute. After the petition to open the gates was moved in the court, the Rajiv Gandhi government ordered the locks on the Babri Masjid gates to be removed, reversing the decision of his grandfather Jawaharlal Nehru. The decision led to Muslim protests in major parts of the country. In Jammu, Firdous Ahmed Baba and his Muslim Action Committee joined the protests, and it had a profound impact on him.

In the subsequent police crackdown, Baba's friends were arrested and lodged in a jail. Baba managed to evade arrest and, for the first time in his life, went in hiding. Later, when he went to meet his friends in jail under a pseudonym, he was introduced to Shabir Shah, who was also lodged in the same jail. Both took an instant liking to each other. Baba remained in touch with Shah and would often go to the jail to meet him. He had now become the eyes and ears of Shah outside the prison.

The allegedly rigged election of 1987 was a tipping point in the lives of many Kashmiri youth, including Firdous Ahmed Baba. When the exfiltration to Pakistan for armed training started, he was increasingly attracted towards the militant way of 'liberation of

Kashmir' and pondered over his moment of reckoning. In 1988, he met Ashfaq Majid Wani – the supreme commander of Jammu and Kashmir Liberation Front (JKLF) – and his life changed. Within JKLF, Ashfaq Wani, along with Hamid Sheikh, Javed Mir and Yasin Malik, formed the infamous HAJY group, an acronym of the first letter of their names. The group was among the first to espouse armed struggle in Kashmir.

Ashfaq Wani gave elementary training to Baba in handling a Kalashnikov rifle. Losing his innocence and yearning to go to Pakistan, the latter returned to Doda and carried out the blast under the bridge, followed by blasting a government jeep. There were other series of low-intensity blasts and incidents of arson in Kishtwar and Doda that Baba carried out.

Along with two close associates of Sabar Siddiqui – a code name given to Shabir Shah by the Inter-Services Intelligence (ISI) – Baba finally managed to exfiltrate into Pakistan in the autumn of 1989. They took a shorter route through a stream in Uri and then trudged on a hillock for three hours. The 'guests' were housed in a safe house in Rawalpindi, and all possible hospitality was extended to them. During their stay, a large number of ISI officials met Baba to chalk out a roadmap to intensify the armed insurgency in Kashmir. He was also enrolled for a three-month training module, but he did not complete it. Instead, he preferred to strategize the 'movement' to follow and Shabir Shah's role in it. He also visited Darra, a nondescript town at the border of Pakistan and Afghanistan, where an American Wild West kind of arms bazaar had sprouted after the Americans started sponsoring the Afghan mujahedeen against the Soviet occupation. The shopfronts lined on either side of a narrow street displayed Russian and Chinese guns along with the ammunition. Though Baba did not buy any arms, he was overwhelmed with what he saw, and his resolve for armed struggle in Kashmir was reaffirmed.

Through the network of other Kashmiri separatists and ISI officials lurking in Muzaffarabad, he was led to Brigadier Farooq in Islamabad. The brigadier saw a lot of potential in Baba since he belonged to Jammu – through him, the militancy could percolate into the Chenab Valley. He even advised Baba to start his own outfit and suggested a name, Al-Madad. The latter scoffed at the idea and remained loyal to Shabir Shah. Anyhow, both worked out a deal for weapons to be carried back. Baba infiltrated through Poonch and carried two Kalashnikovs and five pistols, apart from grenades and ammunition. The rest of the consignment was carried by other cadets from different places at different times.

Baba located himself in Srinagar and perhaps taking a clue from Brigadier Farooq's proposal, formed an organization called Muslim Janbaz Force (MJF) with headquarters in a small house in downtown Srinagar. The outfit was named after the Janbaz Force propounded by Zia-ul-Haq as national militia, modelled after the Chinese Army. It acts as a reserve force for the regular Pakistan Army in times of national emergency or war. Baba became the chief commander or Salar-e-Allah [literally, god's general] and took the nom de guerre of Babar Badar. Soon, the tentacles of the new outfit would spread in the Chenab Valley and Babar would command a formidable force of young radicals.[58]

There may have been varied reasons for the young men to join the ranks of militants, but the story of Nawaz Ahmed of Doda town was different. Nicknamed Dama, he was the son of a forest guard. He was a strapping young lad who played the drums in his school band. Being on the heavier side, he was often bullied by schoolmates. The news of his disappearance and subsequent return after taking arms training in POK had spread around in whispers. With a gun in his hand, he was not to be ridiculed anymore, and the bullies in the school were wary of that.

One day, the local police learnt about Dama hiding in a house on the upper side of the Doda town. A police party, accompanied by a component of the Central Reserve Police Force (CRPF), approached the hideout, and thoroughly searched the whole house without finding anything suspicious. Suddenly a fissure was noticed in the ceiling of the house. When it was parted, Dama was found crouched there, looking visibly terrified and helpless. With the assumption that he carried arms, earnest efforts were made to affect his surrender. Though some villagers also tried their bit, Dama remained stubborn. His sister was called to help with the negotiations. The slander that she smuggled grenades to him, hiding them in her bosom, still prevails. Dama hurled a grenade, and in the ensuing chaos, made good his escape. He trekked up the hill and melted into the forest. In this botched-up operation, a young under-trainee sub-inspector and a CRPF soldier laid down their lives. A few months later, Dama was killed in an encounter in Srinagar.

The year 1991 also saw the first militant casualty in Doda. The police received the information of Aijaz Wani visiting his family in Ghat village, about four miles uphill from Doda town. Wani was trained in Pakistan and was listed as an 'A' category terrorist in the police records. As the house was being cordoned, Wani, along with his sister and two minor brothers, hid themselves in a dried water tank adjacent to the house. In the ensuing firing, Wani, along with his three siblings, was killed. It was later learnt that the presence of Wani was tipped off by his elder brother for a paltry sum of money. This brought into the local parlance the word *mukhbir* or informer, collaborator, someone who 'betrays the cause'. For a long time, the sympathizers in Doda would go on to curse the brother of the slain militant, who even sacrificed his three other siblings for money. He still lives in Ghat with his aged parents; they all lead a normal life, trying to erase the painful memories of losing their kin.

Notwithstanding these initial incidents, the militancy gained dangerous colour in August 1993, when seventeen Hindus were gunned down in the Sarthal area of Kishtwar. A bus headed for Jammu started early in the morning from Kishtwar. On the outskirts of the town, a group of terrorists hijacked it. They forced the driver to take a detour, and after crossing the Chenab, the bus took a link road towards Sarthal.

The area has mixed population and is situated about 18 km away from the highway. The village is famous for its ancient stone temple that houses an eighteen-armed idol, considered as an incarnation of Goddess Durga. According to the myth, the idol was brought here by some devotees from Kashmir, when it was being ruled by Sikandar the Iconoclast, who was infamous for destroying temples and breaking idols. A new temple was built for the goddess by Zorawar Singh, who was an ardent devotee of Sarthal Devi. The devotees bring in tridents as offerings to the goddess and the temple boasts of a huge collection of tridents, some of them being hundreds of years old.

However, on that fateful day, Sarthal Devi did not come to the rescue of the hapless Hindus, who, midway on the road, were segregated and asked to line up before being rained upon with bullets from automatic weapons.

The Sarthal massacre raised a huge outcry in the country. As a result, serious steps were taken to tackle militancy in the Chenab Valley. Large number of security forces were deployed in the region. This led to the sprouting of bunkers, checkposts and security pickets all over the landscape – in the towns and villages, alongside the Chenab, overlooking the spurs, guarding bridges and other vital installations, staring down from buildings, in marketplaces, and at roundabouts. The proliferation of security installations intruded into the ecosystem of the local existence, causing ripples in their daily rhythm of life.

Inaccessibility of the region and the inevitable summer migration to the upper reaches by both Hindus and Muslims made the situation more difficult. It was not possible to provide security to every vulnerable member and house. Therefore, the concept of Village Defence Committees (VDCs) came into being. The retired servicemen in the Chenab Valley readily accepted the weapons, which were mostly archaic Bolt Action .303 rifles, phased out from the police department. Similarly, young men were also enrolled as members, and elementary weapons training was provided to them by the police and the army. The weapons, clubbed with the valour of the wielder, transformed the VDCs as solid deterrents to the free movement of terrorists, though pitted against the war-hardened militants armed with much sophisticated weapons.

Meanwhile, the militancy in Kashmir was getting increasingly criminalized and inflicted with internecine conflicts. Babar Badar had started to question the motives of Pakistan and her seriousness to 'liberate' Kashmir or further the agenda of 'bleeding India with thousand cuts'.[59] However, in 1991, he went on to execute the sensational kidnapping of two Swedish engineers employed at Uri Hydroelectricity Project. These engineers, along with their families, would often visit Gulmarg on weekends. Babar was aware of this routine and he had planned it well. That day, the Land Cruiser of the Swedes was blocked by a truck parked in the middle of the road in Magam. The engineers were whisked away at gun point and taken to an unknown location in the truck that was used to block the road. Another militant drove away the Land Cruiser with a shrieking woman and her child. Twenty km away, he abandoned the vehicle and disappeared.

The MJF put forth their demands, including setting up of a United Nations (UN) cell to probe human rights violations in Kashmir. The sensational kidnapping of the Swedes attracted a lot of international attention. The secretary general of the UNO and the prime minister of Sweden appealed for the safe release of the hostages. While basking in the glory of his deed that day, Babar would soon realize that this moment of triumph would also become his nemesis. The intensified operations to trace the kidnapped Swedes led to Babar being discovered, along with his accomplices, inside a hideout in Ganderbal. His subsequent interrogation also led to the release of two Swedish engineers. Babar would go on to spend two years in jail, which gave him enough time to ponder over his mission, the betrayals and the sheer futility of it all.

Meanwhile, through Track II diplomacy, the retired and serving diplomats, intelligence sleuths, army officers and civil society of both the countries, were looking for a middle way to resolve the Kashmir issue. One of their major successes came in 1996, with the mass surrender of the leadership and cadre of the MJF. It was done surreptitiously without any formal ceremony, showboating or media hype. One by one, about 300 terrorists, mostly from the Chenab Valley, surrendered with their weapons, and it included Babar Badar who reclaimed his original identity of Firdous Ahmed Baba. The government also ensured proper rehabilitation of the surrendered militants. About a dozen of them were given permits and easy loans to buy video coaches. Many others were helped with starting small businesses and retail shops and others were recruited as special police officers (SPOs). A few months after his surrender, Baba was nominated as a Member of Legislative Council of Jammu and Kashmir. From a gun-toting militant, he had become an honourable legislator.

The surrender of MJF, however, did not change the ground reality in the Chenab Valley. The swirling circle of blood continued, becoming more frequent and ferocious.

After the Chamba massacre of 1998 near the Saach Pass, the terrorists had fanned further out in the mountains of Paddar. In May 2001, seven Hindus were killed in Sazaar village of Paddar. To repose faith in the hapless Hindus, the militants purchased a goat from them and even paid thousand rupees for it. They made eight people accompany them to guide them to the adjoining ridge. Here, they sent one individual to the police post with the demand that the post should surrender their weapons. On the refusal of the brave policemen, the militants shot the hostages dead. In July, this was followed by the killing of four Hindus in a pasture in Chatroo, and the next night, eight others in Cherji. Then on 3 August, death knocked at door of the small village of Ladder about 30 km from the roadhead.

The Hindus slept in two *dhokes*,* while their herds roamed in the open, guarded by the domesticated dogs. When the first dhoke received the knock from the muzzle of a terrorist's gun, fourteen-year-old Dev Raj was the first to respond. Pushing the boy aside, two terrorists stormed inside and asked all sleeping men to wake and line up. They scoured the dhoke and carried with them the containers of ghee, maize flour and blankets. Terrorists abducted the sleeping men in both dhokes. One of the survivors recollected one terrorist asking him to light the earthen lamp to ensure nobody was left behind. Seventeen Hindus were killed in cold blood as their sheep bleated nearby.[60]

Dev Raj, who survived the massacre, later divulged the chilling details of the killings:

> 'You know what this is?' a terrorist had asked one of the hostages in Urdu.
>
> 'It is a gun, I know.'
>
> 'Do you know what comes out of a gun?'
>
> '*Goliyan.* [Bullets.]'
>
> 'Take a close look at the bullet,' the terrorist said and shot the hostage dead with fusillade of bullets from the Kalashnikov.[61]

Dev Raj, too, was shot, and was buried under a pile of dead bodies. He feigned death. The next day, a police team from the Atholi police station was the first to reach the massacre site. The dead bodies were brought to Atholi for the last rites on the banks of the Chenab. Hundreds of Hindus from neighbouring villages descended on Atholi town. Many of them were Village Defence Committee (VDC) members who came with their .303 rifles. They were joined by Hindus from Kishtwar and Doda who had been egged on by their leaders. Amidst the anger fuelled by fiery speeches, the crowd enlarged and became unruly. Two shops in Atholi bazaar belonging

* Dhokes are the summer abode of nomadic people.

to Muslims were burnt down. It was alleged that eight shots were fired at the masjid where labourers were engaged in repairing a portion of a wall. The mob alleged that there was a bunker being built in the masjid to be used by the militants.

The carnage had its impact on Doda, Bhaderwah and Kishtwar towns where the Hindus kept their shops shut. In Kishtwar, people took out processions and staged anti-government protests. The angry procession soon spiralled into a violent mob as they threw stones at government buildings and police patrols; a curfew was imposed in the town.[62]

In the following days, helicopters hovered over the Chenab and landed in Gulabgarh and Atholi. L.K Advani, the then home minister, was welcomed with angry sloganeering as he tried to soothe the temper of the people. Within a few days, the Jammu and Kashmir government ordered the imposition of the Disturbed Areas Act in Doda, Udhampur, Samba and Jammu districts, bringing the whole state under the ambit of the act. The mistrust stirred among communities would linger for a long time, with each community threatening to drown the other in the Chenab.

Despite the massacre of Hindus, few of their own youth joined the ranks of the militants. By the late 1990s, about a dozen Hindu militants were operating in the hills of Doda and Kishtwar. The association became more evident when security forces killed Kuldip Singh along with seven Muslim jihadis at Chatter Gali in Doda district in 2001. Another terrorist, Uttam Singh, was also killed. Incidentally, he had been trained in Pakistan and had risen to the rank of a district commander. On the night of his encounter, Uttam Singh along with his team of militants was trying to kidnap a Muslim soldier of the Indian Army.

Jihadis with names like Chattar Singh, Sachan Kumar, Sham Lal, Kripal Chand, Krishan Lal, Dhuni Chand, Bipin Kumar, Bittu Kumar and Virender Kumar were registered in the records of the police stations of the Chenab Valley. Some of them got killed, others were arrested and at least two surrendered.

One of the Hindu terrorists, Subash Kumar Shan, who was son of a constable of Jammu and Kashmir Police, rose to the rank of deputy divisional commander of Hizbul Mujahedeen (HM). In 2001, when he was studying in Class X, he went missing and joined HM, taking the codenames Kamran and Wasif. After being active for a decade, he was killed in the higher reaches of Marwah, along with three other Muslim terrorists. After leaving his home, Subash had never been in touch with his family. His father refused to accept his dead body, and he was buried in the 'martyr's graveyard' by some local Muslims.

Hindus joining the militant organizations was a great victory for the jihadi movement and Pakistan. It was propagandized that the militancy in Jammu and Kashmir had a secular colour. Though the Hindu militants took Muslim codenames, they rarely converted to Islam and continued to follow their religion. These militants were not married to the ideology of jihad but joined the ranks to escape their own drudgery and low social status. Some were lured by their Muslim friends and were subsequently brainwashed. In the case of Subash Kumar Shan, it was said that he was madly in love with a Muslim girl, and that instigated him to pick up the gun to impress her. In a conservative society, his love story would not have attained fruition, yet he continued to carry the gun.

Once they joined the militant outfits, the Hindu recruits were drawn deeper into the quagmire, since any attempt at reneging, would put their families in peril. On the other hand, the familiarity of the Hindu recruits with the terrain and their acquaintance with most Hindu families became advantageous for the militants.

7

The Call of the Muezzin

Continuing with its protracted course, the Chenab passes by the village of Atholi or 'the eight houses', settled on a plateau about a hundred feet above the bank of the river. Over the years, the houses, surrounded by terraced fields, have increased to hundreds and flank both sides of the strident river.

There are about two dozen Muslim houses in Atholi. The advent of Muslims in the Paddar Valley is fraught with diverse opinions. It is said that when Paddar became part of the Chamba kingdom, some Muslims, primarily the porters and blacksmiths, came here to look for work. Some say that they came in 1947, when communal riots swept through undivided Punjab and threatened to spill over to Himachal. Later, many of them crossed over from Kishtwar, which had a large population of Muslims.

When militancy reached the hills of Paddar, inevitable repercussions affected the harmonious existence of Hindus and Muslims. In August 2001, battle lines were drawn between the communities when violence hit Atholi, with the massacre of seventeen Hindus in the dhokes of Ladder. However, stray incidents detrimental to the interests of the two communities were largely settled amicably.

For example, in 2014, an incident involving a Hindu girl and a Muslim boy strained the relations between the two communities. After the love affair was discovered, there was much scurrilous gossip. The girl was found dead one day, and a hasty cremation took place. Though projected as a suicide, many suspected it to be a case of honour killing. Unable to bear the loss of his beloved, the boy died by suicide after a few days. Now the incident stands buried in the sands of time.

In another incident, the two communities joined hands when a major law-and-order problem arose in July 2010. On a pleasant day, two teenaged sisters from Atholi, along with a local boy, were sitting on the banks of the Chenab amidst the lush verdure. Probably, one of the sisters was in love with the boy. In small towns and close-knit societies, love affairs are either secretive or a taboo. A passing patrol of police saw the three sitting by the riverside, and it looked a little unusual to them. The trio was taken to the police station, where they were detained for many hours. The police accused the trio of indulging in immoral activities, which was vehemently denied by the youngsters. The girls were released by evening but they never reached home. The humiliated sisters did not have the courage to face their parents having been brought up in an orthodox culture. On their way back, they held hands and jumped into the Chenab. Their dead bodies were never recovered. The protests broke out in the town after the girls went missing, and the Atholi police station was pelted with stones.[63]

From Atholi, the Chenab flows alongside the Kishtwar road, which almost overlaps with the track used by Zorawar Singh. It is locally known as Ram Rasta or the path of Lord Rama. The Kishtwar–Gulabgarh road became operational in 1991. Before this, the only way to traverse the distance between the two towns – on a track that zigzagged in the mountain, along the riverside – was on foot or mules.

While doing research for this book, I came across many anecdotes narrated by Khalid Hussain, a retired bureaucrat. A Sahitya Akademi Award–winning author of Punjabi and Urdu literature, his short stories and novels are widely read by Punjabi-speaking people of India and Pakistan. In 1988, Khalid Hussain was posted as a project officer of the District Rural Development Agency (DRDA) in Doda. The agency worked as a catalyst to oversee and facilitate the implementation of different anti-poverty schemes of the Ministry of Rural Development.

In June 1988, in connection with one such scheme, the DC of Doda decided to visit Gulabgarh and Atholi along with a team of district officers. The DC, along with Khalid Hussain, Teli (district manager of Jammu and Kashmir Bank, Doda), Anaytullah (assistant project officer, DRDA) and a few other officers set out on a journey that normally entailed two night-halts enroute. The foot journey began from Padaryana, from where the track steeply wounded uphill and negotiated twelve curves – this part of geography is referred to as Baramarori or twelve bends. The undulated path, strewn with pine cones, traverses steeply over the ridge and then climbs down and largely runs parallel to the Chenab. At certain places where the track could not be engineered due to the perpendicular drop into the river, iron rods have been embedded in the rock of the mountain. The rods were then laid over with wooden planks of pine; the arrangement is locally called 'Sabal'. Precariously constructed, even the mules tread carefully over it, and the riders avoid looking at the river with its deadly whirlpools.

The two night-halts were made at forest rest houses in Lidrari and Shashu. On the third day, the team reached the Atholi Dak Bungalow. Several deputations met the DC with their grievances. Under a centrally sponsored scheme, fifty cases were approved for providing yaks, mules and cows to tribals on easy loans and subsidized prices. The next day, the DC and other colleagues had to cut short their visit on account of an official contingency.

Khalid Hussain, along with other officers, stayed put in Atholi for two more days before they began their journey back. As they prepared to leave, a young girl presented Khalid Hussain with kernels of walnuts wrapped in a cloth. Soon after, Khalid Hussain and Anaytullah, astride horses, prepared to leave. Teli also insisted on mounting a horse, despite not being an expert rider. Khalid Hussain discouraged him as it was not easy to control the horse on the treacherous track, but Teli remained adamant. Finally, a horse was arranged for him too.

Horses are intelligent animals and they can sense the confidence of their rider. If someone reeks of fear, the horse can instinctively smell it. Ten kilometres into the journey, to evade an unexpected jutting rock, Teli ducked down and pressed his hand against the side mountain. The horse rose on its hind legs, destabilizing the nervous rider. Teli wobbled, and, in an attempt to dismount the horse, lost his balance. As a result, his right foot got entangled in the stirrup. The horse got excited and lost its footing, tumbling down the cliff, dragging his rider along. Listening to the horror-filled shrieks of their colleague and the panicked neighs of the horse, Khalid Hussain and Anaytullah quickly jumped off their horses. They chased Teli and his horse down the cliff, tumbling through thorny bushes and getting bruised. By the bank of the Chenab, they were able to untangle Teli's leg from the stirrup of the now-dead horse.

Though Teli was not bleeding profusely, he was writhing in pain. He mumbled and asked for water. Khalid Hussain raced towards the Chenab and tried to bring some water in his cupped hands. He tried a few times but the water would leak before he reached Teli. Then he found a battered skull of a dead animal. Filling the skull with the river water, he reached the grievously injured Teli's side and offered it to him. Anaytullah unbound a blanket from the saddle of the dead horse and wrapped Teli with it. After a great struggle, the duo climbed up the steep gradient, carrying their injured colleague. Khalid Hussain fished out the walnut kernels from his pocket and stuffed them into Teli's mouth. Now, Teli wanted to urinate and Khalid Hussain opened the zippers of his trousers and helped him. Teli's skin had turned pale and his eyes dilated and it appeared as if life was being snuffed out of him. Khalid Hussain gazed at his unfortunate colleague helplessly as death embraced him, silencing his heartbeats and pulse.

Devastated at the tragedy, Khalid Hussain asked Anaytullah to watch over the cadaver as he proceeded to Shushoo to seek help. By the time he returned, it was late in the night. He was accompanied by Panchyat Inspector Duni Chand, a peon and few village-level workers. Teli's dead body was tied to charpoy and carried by four men, negotiating the perilous path with makeshift torches made from pine twigs bounded together. The solemn cortege marched amidst the screeching of crickets, clinking of brass bells around the necks of the mules and the roar of the river.

When the dead body reached Atholi, the villagers thronged the Dak Bungalow. The women wailed, beating their chests, shocked to see the benevolent manager who had approved their bank loans just a day before dead. As the morning broke, hundreds of more people from neighbouring villages descended to Atholi after hearing the tragic news. Meanwhile, Khalid Hussain had arranged for a helicopter to transport the dead body.[64]

In his autobiography *Main Ek Zinda Adami Hun* (2021), Khalid Hussain has painfully recounted the traumatic incident. Teli was fortunate to have landed on the bank of the Chenab; his body could be retrieved for a dignified burial. There have been many incidents where the strong currents of the Chenab have washed away unfortunate people, with their families and friends looking on helplessly. The locals blame it on destiny, with a stoic belief that nothing can be done while facing the fury of the river.

It is apparent that you cannot fight or resist a river as strong as the Chenab. You cannot shoot her down with a gun or dismember her with a sword. You cannot intimidate her, bribe and file a complaint against her. A large river like the Chenab never dies; eventually, she becomes a part of an ocean and continues to live, even after surrendering her identity.

~

Along the Ram Rasta, the Chenab flows past Kijai, a Muslim village, where another nullah meets the river. The minarets of the village mosque loom in the sky, as if waiting to catch a glimpse of the beautiful river and welcome her. The river had been welcomed similarly by the Buddhist gompas and Hindu temples in the past. Perhaps this is for the first time that the muezzin's calls blend with the hum of the Chenab.

A nondescript village, Kijai came to prominence when Azad, a local boy, joined the ranks of the militants. The son of a village-level worker, he crossed over to Pakistan for arms training but never returned. A little above on the mountain, another Muslim village of Afani sits, overlooking the Chenab. A boy named Bilal of this village also joined the militants, and he was killed in an encounter somewhere in the Kashmir Valley.

Not too far from the Muslim villages, the Chenab reaches the Hindu village of Kundal, which is perched on the left bank of the river, where Ladder Nullah joins the flow. Though the muezzin's calls from Kijai and Afani reach Kundal, the village has its own spiritual calling affiliated with the nearby village of Tatapani.

Tatapani, literally meaning 'hot water', is replete with hot springs. As per local folklore, Balram, Lord Krishna's older brother, had visited the place as an itinerant sage known as Sheshnag. He requested the local ruler Ruti for a piece of cultivable land. The enraged woman apparently hurled a spade towards the sage, hitting him in the eyes. In retaliation, Sheshnag impaled his trident in the land. When he retrieved it, water gushed out, flooding the land and destroying Ruti's kingdom.

A local ruler came forward and begged for forgiveness from the Sage. Sheshnag replied that he was leaving for his penance and asked the king to construct a temple at a specific spot, where a stone would miraculously appear along with hot water springing from the mountainside. True to the word of the Sage, the stone appeared the next day along with a hot spring. The local king also kept his promise and built a wooden temple at the spot. The temple today houses the stone of Sheshnag along with a 3-inch-tall Buddha statue, conch shells, ritual bells, tridents and holy water.

From the main spring in front of the temple, the bubbling sulphurous water is diverted to two adjacent rooms, forming warm pools for bathing. The devotees rush here for the blessings of Sheshnag to get their skin disorders and rheumatic pains cured, since the water is believed to have healing properties.

The legend of Sheshnag further unfolds: After establishing the spring, he had purportedly gone to Chitoo, requesting for help in cleaning the springs. There he met Chitoo Mata, along with five other villagers, who agreed to carry out the cleaning. Following the ritual, once every three years, a family from Chitoo comes to clean the springs after midnight. This is followed by a big fair.

The Chenab gurgles over the rocks on its way to Kishtwar. About 15 km short of Kishtwar the river reaches Bandarkoot. Here, the turbulent Marsudar – a river that originates in Wadwan Valley – converges with the Chenab. The purists say that this is the point where the Chandrabhaga becomes the Chenab and not at Sansari Nullah where the river enters Jammu and Kashmir. They base their theory on the quantity of water that Marsudar carries, which, in their opinion, is more in volume than the Chenab.

There are no inhabited houses at Bandarkoot, yet many people visit the place. They are attracted by the confluence of the rivers as well as the *ziyarat* at the foothill and an ancient temple on the other side of the river. On Baisakhi festival, a big fair is held here. After a dip in the confluence, the devotees pay obeisance at both the temple and the ziyarat.

The ziyarat is attributed to Sheikh Zain ud Din Wali, who lived in the fifteenth century. He was the chief disciple of the leading Sufi saint of Kashmir, Sheikh Nur ud Din Wali, popularly known as Nund Rishi.

Sheikh Nur ud Din Wali's father, Salar Sanz, was a Hindu, with his family roots in Kishtwar. It is said that after having a dispute with his family, Salar Sanz shifted to Kulgam in Kashmir. Here, he embraced Islam under the influence of a Sufi saint and was rechristened as Sheikh Salar ud Din. At the insistence of his spiritual master, he married a widow who had been brought up by the village watchman after she was orphaned at a young age. Through this union, Nur ud Din Wali was born in 1377 in the Qaimoh village of Kulgam. As per the folklore, he did not suckle at his mother's breast for three days after his birth. Lalla Arifa, a local woman who used to take care of his pregnant mother, was the one who breastfed the young child. Lalla Arifa would go on to become one of the greatest Sufi poetesses of Kashmir, popularly known as Lalleshwari or Lal Ded. Sheikh Nur ud Din Wali would transform into a greatest mystic, poet, philosopher and preacher from Kashmir. 'Shruks', the excerpts from his poems, four to six lines usually, which encapsulate his teachings, continue to echo all over the region. Sheikh Zain ud Din turned out to be his most important disciple.[65]

Zain ud Din Wali was born in a Rajput family as Zia Singh or Zaina Singh. His father ruled a small principality near Bandarkoot, who was assassinated when Zia was thirteen years old. As luck would have it, Zia was afflicted with a serious ailment. Despite all possible treatment, the disease turned serious, with no chances of recovery. At that point, Sheikh Nur ud Din Wali was passing by Kishtwar. Zia Singh's mother pleaded with him to save her son. He agreed but on a promise that Zia would meet him in Kashmir after his recovery.

However, the legend goes that Zia's mother did not keep her promise and her son took ill again. His mother kept crying until she was visited by a dream reminding her of the unfulfilled promise. She resolved to rectify her mistake and, along with Zia, proceeded to Kashmir to meet Sheikh Nur ud Din. Zia and his mother adopted Islam, and they were renamed Zain-ud-Din and Zoon Ded, respectively.

Another story suggests that it was Nund Rishi who while passing through Bandarkoot happened to see Zain Singh. He asked the young man to accompany him to Kashmir. For this purpose, he threw his *jai-e-namaz* (prayer rug) in the Chenab and started off for Kashmir. Though the Chenab does not go to Kashmir, but Zain Singh tossed his own prayer mat in the river and followed Nund Rishi's path. Apparently, Nund Rishi did not like Zain Singh's gesture of travelling independently. Therefore, he directed him to carry out his meditation at the same place. Zain Sigh complied and stayed in a Bandarkoot cave to meditate for twelve more years.

Later, in Kashmir, Zain ud Din took allegiance to the order of Nund Rishi and spent the rest of his life spreading his message.[66] He meditated in Sopore, north Kashmir, for a long time and attained spiritual perfection. At this stage, Nund Rishi directed him to shift to a cave in Aishmuqam and meditate there for the rest of his life. On his arrival, Zain ud Din found that the entry to the cave was obstructed by snakes and scorpions. It is said that the saint carried a club with him that was given to him by his master. Seeing the serpents, he placed the club on the ground, where it instantly transformed into a dreadful cobra with majestic fangs. The snakes in the cave were awestruck and immediately surrendered and left the cave. Zain ud Din spent many years in the cave, meditating, surviving only on dry walnut kernels. He led a life of great simplicity and spread the message of love and social equality.

After his death in 1140–41, he was buried in Aishmuqam, where a great mausoleum came up. At the same place, there are twenty-four more graves of his relatives and closest disciples. The shrine also houses some relics associated with the saint, namely, a pair of patten, a rosary, a wooden club and a copy of the Holy Quran.[67] The *Urs* or the anniversary of the saint is celebrated in mid-April with congregational prayers, and is attended by thousands, exhibiting a picture of inter-faith existence and the shared heritage of Kashmir. On this occasion, torches, locally known as zool, are lit on the surrounding hillocks.

There is a very interesting story behind the burning of torches, which is evocative of the famous story in the Mahabharata of Bhimsena and Bakasura's battle at Ekachakra. Many centuries back,

Aishmuqam village was under the terror of a local demon. There was hardly any day when someone from the village was not preyed upon by the demon. One day, the villagers approached the demon and requested him to eat them one by one. The demon agreed on a condition that the villagers would offer him bread every day. After a few months, it was the turn of a young Gujjar orphan called Bumisad to be the demon's victim. The boy's turn to be devoured by the demon coincided with the day of his wedding. Bumisad approached the demon with the offering of bread. The boy started munching on the bread instead of proffering it to the demon. The outraged monster yelled, 'Why are you eating my food?' He replied nonchalantly, 'The food I eat would eventually become your food too.' He was audacious enough to challenge his enemy in a fight. Finding an easy adversary, the demon agreed to the challenge, vain about his own strength. Surprisingly, the fight continued for a week and, finally, Bumisad was able to vanquish the demon.

When the news of killing of the demon reached the villagers, they emerged from their homes carrying torches made of burning zool. When the light of the zool fell on the dead body of the demon, bloodied and battered, a joyous wave of victory spread all around. From that day of the triumph of Bumisad, the zool festival of torches is celebrated during the Aishmuqam ziyarat.

In 2015, a Hindi movie starring Salman Khan, called *Bajrangi Bhaijan*, was shot here. It was the first movie that was granted permission to shoot inside the shrine and featured a Qawwali sung by Adnan Sami.

Ahead of Bandarkoot, at a place called Dul, the river Chenab is tamed, by a run-of-the-river hydroelectricity project of 390 megawatts (MW). While a dam stores the water here, the powerhouse and headrest tunnel are at Hasti, about 20 miles away. Therefore, the project is called the Dul–Hasti power project. The project was brought to Kishtwar because of the efforts of Om Mehta, a towering personality of Kishtwar. Om Mehta's sister Krishna Mehta had fled from Muzaffarabad when the Kabalis had ransacked the town in 1947 and killed her husband, who was the DC.

Being the chairman of the Chamber of Commerce Co-operative Society of Kishtwar, Om Mehta had managed to win popularity across the communities. He dabbled in politics and rose to become the country's home minister in the early 1970s under Indira Gandhi.

Prime Minister Indira Gandhi laid the foundation stone of the project in April 1983 in Shalimar, where a National Hydroelectricity Power Corporation (NHPC) colony was constructed. Being the lowest bidder in the global tender, a French consortium, Dumez Sogea Borie Sae (DSB), was allotted the contract. The actual work started in 1989, five years after the assassination of Indira Gandhi. With the lack of a proper road network, at times, cement, wood, stone and steel had to be hauled via a helicopter. With terrorists lurking on the nearby hills, the work kept stumbling over one roadblock after another.

One evening in 1991, the jeep of Mosio Antonio Silva, the French engineer associated with the project, was blocked by a truck on a narrow road near Bandarkoot. A group of terrorists stormed out of the truck and kidnapped the engineer. They pushed the jeep down a gorge, which rolled down but stopped short of the Chenab, its chassis and wheels destroyed. The terrorists disappeared with the engineer into the forests of the nearby mountains. The jeep had been sabotaged in order to give the impression of the engineer meeting with an accident; his body presumably being washed by the torrent of the river. However, the team of French mechanical engineers who carefully studied both the scene of crime and the damaged vehicle ruled out accident as a possibility.

The police swung into action and arrested the driver of the truck used to waylay the engineer. A local contractor was soon traced, who admitted to conspiring with the terror outfit Al Fateh to abduct the engineer. The kidnapping created a general fear psychosis, leading to the French consortium abdicating their contract. After repeated negotiations, the engineer was released on payment of a handsome ransom. For the next four years, the project was stalled. After many tenders and allurement of the foreign companies, the project was finally taken up by M/S Jai Parkash Associates Limited, a Delhi-based business conglomerate, popularly known as the Jaypee Group. Despite many impediments, the work on the project continued at a slow pace and the first phase of the project was finally commissioned in 2003.

Further tapping the tremendous hydel capacity of the rivers in Jammu and Kashmir, 10 miles away from the Dul–Hasti project, one of the biggest hydroelectric projects of 1 gigawatt (GW) is under construction on the river Marsudar. Pakistan had vociferously objected to the project, arguing that it violated the Indus Water Treaty.

The Indus River system has been vital for the irrigation of Punjab from time immemorial. The Mughals built an efficient canal system, drawing water mainly from the five rivers of Punjab. In the nineteenth century, the British further elaborated the system by not only laying new canals but also reviving and modernizing the old ones. After Partition, water sharing became a major point of dispute between the two countries. The rivers in the Indus system originated from the Indian Himalayas or Tibetan glaciers and flowed through the undivided Punjab to finally drain into the Arabian Sea. Boundaries can be marked on land but not on the water.

The Indus Water Treaty was signed by the two countries in 1960. Brokered by the World Bank, the preamble of the treaty recognized the rights and obligations of each country for optimum utilization of the Indus system in the true spirit of goodwill, friendship and cooperation. According to the treaty, the control of the water of three eastern rivers – Beas, Ravi and Sutlej – was given to India; similarly, the control of three western rivers – Indus, Chenab and Jhelum – was given to Pakistan. Most experts felt it was a fair treaty, and India has been generous enough to share the waters in a just manner.

The treaty constituted a Permanent Indus Commission, having a commissioner from each country, to bilaterally solve any future disputes arising in the sharing of waters. Most of the issues have been settled through legal procedures provided within the framework of the treaty, and despite three wars and numerous skirmishes between the two countries, the treaty remained unscathed.

However, now and then, when tensions flare up between the two countries, the sanctity of the Indus Water Treaty is also questioned. After the Uri attack of 2016, Prime Minister Modi had said that water and blood cannot flow together. In 2019, after the deadly Pulwama attack, a senior Indian minister, Nitin Gadkari, proposed that India should stop sharing waters of the eastern rivers with Pakistan. On the other hand, Pakistan has often accused India of violating the provisions of the treaty, often harping about the construction of new hydel projects.

In Pakistan, terrorist organizations like Lashkar-e-Taiba, have called for war against India over water rights. Spitting vitriol against India, Lashkar-e-Taiba chief Hafiz Saeed once claimed that fields across the Punjab province in Pakistan were turning to dust because of India's 'water terrorism'. He was adamant that the Hindu India was building dams in Kashmir to choke Pakistan's water supply and cripple its agriculture. Intermittently, India threatens to withdraw from the treaty, alleging that unequal benefits are accruing to Pakistan.

Though the banks of Chenab thrum with spiritualism, her water has been vulnerable to disputes. However, no one can stop the river on her forward journey, her waters resonating with the wisdom of saints and lunacy of politics.

8

The Land of Saints

A few miles from Bandarkoot, the Chenab takes a major bend to change its course and passes on the outskirts of Kishtwar town. The etymology of the name 'Kishtwar' has many theories. Some say that the name 'Kishtwar' is derived from *kaasht* or *kaath*, which means wood. A possible analogy for this premise is that Kishtwar is surrounded by dense forests all over.

As per an ancient legend, once, a massive flood occurred in the Chenab and the Marsudar Rivers, submerging a large area in and around Kishtwar, converting it into a vast lake called Govardhansar. Thousands of years later, a series of earthquakes tore apart the mountains and drained the water. The Earth dried up and the forests grew anew. Today, amidst Kishtwar town, there is a sprawling grazing field called Chaugan spread over an area of 165 acres. It is one of the biggest grounds in North India. Once upon a time, the ground was used to play horse polo, a game cherished by both kings and commoners.

During this time, a saint, Sherpal, sat down on the edge of the Govindsar Lake to meditate. He built a temple and started worshipping Goddess Maha Kali. The saint's fame spread far and wide; a lot of people started to settle down here, and the place came to be called Mahakal Garh. Soon differences started to develop between the followers of Sherpal. Seeing the bitter internecine strife, Sherpal disappeared one day. In his memory, the place came to be known as Sherkoot. Today, on the outskirts of Kishtwar, a village called Sarkoot exists. The people of Sarkoot started saffron cultivation in large tracts of land that came to be called Lohit Mandal or Pargana-e-Zaffran, the land of saffron. The Mahabharata records: 'After this Arjuna conquered Kashmiri armed forces and kings of ten Mandals including Lohit Mandal.' The area where saffron grows is still called Mandal.

Despite the happiness evoked both by the saffron and spirituality, another theory propagates Kishtwar as a place of suffering. In Hindi, *kasht* means affliction and *waar* is a place. Therefore, Kishtwar is a place of sorrow and pain, validating the belief that anyone staying here shall face starvation during the day and cold at night. Another view says that when the Rathers and Ganais of Kashmir settled here, they held sway over large territories abutting Doda and ruled from Cherhar. They planted apricots in a large area, and the fruit was soon available in abundance. During this time, the traders of Punjab, popularly called Panjsansis, would visit to trade their merchandise of salt, jaggery, cotton and decorative pieces. In return, they took saffron, cumin seed, clarified butter, medicinal herbs and apricots. The dry skin of apricots is called *kushta* in Punjabi and, hence, the area started to be called Kishtwar instead of Cherhar. Even today, there exists a small village called Cherhar that has now been assimilated in the fast-growing town of Kishtwar.[68]

For a major part, Kishtwar has been ruled by Hindu kings, till Raja Kirat Singh converted to Islam in the seventeenth century. The Raja was impressed by the policies of Aurangzeb, who gave him a new name – Raja Sa'adat Yar Khan. Some historians believe that this conversion was an outcome of pressure exerted by the kings of Kashmir, who threatened annexation if he failed to convert. By this time, the majority Hindu population had shrunk because a large number of Muslim Kashmiris started settling here in the town and villages. The reason for this migration has not been clear, yet a view persists that some were poor peasants who escaped the persecution of the feudal classes of Kashmir.

Despite various views by historians, it seems that the Raja, along with hundreds of followers, voluntarily converted to Islam, deeply impressed by the teachings of a Sufi saint named Mohammed Farid-ud-Din Baghdadi.

Early in the seventeenth century, Farid-ud-Din Baghdadi, along with his wife Shehzada Bibi and four disciples came to India from Iraq. He was hosted by the Mughal King Shah Jahan in Agra and Delhi, before he embarked on further travels. Leaving his wife in Delhi, he entered Jammu and Kashmir from Bhimber and, travelling through the hills of Pir Panjal, reached a place called Deng Batal in Gool Valley. He propagated religion here. The local Hindu chieftain was so impressed by his preaching that he gave his daughter in marriage – called Roshan Dil after converting to Islam – to stop the resolute saint from moving further.

However, the saint once again left his wife behind, and moved on and reached Ramban, where he preached Islam for a few weeks. Finally, he reached Doda and took in his third wife, Mai Malhat – a daughter of a village official from Nagri. After a stay of two years in Doda, he moved towards Kishtwar.

On hearing of the arrival of the saint and to deter his entry in the town, the Raja of Kishtwar ordered the closure of the bridge at Bandarkoot. Farid-ud-Din had to resort to his miraculous powers to cross the river. He spread his prayer mat on the river and, along with his followers, rode the mat and crossed the Chenab easily. In Kishtwar, he took shelter in a small thatched hut.

In the next few days, the news of the arrival of a great saint spread all around, and many people thronged the cottage he was staying in. The news also reached the local raja who sent his spies to find out about the stranger. Due to divine intervention, when the raja slept at night, he dreamt of the Sun and the Moon, accompanied by four bright stars. His cot overturned and he saw a saintly figure under a thatched roof. He immediately woke up and ran to the saint asking for forgiveness. The raja built a house for the saint near his palace, where Farid-ud-Din stayed for a long time. At different intervals, his three wives joined him here.

For many years, Farid-ud-Din preached in Kishtwar and became popular as Shah Sahib. He transformed the social and religious milieu of Kishtwar and the town became a great spiritual centre. Soon Islam spread all over the Chenab Valley.

Shah Sahib was blessed with two sons from Shehzada Bibi and Malhat Mai – Syed Asrar-ud-Din and Syed Akhyar-ud-Din, respectively. Another son born to Shehzada Bibi died in infancy. Both Asrar-ud-Din and Akhyar-ud-Din had innate saintly qualities, inheriting the divinity from their father. Akhyar-ud-Din travelled widely in Punjab and Kashmir to preach Islam. The stories about his piety, worship and asceticism vouch that he did not sleep on a bed for forty years and instead squatted all the time, reciting from the Holy Quran.

As per popular legends, the infant Asrar-ud-Din started speaking to his mother right from the womb, and on his birth, he exuded the fragrance of roses and possessed a halo, luminous like the full moon. He was blessed with miraculous powers to cure the ill, grant sight to the blind and foretell the future.

Asrar-ud-din often played polo with a Hindu friend in Chaugan. One day, having lost a game to his friend, Asrar-ud-Din promised to square up with him the next day. While on his way to Chaugan the next day, he saw a cortege of mourners carrying the mortal remains of his Hindu friend. He found out that his friend had died the previous night due to cardiac arrest. Asrar-ud-Din asked the mourners to lay down the bier. Pointing at the corpse with his staff, he commanded, 'Rise by the order of the God. You have to still repay my turn in the game.' To keep his promise, he resurrected his dead friend, had a game with him and defeated him. His Hindu friend went on to live for forty more years. After the miracle, the whole family of the Hindu friend converted to Islam.

As per another story, Asrar-ud-Din saved a man from getting murdered. According to this tale, a woman came to him and fell at his feet, weeping. Her husband had gone on a business trip, but nothing had been heard of him for many days. The saint told her, 'Your husband is on his way to Delhi and is sitting under a tree right now. However, after two more stages of the journey, he would be beheaded by robbers.' When the woman started wailing, the saint asked her to hurry along to her home. On reaching her house, the woman was astounded to see her husband, alive and happy. He was narrating how, during his journey, while he slept under a tree, an invisible hand had lifted him and brought him home. When he was told the reality, he decided to serve the saint all his life. But that was not to happen for long, since Asrar-ud-Din would die at the age of eighteen.

Disapproving Asrar-ud-Din's miracles, which he firmly believed to be exclusively in god's purview, his father prayed to god for calling back Asrar-ud-Din to his abode. Apparently, one day Farid-ud-Din ordered a bowl of candy syrup, whispered his prayers over it and asked his son to sip it. When Asrar-ud-Din drank the liquid, he fell down dead. He lay facing the Kaba for three days. Farid-ud-Din spoke to his dead son, emphasizing the benefits of returning to the world of seers, far away from the mortal world. Many heretics would receive guidance and attain serenity due to him and he had reached an exalted stage, Farid-ud Din further propounded.

There was a deep mourning after the death of Asrar-ud-Din. Both animals and humans wailed in unison. A shrivelled tree, which had once bloomed at the sight of the young saint, withered again. It was cut down and the wood was used for crafting his coffin. Apparently, when the last prayers were being offered, red and green birds filled the skies, reciting holy prayers. These birds shaded the coffin with their wings spread fully. When the coffin was being carried through Chaugan, it suddenly became heavy. The oracle proclaimed that it was the ideal burial place. Asrar-ud-Din was buried reverentially at the same spot. His disciples later built a mausoleum which is now known Asthan-e-Payeen – Choti Ziyarat or the Lower Shrine.

Some accounts suggest that Farid-ud-Din went on to live for a staggering 181 years. When he died, his devout followers constructed a shrine in his honour, where he lies buried along with his three wives, disciples and infant son. The mortal remains of his elder son Akhyar-ud-Din, who died in Kashmir, were also brought here and buried next to him. Asthan-e-Bala – Badi Ziyarat or the Upper Shrine – is a revered place. Every year in June, an impressive Urs takes place at the ziyarat, which is attended by thousands of Muslims and Hindus from all over the Chenab Valley. Besides religious discourses and special prayers, the sacred relics of the Saint and his sons – a sword, clothes, sacred hair of all three of his sons, a comb, turbans and a prayer cap, quilt and a stick he used all his life – are also displayed. The descendants of the Hindu wife of Farid-ud-Din, who are still Hindus, continue to have a special role in some rituals associated with the shrine. Similarly, at the Choti Ziyarat, many Hindu farmers unfailingly leave a part of their first harvest at the doorstep of the shrine as an offering. There are a bunch of friends – Hindus and Muslims – who registered a charitable trust called Faridia Charitable Trust, named after the saint. They raise resources to help poor patients at the local government hospital.[69]

Another institute associated with the Badi ziyarat is the Islamia Faridia Higher Secondary School, which was founded in 1905. Starting as a boys' school, it has been imparting modern education and is now a most sought-after co-educational institute. For a long time, the school was ably run by Darvesh Mohammad Ishaq Bazdar, one of the most popular saints in the area. Commonly known as Ishaq Sahib, his Kashmiri poetry became very popular and is still recited in literary gatherings and on radio and television programmes. The followers of the paralysed saint would usually flock around him, seeking his blessings, as he sat in his wheelchair.

Darvesh passed away in 1999 and is buried in the complex of Malik Manzil in Kishtwar town.

Being a mosaic of composite culture and plural ethos, Kishtwar remained a cradle of religious tolerance. The fragrance of Sufism, preaching the values of piety, compassion and peace were imbibed by all the communities. In 1947, when communal riots broke out in Jammu, Bhalesa, Bhaderwah and other places, Kishtwar remained aloof from all the mayhem. The town's inhabitants had formed joint Hindu–Muslim patrolling teams to prevent rioters from entering Kishtwar. Because of these collective efforts made by the elders, many Hindus and Muslims of distant villages sought refuge in Kishtwar.

This strong inter-community bond continued for next many decades and remained the hallmark of collective triumphs and travails. In 1969, a strong agitation for the opening of a degree college was started by the students in Kishtwar. The demand was genuine because due to lack of higher-education facilities, the students had to go to either Doda or Bhaderwah to pursue their studies. The agitation abated after a while due to lack of response. The agitation was revived in 1974 under the umbrella of Kishtwar Welfare Front. This movement gained more momentum because of its backing by the political leaders irrespective of their party affiliations. On 13 June 1974, a protest march turned violent and police resorted to firing to handle the rampaging crowd. Four protesters – two from each community – got killed in the firing. After the incident, a complete civil-disobedience movement started in the town, which lasted for one month. Ultimately, at the intervention of the highest authorities, a job-oriented college was promised. Finally, the Degree College was established in Kishtwar in 1986.

As a salute to the college, a memorial in honour of the four martyrs – the names embossed in gold on a black slab – still exists in the town. In 1982, another name was added to the memorial: A

Muslim, who had fallen prey to the police bullets while agitating for the demand for the separate district of Kishtwar. This agitation was once again spearheaded jointly by the Hindus and Muslims.

However, with the advent of militancy, all the inter-community camaraderie started to deteriorate in the 1990s. The violence perpetrated through a spate of selective killings, during this period, sowed the first seeds of mistrust.

On 10 May 1993, a popular leader and the general secretary of the Hindu Raksha Samiti, Satish Kumar Bhandari, was shot dead in broad daylight outside his shop in Kishtwar town. Bhandari was a true nationalist and a vociferous opponent of militancy. These were good enough reasons to antagonize the terrorists.

Apprehending communal tension, a curfew was imposed in the town. Defying the curfew, thousands joined the funeral procession of the slain leader. The anger among the Hindus was palpable as they torched a few Muslim houses and the Sir Iqbal Academy. Then, in a tragic incident, Abdul Qayoom Dar, a civilian, was burnt alive in his brother's house. Dar's brother lived close to the Hindu-dominated area of Kuleed, and Dar, after shifting his brother's family to a safer area, had returned to secure the house. The marauding Hindu crowd set the house on fire and he was burnt alive. This was followed by communal clashes resulting in the looting of shops and destruction of properties of both communities on a large scale.

Despite the army presence and strict curfew, the stalemate continued for weeks. In the following days, there was more violence and killings including an ambush on a patrol party of the BSF leading to the death of an official. The next day, three Muslim employees of the Public Health Engineering department, including an assistant executive engineer, were found dead.

The communal schism caused by the assassination of Satish Bhandari and the subsequent violence left a deep impact on the relations between the two communities. The seed of mistrust was continuously watered by the armed militants, and the festering wounds of hatred were not easy to heal. The day of Bhandari's killing is observed as martyr's day, and a function is organized at the Gauri Shankar temple to honour him and other Hindus who fell to the bullets of the terrorists.

Despite an uneasy calm, the two communities continued to coexist peacefully and mutually engaged in businesses. However, all this got another jolt on 9 August 2013, when the air was joyous with the celebration of Eid.

The *namazi*s had started to arrive early at the Chaugan ground for prayers. After the holy month of fasting, the mood was effervescent with celebration. Most of the men were dressed up in new clothes, and prayer caps sat proudly on their heads. The young boys in their new finery, their pockets heavy with eidi or the money given by their elders, looked ecstatic. A large number of handcarts and wheelbarrows had formed a little makeshift bazaar on one side of the ground. They sold baubles, sweetmeats, fritters, ceramic vases and skullcaps. A line of crippled beggars sat anxiously, seeking alms. Amidst this festivity, at various spots, policemen stood alert with their truncheons and guns.

Most riots give rise to multiple stories about their beginning. On that Eid day, it was said that the violence started from the Hindu-dominated Kuleed Chowk. As per this account, a strong procession of the Muslims, while passing by the locality, started raising provocative slogans. This led to stone-pelting by the resentful Hindus, resulting in scattering of the procession. Another view says that a motorcycle rider, who happened to be a prominent Hindu leader's bodyguard, was trying to wade through the procession. In the melee, he landed in a heated argument with some members of the procession. The argument soon turned into fisticuffs and, allegedly, the bodyguard was beaten up by the crowd. This provoked the Hindu neighbourhood and people started pelting stones at the procession. Word spread, and the Muslim crowd, supplemented by the Eid namazis soon swelled to thousands. The Hindus also grouped up and both communities started throwing stones at each other in the sprawling Chaugan.

A large component of the crowd charged towards the main market, where it started to loot and burn shops. In that frenzy, business establishments and vehicles were set on fire. Soon, black smoke billowed all over Kishtwar town. In the ensuing chaos, a private armoury was looted, which included forty guns and thousands of cartridges. The army was ordered to march into the town. By this time, an unemployed Hindu youth's body was riddled with pellets and a middle-aged, handicapped Muslim was found charred to death.

The next day, massive protests were carried out in the rest of the Jammu province. In Atholi, both communities came face to face and pelted stones at each other. It was also alleged that some VDC members fired their official weapons. The injured were taken to the hospital, from where the grievously injured were referred to be shifted to a Jammu hospital. When one of the ambulances reached the helipad in Gulabgarh, a violent mob broke down the fence and entered the area. They attacked the ambulance, and pulled out an attendant and beat him to death. It was also alleged that two other men had gone missing and they could never be traced. In a town where a river as thunderous as the Chenab flows, one can imagine where these 'disappeared men' have gone.[70]

Except for the massacres of the minorities, communal conflagrations and sapphire mines, the far-flung Kishtwar mostly remained out of sight and mind of the national milieu. However, this changed in September 2011, when terror descended from the towering hills of Kishtwar and exploded right in the heart of Lutyens's Delhi.

After the scorching heat of the preceding months, September started to usher in pleasant weather in Delhi. During this time of the year, the wide avenues of South Delhi and its various mansions started to blossom with dahlia, chrysanthemums and petunia. On 7 September, the Delhi High Court complex, showcasing elegant Indo-British architecture, had begun to bustle with people – the plaintiffs, lawyers, judicial clerks, public witnesses and others. The maximum rush was at the reception counters between gate numbers four and five. Four long queues of people – two for men, one for women and the last for the senior citizens – were present in front of four desks. These desks were manned by the court employees who were busy stamping the mandatory visitor passes required for entry inside the court complex. Wednesday, being the day of public interest litigation hearings, drew a huge footfall.

Amidst this hustle, a deafening explosion ripped through the space, with a rising ball of fire, followed by plumes of smoke choking the air. Within a few seconds, a huge crater emerged, at the place of the blast. All around, broken tiles, shreds of glass, shattered furniture, mangled metal, mobile phones, files and bloodied human flesh lay strewn. The impact of the blast was so severe that some limbs and tatters of clothes were seen hanging on the branches of the nearby trees. Fifteen people died in the blast and scores were injured.

Within a few hours of the blast, media houses and news studios received two e-mails claiming responsibility for the blast. Two days later, two more e-mails claimed that the blast was carried by an indigenous terrorist organization called the Indian Mujahedeen. However, the investigations by National Investigation Agency (NIA) proved that two of the e-mails were hoaxes. These were eventually traced to two pranksters, one of them only fifteen years old.

The first e-mail from harkatuljihadi2011@gmail.com was received by popular news channels Aaj Tak and NDTV, and in a crisp message, it said:

> We owe the responsibility of today's blast at High Court Delhi... Our demand is that Afzal Guru's[71] death sentence should be repealed immediately else we would target major high courts and THE SUPREME COURT OF INDIA.

The NIA investigators traced the e-mail to Kishtwar and the Internet protocol address further tracked it down to the Global

Internet Cyber Cafe located in the Kishtwar market. The telephone lines between Delhi and Kishtwar got busy, and a case was registered in the latter.

The police immediately swooped on the Internet cafe and subjected its owner to questioning. On its first floor, the cafe had six computer terminals installed inside small chambers made of plywood. The CPUs of all computers were seized and their hard discs were scanned. The web history of the computer in the third chamber revealed the URL for the creation of a new Gmail account.[72]

The cafe had not followed the standard instructions, mandated by law, of maintaining user details in a register, including the complete addresses of the visitors. These instructions are often ignored by most Internet cafes across the country.

The cafe owner gave the Descriptive Roll of the users of the third chamber that day. With the earnest efforts of police and analysis of the bulk data of the mobile tower in the vicinity, finally, a user – a local Hindu – was traced. Though his interrogation revealed that he had nothing to do with the e-mail, he gave the useful tip of having seen two young men hurriedly coming down the staircase of the cafe while he was going up. One of them wore a red-coloured half-sleeved shirt. This was corroborated by the owner, who affirmed that the two men had visited the cafe and they were allotted two separate chambers, the third and the fifth. Later they were together in the third chamber for some time.

The hunt for the 'red shirt' was carried out extensively for two days in the bazaars, streets, squares, mosques and Chaugan. About half-a-dozen men wearing red shirts were randomly picked up by the police. Finally, Abid Hussain Bhawani – a Class XI student at the Islamia Faridia Higher Secondary School, Kishtwar – broke down and admitted to having written the e-mail. Through his disclosure, his accomplice was also identified and picked up, but was later released since his role in the conspiracy was not established.

After the sustained questioning of Bhawani, the name of Amir Abbas Dev came up. Amir was a distance-learning BA student at the Kishtwar branch of the Maulana Azad Urdu University, Hyderabad. He was highly radicalized and spent a lot of time at the Mohammadia mosque in Kishtwar. Later, the investigation revealed that Amir had motivated Bhawani to send the e-mail to claim the blast. Along with studying in a school, Bhawani was also taking computer classes at a local institute and, therefore, was ideally suited to handle a computer and the Internet.

Amir Abbas Dev's arrest cracked open the whole plot. Soon, the name of Wasim Akram Malik surfaced, who turned out to be the chief conspirator. He belonged to a well-off family, and his father had shifted him to Jammu for his schooling. There, Wasim got in touch with Salim Wani, who was associated with Jaish-e-Mohammed. Influenced by Wani and his associates, Wasim was introduced to online jihadi literature and read extensively about the Al-Qaeda leader Osama Bin Laden and the Taliban chief Mullah Omar. He was particularly impressed by Bin Laden, who chose an austere lifestyle, giving up luxuries for the sake of Islam. Once, while roaming around in Jammu along with Salim Wani, Wasim was detained by the police. However, being a juvenile, he was let off after a few days. Finding his son straying towards radicalization, Wasim's father enrolled him to study Unani medicine at a medical college in Sylhet, Bangladesh.

Meanwhile, the years of militancy and communal undercurrents in Kishtwar had its impact on the Malik household. In 2010, Wasim's younger brother, Junaid Akram Malik, a student of Sir Iqbal Academy, Kishtwar, vanished into the forests of Chatroo and joined the ranks of the HM.

In Bangladesh, Wasim met a lot of Kashmiri students and other like-minded men. Some were from his college and others from the nearby medical college. He got associated with a religious organization called the Islami Chitrashibir (Islamic student organization in Bangladesh). It was a forum of vigorous debate regarding issues pertaining to the Muslim community throughout the world. The topic of secessionism in Kashmir was often discussed.

In 2011, when the American marines killed Osama Bin Laden in Abbottabad, Wasim accompanied his friends to a local mosque to offer funeral prayers in absentia to honour the 'martyrdom' of Bin Laden. Wasim started to revere Ayman al-Zawahiri, an Egyptian doctor and the successor to Osama Bin Laden. At the expense of his studies, Wasim's belief in jihad grew stronger by the day. He failed in a number of subjects, and the chances of successfully completing his medical studies looked bleak. However, the turning point in his life came in August 2011, when the home ministry of India rejected the mercy petition of Afzal Guru and sent a letter to the president of India recommending the death penalty. Since he was a doctor too, Wasim, the medical student, deeply sympathized with him and wanted to do something spectacular to avert his impending execution.

In June 2011, Wasim entered India from the Haridaspur border checkpost and drove to Kolkata. Taking the Rajdhani Express from Kolkata, he reached Delhi. Resorting to subterfuge, he deposited his luggage in the cloak room of the Old Delhi Railway Station. Then he took an auto rickshaw to visit the High Court complex, where he carried out a reconnaissance of the premises. Later, he collected his luggage and took a night bus to Jammu.

After spending some days in Jammu, he reached Kishtwar. Through a common friend, Wasim contacted Amir Kamal, the area commander of HM. Amir and Wasim had been classmates in school and were good friends. Through Amir, he also got in touch with his militant brother Junaid Malik and Shakir Hussain Sheikh alias Chota Hafiz, the elusive divisional commander of HM. Although militancy was on the decline, Chota Hafiz had been evading the security forces since 2005. Along with Junaid Malik and Amir Kamal, he was mostly operating in the far-flung areas of Wadwan Valley and Chatroo region.

Wasim was given a code name: Amzad. He stayed in touch with the three militants on phone. Subsequently, he revealed his plan of trying to stall the death sentence of Afzal Guru. 'Think big and beyond Kishtwar,' he told the militants. After getting convinced of Wasim's unflinching commitment towards jihad, Chota Hafiz agreed to meet him. He met the trio in the second week of June 2011 at Hullar Hill, on the outskirts of Kishtwar town. Wasim ridiculed the militants propagating what he called '*chillar* jihad' or petty jihad. Then he revealed the diabolical plan of causing a big explosion in the Delhi High Court to thwart the execution of Afzal Guru. He gloated that it would garner national and international attention. Wasim proposed to rope in non-Kashmiri–looking boys, as an added safety, for executing the task. Chota Hafiz and others seconded the proposal and took on themselves to prepare the improvised explosive device (IED) and arranging the non-Kashmiri recruits. It was also decided that an e-mail would be sent to the media houses to claim the responsibility of the blast. For this purpose, Junaid roped in Amir Abbas Dev, whom he met at the Mohmmandiya Masjid sometime in the first week of July. Amir and Junaid were friends as they had studied in the same school. Without revealing the details, Junaid tasked Amir to look for a computer-knowing fellow who could be entrusted with an important task. This is how Abid Hussain Bhawani came into picture – he was the first to be picked up after he had sent the e-mail from a local cyber cafe.

The preparations for the blast had to be temporarily suspended since Wasim Malik had to return to Bangladesh. His father had forced him to rejoin college after he had received a letter regarding Wasim's shortage of attendance. One month later, in the last week of August, Wasim flew back to India during Eid holidays. After celebrating the festival with his family in Jammu, he came to Kishtwar. The very next day, as the Sun dipped behind the mountains, Wasim reached the Dashanwajan playground, located on one side of the Kishtwar town. Chota Hafiz and Amir Kamal, carrying pistols under their clothes, were already waiting there, stealthily sitting amidst a dense copse of trees. In a little while, two Pakistanis – Abu Saifullah and Abu Bilal – also appeared. They were the two non-Kashmiri–looking militants who were tasked to plant the bomb. The investigation later proved that the two Pakistanis were experts in fabricating explosives and they had been active in Kishtwar for a few months.

On 3 September, Junaid and Wasim introduced the two Pakistanis to Amir Abbas Dev in the Mohammadia Mosque. In order to hide their identities, Wasim introduced them as colleagues from Bangladesh. After the meeting, he bought some food from a local restaurant and, along with Amir, took the two Pakistanis to his house. Next day, early in the morning, Wasim and Amir drove the two Pakistanis to the Kishtwar bus stand, from where they took the solitary bus for Delhi. As per the plan, Junaid met the two Pakistanis in Kud and handed them a briefcase, heavy with an IED primed by detonators and circuited with wires.

On 5 September, Wasim summoned Amir Abbas Dev and Abid Hussain Bhawani to the Mohammadia Mosque to finalize the contents of e-mail. He wrote the text on a piece of a paper and also noted down the e-mail addresses of media channels like NDTV and Aaj Tak. Further, he wrote step-wise instructions required for creating a new Gmail account. Bhawani was asked to follow the news channels on 7 September and to send the mail a few hours after hearing about the blast. He was also directed to destroy the piece of paper after sending the e-mail.

Thus, a conspiracy hatched in Kishtwar and was executed by two Pakistanis aided by local terrorists, resulting in a massive explosion when the Delhi High Court was brimming with people. Wasim Malik, who had reached Jammu on 5 September, heard about the blast on the news channels. He pretended everything was normal, avoided any talks on the telephone about the success of the sinister mission and went about his routine. After five days, he took a connecting flight to Kolkata and reached Bangladesh, returning to his life as a medical student.

Oblivious to the breakthrough made by the investigating agency, Wasim was arrested from the Indira Gandhi International Airport on 7 October, as his flight landed from Dhaka. The NIA and state government offered INR 20 lakh as prize money for aiding the capture of Chota Hafiz, Amir Kamal and Junaid Malik. The hot pursuit by the security forces led to the killing of two terrorists in Trothil forest in August 2012. One of them was identified as Amir Kamal. Knowing that the security forces were zeroing on him, Junaid Malik had started to contemplate surrender. Due to this, Chota Hafiz felt betrayed, and it was alleged that he got Junaid killed. It seems logical since nothing has been heard about Junaid since then.

Agencies believed that at one point, Chota Hafiz was thinking of surrendering too. He released a video message in this regard wherein he denied his involvement in the high court blast and alleged that he was being wrongly implicated. In the 1.21-minute-long video, shot on an unknown mountain, he was sending feelers for his conditional surrender. Sporting long hair and beard, wearing a gun pouch and a black bandana, Chota Hafiz pled his case:

> I am a soldier of Hizbul Mujahedeen. My name is Shakir Hussain alias Umar Ilyas. We haven't done this. In case there was any involvement, we would have been executed by our seniors across the border or those sitting in Jammu and Kashmir. We are small-time mujahedeen.[73]

Despite his half-hearted offer to surrender, the relentless pursuit of Chota Hafiz continued. There were reports that he might visit Palmar since he had been blessed with a boy. Finally, in December 2012, the security forces got a tip off of his likely visit to village Qadrana, in the remote mountainous region of Navapachi in Kishtwar. As the twilight set on the mountains, Chota Hafiz crossed a small wooden bridge over a shallow rivulet to enter the village. Here, he was ambushed by a team of soldiers who were anticipating his arrival. He lay dead by the side of the stream after a few gunshots.

All three local terrorists involved in planning the Delhi High Court blast were dead. Amir Abbas Dev turned approver in the case and was released after spending few months in prison. Being less than 18 years of age, Abid Hussain Bhawani was tried in a juvenile court and convicted. Wasim Malik, the would-be doctor, has spent more than ten years in jail and still awaits his fate. Nothing has been heard about the two unknown Pakistanis who planted the bomb.

From that fateful day of Eid in 2013, Kishtwar has moved a decade forward. Chaugan, carpeted in lush grass and skirted by deodars and chinars, gives a spectacular look at the fore drop of snowy mountains. People from both the communities gather here for morning and evening walks or to leisurely sit under the trees. Polo has paved way for cricket and football. In the south of Chaugan, the shrine of Asrar-ud-Din Baghdadi, and in the north, the ancient temple of Gauri Shankar both coexist peacefully. According to the myth, the original idol in the temple was made of sapphire, and when one looked at the idol, one could see the details of their previous life.

There is an interesting story about the queen of Kishtwar. She saw the idol and had the vision of a monkey! Outraged, she hurled the idol into the lake and, apparently, it turned black.

The modern Kishtwar retains her erstwhile glory; the soil is permeated by myths, legends and the teachings of saints. The picturesque village of Pochhal and the surrounding hamlets render captivating beauty to the region of Mandal, just 2 miles away from Kishtwar town. During the season, the sprawling saffron fields of Mandal resemble a purple blanket, spread on earth. The families that own these fields, clad in colourful dresses, engage in flower picking in the fragrant ambience, extending a mystic charm to the place. Though it is one of the most remote districts of the nation, the summers have now started to buzz with bikers, trekkers, adventurists and pilgrims. Occasionally, the NIA sleuths drop in to search for militants spilling blood in Lutyens's Delhi.

9

The Hill of Poppies

Outside Kishtwar, the Chenab passes by Shalimar – a colony established by the National Hydroelectricity Project Corporation when the Dul–Hasti project was commissioned. The colony, with its green-topped buildings, comprising both offices and residences of the professionals associated with the project, exists serenely, under the watch of the majestic mountains. Since it included a lot of foreigners, it remained under grave threat during the peak of militancy. At Hasti, from a single-lane bridge, a muddy track winds up the hill to the Sarthal temple. Each year in July, the path is taken by the devotees who have almost forgotten about the Hindu blood spilled here in 1993.

Flowing through a narrow gorge, the Chenab spurts westwards, travelling parallel to NH-244, making its way to Doda. On both sides of the river, the landscape is dotted by a sporadic spread of flat-roofed and sloped houses. In some patches of terraced flatlands on the hills, maize crop swirls, gaining a height of 10 ft at its peak. The highway and the river glide by small towns before entering the Doda district at Thathri.

Thathri has deposits of marble and is also known as the Marble Town. In the old days, when the Chenab was a major mode of transportation of wood, Thathri was one of the main collection points. The main bazaar of the town is fragrant with *nun* chai or salty tea because the town is predominantly Kashmiri. They settled here hundreds of years ago, after escaping repression of the feudal class in the Kashmir Valley. Initially, there was enough land available for paddy cultivation, nourished by the mountain brooks. However, after the onset of militancy, many families of both Hindus and Muslims migrated from the higher reaches and settled down in the town. Therefore, the cultivable land made way for residential areas. The new constructions have been so erratic that many of these houses have been built down the slope towards the Chenab, thus making them vulnerable to flash floods as the town often gets peppered with boulders and other debris.

From Thathri, a macadamized road leads to the beautiful town of Gandoh. The beautiful valley of Bhalesa–Gandoh witnessed much bloodshed in the darkest days of militancy. These killings were not restricted to one community, and the Muslims, too, faced the wrath of this gore.

In April 2002, as the twilight engulfed the mountains, a group of terrorists barged into a house in Dudwar Nagni in the Gandoh area. The house belonged to Ibrahim Gujjar, who had been abducted by the terrorists the previous year and was never heard about again, presumably killed and buried somewhere in the forest. When the militants came visiting second time, Ibrahim's widow Beeran was cooking a special dinner at the hearth. Her sister with her three grown up children were visiting. Beeran's daughters, ten-year-old Fatima and five-year-old Gulshan, were huddled with their cousins. The militants corralled the family into one room and enquired about the men folk. On not finding any men, they indiscriminately sprayed bullets, killing Beeran, her sister and her three children. Fatima and Gulshan were perhaps spared but they, too, got injured in the shootout. The two young girls spent the whole night amidst five dead bodies before they were found by the neighbours the next morning.

These killings could have easily been passed off as another mindless massacre by unknown militants. However, the police investigation established the link of this murder to a land case. Mohammad Akhtar, belonging to Dudwar Nagni and working as SPO with the Kishtwar police, was arrested. Akhtar had a chequered past: Three years before, he, along with four other SPOs, had deserted the police camp and defected to HM. After a few weeks, Akhtar, along with another SPO, surrendered and rejoined the police force.[74]

Akhtar's father-in-law had a long-lasting dispute with Ibrahim Gujjar's father. Beeran suspected Akhtar of having plotted her husband's killing due to the dispute. To follow up on the case, she had often visited the Special Operations Group (SOG) camp and allegedly developed intimate relations with one of the constables. This irked the militants who sided with Akhtar and carried out the killings. Akhtar denied the allegations, but he was arrested and tried in the case. After a long trial, he was acquitted of all charges.

Not all killings were carried out by the terrorists, as is evident from the communal madness of 17 March 1998.

One day before the parliamentary elections of the Udhampur-Doda constituency, a tragedy brewed in Karara, a small town on the bank of the river Chenab. The main bazaar was decked with party flags and posters. The political activists were busy in last-minute wooing of the voters.

The same day, a local political activist from Karara, Suresh Kumar, and an accomplice were caught by the Muslim men in Panasa village on allegations of molesting a local Gujjar girl. Kumar was severely beaten up, but his accomplice managed to flee. Kumar also had a history of few minor crimes and violent behaviour, present in police records. However, for the Hindu community of Panasa and other villages in the vicinity, he was a hero and a crusader against militancy and fundamentalism.

In the local hospital, Suresh Kumar writhed in pain, while outside, tension was simmering. His condition deteriorated, and he was shifted to Doda, where he succumbed to internal injuries on election day. The authorities were still busy collecting the ballot boxes and the forces were returning from the booths when Kumar's funeral procession to the bank of the Chenab began from his village. Many angry Hindus of neighbouring villages had come down from the hills and assembled at the cremation site.

Unfortunately, eight members of the Muslim community, including three women, encountered a belligerent group of Hindu mourners. The men were heckled and abused, while the women were set free after a while. An aged man, severely roughed up, managed to flee. Four others were beaten and bludgeoned. One, desperate to escape, raced down the path heading to a precipice overlooking the Chenab. Few members of the bloodthirsty mob pushed him down the cliff. The rest were frog-marched down the hill, tortured all along the trail to the riverbank. By this time, the three men were profusely bleeding and crying in pain. Soon, they were relieved of their ordeal and pushed into the Chenab. Not far from this spot, Suresh Kumar's pyre was lit amidst frenetic wails and nationalist slogans. The dead bodies of the four Muslims were recovered four days later, about 50 km from Thathri.

For criminals, there cannot be a better crime scene than the Chenab. A felony committed here leaves minimum evidence: no fingerprints, no maps, no chances of forensic investigations and, in most cases, not even a corpus delicti. The river remained an unwitting accomplice in such brutal crimes. In Doda, whenever someone goes missing, most eyes turn to the Chenab.

That black day, when the police responded to the Muslims' distress calls, they did not find anything amiss. In Karara, people were busy with political discussions, speculating about potential winners of the election. But when more witnesses corroborated the lynching, the police sensed the gravity of the situation. There was a blood trail on the gravelled path that curved down the mountain, ending at the bank of the Chenab.[75]

About 15 miles from Karara, the Chenab flows past Premnagar, a village with mixed population of Hindus and Muslims. A dilapidated wooden walk-bridge was recently replaced by a concrete motorable bridge at Shiva, a mile ahead of Premnagar. Before the bridge came, the only mode to cross the Chenab at Shiva was the cradle box – a small carriage for four people, running on a cable and propelled by pulleys and a motor. The villagers, along with their goats and goods, would take this precarious crossover for mere pittance.

On the lookout for exotic locations, one fine day in 1980, Rajshri Productions – a movie production unit from Bombay – landed up in Shiva. They shot the climax scene of an action movie *Khoon ka Rishta* (1981) on the cradle box.

On the bank of the Chenab, Amjad Khan, along with his cronies, stand on a rock, with a revolver pointed at Neetu Singh, who plays Jeetendra's girlfriend. On the other end, Jeetendra has taken Pran, a close partner of Amjad Khan, as a hostage. Two cradle boxes ply parallel between two banks of the river. Amjad Khan makes the deal of exchange of hostages on a megaphone. After a count of three, both the hostages sit in the cradle box to crossover to the other side. Underneath, the dark-coloured waters flow with great ferocity. Midway, when the two cradle boxes meet, Pran lifts Neetu Singh from her box and pulls her into his own. Jeetendra quickly pulls the cable to bring back the cradle box. Angered by the deceit of Pran, Amjad Khan fires at the cradle box carrying the two people and then tries to break the cable with a hammer. Amidst great suspense and dramatic music, the cable crumbles and the box falls into the river. The two hostages desperately clutch to the cradle box, trying to avoid being swept away by the river. But like all heroes in Indian movies, Jeetendra succeeds in heroically pulling the cradle box onto the riverbank. Suddenly, Amjad Khan is shot in his leg – the police appear from nowhere to encircle him.

It was a full day's shooting and was watched by hundreds of enchanted villagers. Many of them sat perched at vantage points on the surrounding hills making it look like a grand festival.

Despite the beauty of the Chenab Valley, it comes as a surprise that not many Hindi movies have been shot here, as the Bombay filmmakers always preferred Kashmir. In 1979, *Noorie*, produced by celebrated filmmaker Yash Chopra, became the first movie to be shot in Bhaderwah. The main characters of the movie Farookh Sheikh and Poonam Dhillon played the local lovers in Bhaderwah, and the movie artistically showcased the beauty of the place. Being a major hit of the year, *Noorie* was expected to bring Bhaderwah on the national tourism map. However, this did not happen, and after *Khoon ka Rishta*, no other movie was shot in the Chenab Valley. There was a lack of road network, good hotels and uninterrupted electricity, which could have been the reasons for difficulties in film shoots. However, the locals blamed it on the Kashmir leadership who would never let the filmmakers go outside Kashmir Valley – film shootings meant employment and boost to the local economy.

The hillock of Premnagar has a large number of mixed villages, scattered at inaccessible heights. In June 1998, about a month after the Karara killings, the communal harmony of the area was jolted in such a manner that it left a perpetual scar. Chapnari village of Premnagar area is located 7 miles from Doda, connected by a dilapidated road. The road would often remain cut off due to landslides, and Chapnari would become the last motorable stop.

A modest house in the village Korda of Premnagar was brimming with happiness. The house basked in the festivity of weddings of three siblings. Sesh Ram was the first to marry; he was wedded to Dugdi Devi belonging to a nearby village. Two days later, Sesh Ram's younger brother Khem Raj's wedding procession proceeded to the uphill village of Kadlal. It was a night of feasts and celebration at Kadlal. The next day, Om Parkash's procession was to proceed to Korda. Khem Raj and Om Parkash had decided to marry each other's sisters – Leela Devi and Bimla Devi.

Accompanied by a local band of drums, tambourines, clarinets and cymbals, Khem Raj's and Om Prakash's wedding parties walked from the village Kadlal to the roadside of Chapnari. From here, they

Gondhla Castle, the House of Thakur

Tandi, the confluence of the rivers Chandra and Bhaga

Tholang village, on the bank of the Chandrabhaga

Ghemur Khar, Jispa

Mrikula Mata Temple, Udaipur, Lahaul

Todd Bungalow, Purthi

The Chandrabhaga flows through the Pangi Valley

Killar Town, Pangi Valley

Killar-Paddar road – the world's most dangerous road

Sheenderi nullah; the wooden bridge leads to Chitoo Mata

Kaal Khappar, the old monument at Sohal village

Sohal village, Paddar

Kaban village, Paddar

Confluence of Chenab and Bhot Nullah at Gulabgarh

Suncham, the last inhabited village of Paddar, in the footsteps of the Sapphire Mines

Machail Mata Temple

The Chenab at Bandarkoot

Chowgan, Kishtwar

Choti Ziyarat, Kishtwar

Vasuki Nath Temple, Bhaderwah

The memorial of the Kishtwar agitation

Pul Doda, where the Chenab meets the Neeru

Chenab flows by Ramban town

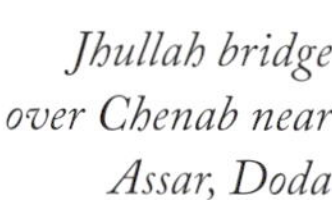

Jhullah bridge over Chenab near Assar, Doda

Sumbar village, once notorious for militancy

The only photograph available of Mohammad Rafiq alias Billoo Gujjar, the dreaded terrorist

House in Manglogi village where Billoo Gujjar was killed

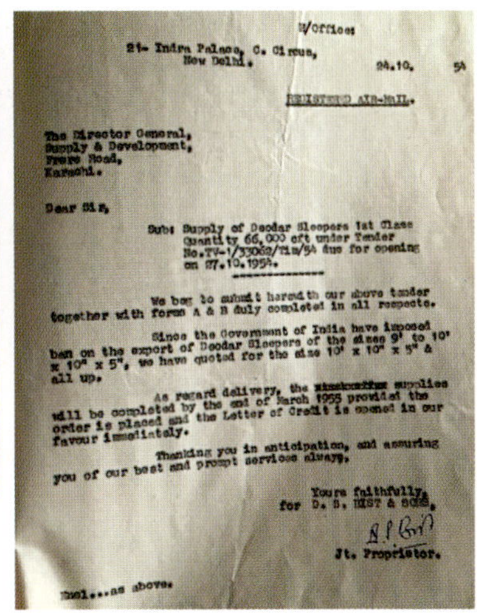

H/Office:
21- Indra Palace, C. Circus,
New Delhi. 24.10. 54

REGISTERED AIR-MAIL.

The Director General,
Supply & Development,
Frere Road,
Karachi.

Dear Sir,

Sub: Supply of Deodar Sleepers 1st Class Quantity 66,000 cft under Tender No.TV-1/33062/Tim/54 due for opening on 27.10.1954.

We beg to submit herewith our above tender together with forms A & B duly completed in all respects.

Since the Government of India have imposed ban on the export of Deodar Sleepers of the sizes 9' to 10' x 10" x 5", we have quoted for the size 10' x 10" x 5" & all up.

As regard delivery, the [illegible] supplies will be completed by the end of March 1955 provided the order is placed and the Letter of Credit is opened in our favour immediately.

Thanking you in anticipation, and assuring you of our best and prompt services always,

Yours faithfully,
for D. S. BIST & SONS,

Jt. Proprietor.

Encl...as above.

Supply order of deodar sleepers to Dan Singh Bist

The Chenab flows by Reasi town

The highest railway bridge in the world over the Chenab in Reasi district

George Harrison's remarks on the Guest Book no. 4 of Butts Clermont

Jia Pota Ghat and the Akhnoor Fort

Ambaran Buddhist site on the banks of Chenab ▲

The steel bridge over the Chenab in Akhnoor

Chenab on her way to Pakistan

were to board a bus, which had been hired in advance. Even after the wait for the bus turned unexpectedly long, everyone continued to look happy. The men sipped tea from a roadside stall and the women, with their faces shrouded by the loose end of their bright dupattas, huddled around the bride's gilded palanquin and dowry items.

Suddenly, a Maruti van ground to a halt near the tea stall. Few elderly men tried to negotiate a deal for hiring a ride for some members of the wedding party. But due to the high-price quoted by the driver, the van moved on towards Doda.

After some time, the van came back to Chapnari, and five bearded men wielding Kalashnikovs jumped out. Three of them wore olive uniforms. The militants ordered some Muslim men present in the vicinity to leave the spot. 'All Hindus come on one side – how many of you are VDC members?' they asked. While the Hindus started obeying the order timidly, one was held back by his Muslim friend, 'Where are you going? They said Hindus, not us?' There were three primary school teachers in the wedding procession. Two Muslim teachers had been invited to the wedding by their colleague Raj Bishan, who was the uncle of the grooms. The Muslim teachers had come to the rescue of their Hindu counterpart.

After sorting out the men, the militants approached the group of women who helplessly cowered at a small distance. The women were asked to hand over their belongings – jewellery, money, and other small things they carried. The two brides parted with all their jewellery. The men folk were also looted of their cash, watches and other meagre valuables.

A few minutes later, the rattle of the guns shattered the afternoon quiet, and twenty-five dead bodies piled up. The women ran down the cliff and some of the men also manage to flee. One of the survivors included fourteen-year-old Pishori Lal, who, with his wiry frame, managed to squeeze out from the pile of fallen bodies. The dead included grooms Khem Raj and Om Prakash as well as Sesh Ram who had got married two days back. Dev Raj, the brother of Sesh Ram and Khem Raj, was also among the dead. When the police reached the spot, it found a gory scene, with blood-soaked bridegrooms and other *baratis* lying dead. Their belongings – boxes of sweets, garlands, turbans and footwear – lay strewn on the road. The heavier items of the dowries remained piled up on one side, unscathed but with a few blood stains on them. At a short distance, the women and children wailed, sitting forlornly. The hennaed palms of the two brides were wet with tears.[76]

The massacre brought a pall of gloom all over Premnagar. A house brimming with festivity of three marriages was now left with the wails of three widows. The incident sent shockwaves throughout the country, and strikes were organized in Doda, Kishtwar, Bhaderwah and other major cities of Jammu province. The next day, three helicopters carrying the then home minister of the country, L.K. Advani, and other security officials hovered over the Chenab. Advani was driven up to the spot before he addressed a public meeting in Premnagar. 'These poor people have no option but to migrate from their villages. Or give them modern weapons to defend themselves,' Anil Parihar, the then president of the youth wing of the BJP thundered amidst anger and wails of the women. Advani, rendered numb by the tragedy, promised strict action against the perpetrators of mindless violence.

In November 2018, twenty-two years after the Chapnari incident, Anil Parihar, along with his elder brother Ajeet Parihar, was shot dead in a street in Kishtwar. The brothers were coming home after closing their stationary shop when militants ambushed them and shot them at a point-blank range, killing the brothers on the spot.

The uproar against the dastardly incident at Chapnari continued for many days. Some speculated it as a revenge for Karara killings, to send a clear message to the Hindus. Later, Dugdi Devi told the investigators that one of the militants who had looted them looked familiar and was a local. He was identified as Gullah, from a nearby village of Breswana. Amidst all the immitigable gloom, it would be noteworthy to discuss a positive story of the village Breswana.

A trek of 2 miles from Premnagar leads one to the predominantly Kashmiri village of Breswana. Being affected by backwardness and militancy, education and development in the village became major casualties. Though there was a government school in the village, the standard of education was very poor.

The mantle of education had been taken by a Hajji family of the village, which had shifted to Dubai in late 1970s. Sabah Hajji, a twenty-six-year-old from the family, who did her early schooling in Dubai and graduation in commerce from Christ College, Bangalore, returned to Breswana in 2008. She was appalled to see the education standards of the government schools. Backed by her mother, who had been a teacher at the schools in Dubai, Bangalore and Doda, Sabah resolved to educate underprivileged children. Her will to succeed was so strong that many villagers stepped forward in her support. They helped build the school brick by brick on the family land donated by the Hajjis. Sabah's mother was designated as the first principal, and the kindergarten started functioning in 2009 out of two rooms.

Sabah continued to raise funds through private donations and social-media campaigns. Today, the school has a three-storeyed building with a library, computer room, a basketball court and recreational facilities. It is the most sought-after school in the region, with the reputation of not having a single dropout since its inception. Sabah invites volunteers to teach in the school, and in the past, about sixty personalities from countries like Canada, Singapore, the United States, South Africa and France have taught here. Among Indians, Rana Safvi, a famous historian and writer, has taught in the school. Similarly, Madhuri Vijay, an Indian American, stayed and taught in the school for two years while she was writing her multi award–winner novel, *The Far Field* (2019).

Despite the philanthropy and spearheading of a great humanitarian cause, Sabah Hajji was arrested in December 2021. Purportedly, she had posted a provocative message on social media. General Bipin Rawat, a celebrated Indian army officer and chief of defence staff, had died in a helicopter crash and Sabah had called the late soldier a 'war criminal', which had invited a hate campaign against her. The netizens across the country demanded legal action and the closure of the school. After spending four days in custody, she was released after tendering a written apology.

Khalid Hussain wrote a story: 'Adami mein Chupa Ek Adami' ['A Man Hidden Inside a Man'], which was published in his book of short stories, *Satisar ka Suraj* (2011). The story, inspired by a true incident, happened during the heyday of militancy. Khalid Hussain was on an official visit to Paddar, but before finishing his task, he had to rush back to Doda. He instructed his staff to finish the work in his absence. After doing the needful, the subordinate staff, comprising the veterinary doctor Latif, his assistant Zameer and the driver of the official gypsy Tej Ram, reached Kishtwar late in the evening. At the Kishtwar guest house, Zameer longed for the comfort of his home, hearth and family. He insisted on continuing the journey to Doda, which was about two hours away.

Born in Bhaderwah, Zameer was raised in an atmosphere fraught with simmering communal narratives. The debates would flare up intermittently on the roadsides, busy bazaars, public parks and the Government Degree College, Bhaderwah, from where he did his graduation. A devout Muslim, he would not miss a single prayer of the day and was well-versed with the Holy Quran. Zameer could quote many *ayat*s [the holy sayings]. With the advent of militancy in the Chenab Valley, his beliefs were further radicalized and he became quite vocal about them, often propagating jihad and extermination of the non-believers.

Zameer prevailed upon his fellow travellers, who all were tempted by the prospective warmth of their own beds. In those days, there was almost no vehicular movement on the dangerous roads after sunset. The gypsy revved on the road to Doda. The Moon hung in the sky to shine over the Chenab, and the crickets chirped their nocturnal song. The vehicle drove past the dangerous spots as well as the security pickets in the Thathri town.

It seemed that danger had been evaded. Doda was not far now. A little further, a gunman dressed in army olives emerged from behind a roadside boulder and waved at the gypsy to stop. Observing the gleam of the Kalashnikov in the light of the headlights, Tej Ram wanted to ignore the signal and accelerate. Zameer asked him to stop and respect the Indian Army man. As the gypsy came to a halt, two more gunmen stepped out of the dark. It was apparent that these were terrorists commanding the highway.

'Empty your pockets and keep your belongings on your seats and get out of the vehicle,' a gunman dictated in an accent which was not local. The gypsy was parked by the hillside, and the Chenab roared on the other side. Identity cards, wallets, pens, currency notes and a few slips sat on the seats as the three occupants came out. 'Call out your names,' a terrorist who seemed to be the commander barked. 'Dr Latif, Zameer, Tej Ram.' Tej Ram was moved aside and the other two were asked to recite the *kalma* (a statement signifying a declaration of faith in Islam), which they did.

Tej Ram, the poor driver and the father of five daughters, might not have escaped because of his identity card and inability to recite kalma. 'We are not even going to waste a bullet on your wretched self; we'll slaughter you,' a terrorist threatened. Tej Ram shivered, his heart pounding fast. Looking at his visible unease, Zameer stepped forward and exhorted the terrorists, 'You cannot harm an innocent soul, and the Holy Quran says that we must feed our neighbour if he has been visited by the pangs of hunger, even if he is a non-believer.' On the hills overlooking the Chenab, dim bulbs flickered from army posts. Crickets continued to chirp, adding to this conversation. Zameer was clearly in a confrontationist mood even when Dr Latif kept quiet.

A militant, annoyed by Zameer's insistence on debating about Islam, asked him to shut up. *'Aap mimbar ki lakdi ho, na jal sakti ho, na bechi ja sakti ho* [You are the wood of mimbar* that cannot be

---

* A mimbar is a pulpit in a mosque where the maulvis stand to deliver sermons. The steps leading to this pulpit are made of a kind of wood that is considered to be sacrosanct and cannot be sold or burnt.

sold or burnt].' The words spoken by Zameer were strong and it was evident that 'the man inside the man' had truly arisen. Despite his radicalized views, Zameer saved the life of Tej Ram.

'Alright, drop us back on your gypsy,' one of the terrorists demanded. When the vehicle was reversed back towards Thathri, two more terrorists descended from the mountain and got inside the gypsy. The five of them got down near a nullah and climbed up the hill to get back to their hideout. Within a month, in a fiercely fought gun battle in a village, not far from Thathri, these five terrorists were killed and their dead bodies were brought down the hill. Tej Ram lives a happy retired life after getting his five daughters married.

At Pul Doda or the bridge of Doda, the journey of the Chenab is temporarily halted. Here, the water is stored in a large lake called Chandrabhagha, which is actually a reservoir backing the Baghlihar Hydroelectricity Project (BHEP) in Chanderkote in Ramban district.

Pul Doda became a busy junction and a lot of commercial activity started around the place. Over the years it turned into a small, bustling town with residential houses alongside business establishments. The creation of the lake necessitated the submergence of these structures in 2008. The town of Doda, on a plateau overlooking the river, was witness to this slow submergence. As the water rose, it also took away with it a mosque and a temple that used to stand next to each other. The dome of the mosque and the inverted lotus on the pinnacle of the temple submerged inch by inch, day after day.

During those days, a single-lane steel bridge laid over the Chenab was the only link to Doda town. Probably it was a good spot to lay a bridge as was evident from a rope bridge described by G.T. Vigne in his 1829 travelogue *Travels in Kashmir, Ladakh, Iskardo*:

> I travelled from Bhaderwah towards Doda along a rocky nullah, which joins Chenab. Over there I crossed over one of the dangerous bridges I had seen in the Himalayan range. The bridge is fastened by strong ropes, about fifty feet in height over the river.

Vigne's description is similar to the jhulla bridges of the Pangi Valley, and the nullah he is talking about is the Neeru River that joins the Chenab at Pul Doda. The river originates from a perennial glacier on the top of Ashapati Mountain. On her journey through the forested valleys, Neeru is joined by many other mountain streams. The river, with her blue-coloured water, tosses over the cragged boulders and flows through the heart of Bhaderwah town.

The Neeru is the lifeline of the villages of Bhaderwah for potable water and trout. There is folklore that speaks about the Pandavas bringing Ganga water to these parts. This story has links with an ancient Shiva temple called the Gupt Ganga Temple on the Neeru's banks. *Gupt* means secret or hidden.

A little further from Gupt Ganga, on the left bank of the Neeru, the most revered temple of Vasuki Naag is located. Vasuki Naagor the 'king of serpents' was the son of Sage Kashyap – after whom Kashmir is said to have been named because he drained the water out of the huge lake – and his first wife Kadru. After the water was drained, a big water-borne dragon named Jallodbhava emerged and started to eat the Naagas. In order to escape the dragon, many Naagas escaped to places like Kishtwar and Bhaderwah. Bhadarakali, the elder sister of Vasuki Naag, was one of them, and she became the first queen of Bhaderwah.

The death of Sage Kashyap in Kashmir led to a war of succession between his sons from two wives, namely, Kadru and Vinata. Garuda – the divine vehicle of Lord Vishnu – was born to Vinata and wanted to kill Vasuki Naag and his two brothers. To safeguard her brothers, Bhadarakali called them to Bhaderwah and divided her territory between them. Garuda also reached Bhaderwah in pursuance of the three brothers. Vasuki Naag refused to fight with Garuda, retreated high in the hills and made his abode in Kailash.

Between the eighth and ninth centuries, the king of Bhaderwah initiated the construction of the Vasuki temple on the bank of Neeru. While the work was in progress, he failed to place the idol in the sanctum sanctorum. On consulting the learned priests, he was told about an evil spirit dwelling in the place, dissuading the installation. Apparently, the only way to get rid of the spirit was to sacrifice a Brahmin to the gods. The king, who was disheartened at the solution, was told about Dev Raj and Bodh Raj, the Brahmin brothers who had recently arrived from Sialkot.

The king's soldiers were able to locate Bodh Raj, who sat in deep meditation. When one of the soldiers raised his sword to behead the Brahmin, his hands froze. Bodh Raj woke up from his trance and, after knowing about the purpose of the visit of the soldiers, volunteered to present himself to the king. He offered to sacrifice his life on a condition: 'I shall cut my head with drub grass. But all the land that my body travels afterwards shall be gifted to my brother.'

The king readily agreed to Bodh Raj's condition, internally scoffing at the travelling abilities of a decapacitated body. Bodh Raj kept his word and beheaded himself. As per the lore, the body awakened, took a few steps and walked further. Soon, he was traversing through the kingdom of Bhaderwah without signs of exhaustion. Startled at the miracle, the king regretted underestimating the mystical powers of the Brahmin and sought help from Vasuki Naag. The king of serpents obliged and miraculously appeared in a cow's form and blocked Bodh Raj's body at Pasri. Here, the last rites of Bodh Raj were performed. Displeased at the turn of events, Dev Raj declared that his family will never enter the Vasuki Naag temple or offer prayers to the deity. Even today, the soil from the cremation site of Bodh Raj is used to mark the holy symbols of 'Om' and tridents on the doors of Vasuki temple.[77]

Vasuki Naag is the presiding deity of Bhaderwah. In August, the annual pilgrimage to Kailash Kund commences from the temple.

Taking bath and donating something to the poor at Kailash is considered a sacred and noble deed. The significance of Vasuki Naag is stated in the Bhagwat Gita (Chapter 10, Verse 28), where Lord Krishna explains his omnipresence by proclaiming, 'Of weapons, I am the thunderbolt; among cows, I am Surbhi. Of causes of procreation, I am Kamadeva, and of serpents, I am Vasuki.' Kailash is a source of seven rivers including the Neeru and the Tawi, and both end up joining the Chenab.

For much part of its history, Bhaderwah has been an independent principality. Raja Nagpal, who ruled Bhaderwah in the sixteenth century, was an ardent devotee of Vasuki Naag and was bestowed with an elevated, spiritual state of mind. During this period, Emperor Akbar annexed Kashmir and came to know about the miraculous powers of Nagpal. He summoned the Raja to Delhi.

As per popular story, Nagpal entered the Mughal durbar and took his seat without bowing to pay obeisance to the Emperor. This act of disrespect offended Akbar and his courtiers. Next day, Nagpal was asked to pass through a small window to enter the durbar, which would have compelled him to bow automatically. However, Nagpal manoeuvred his body through the window in such a way that he entered the durbar with his head held high. This enraged Akbar, who challenged him to exhibit his spiritualism to evade punishment for his misdemeanours. In a state of dismay, Raja Nagpal concentrated his mind on Vasuki Naag and prayed for the solution to his problem. His wish was granted, and a multi-headed serpent sprang from his turban. Akbar was impressed and exempted the Raja from the annual tribute. Nagpal was bestowed with precious stones and costly velvet robes embroidered in gold and silver before he returned.

In Bhaderwah, Nagpal was given a rousing welcome and was paraded in an extravagant procession. Till date, the event is celebrated in form of a three-day fair called Mela Patt. Dedicated to Lord Vasuki Naag, the fair is attended by both Hindus and Muslims. An impressive procession is taken out amidst music and dancing. The procession is led by an energetic person who carries the *patt* [a bundle of silk] on his head.[78]

Nagpal was succeeded by some timid rulers and Bhaderwah often came under the aggression of Chamba and Kishtwar principalities. Finally, it became part of the Dogra kingdom in 1846 under Maharaja Gulab Singh.

Bhaderwah once had a strong fort perched on a hill. Vigne, who travelled through Bhaderwah town in 1839, wrote about the fort:

> The direction of the main market is towards the south and the fort protects the town from the north. The fort is big and square made of slate and big stones. The stones are available in and around it. This is a strange place as compared to other hilly forts. On the back side of the fort; forests protect it.

In 1919, the fort was turned into a jail and the famous freedom fighter Sant Singh Tegh was imprisoned here. Tegh was born in a prosperous family of transporters in the Hatian village of Muzaffarabad, now in POK. At the age of ten, he was a witness to the Jallianwalla Bagh massacre in Amritsar, and that kindled the spirit of nationalism in him. Starting his political career at the age of twenty, in 1933, he was elected as the president of the Kisan Sabha. In the same year, he joined the National Conference of Sheikh Abdullah. Before Independence, he started a crusade against the Sikh clergy: The Mahants who held control of the gurdwaras in Kashmir and other places. The Mahants conspired against him and even tried to get him killed. But Sant Singh Tegh was able to free the gurdwaras from the centuries-old hegemony of the priests. After Independence, he became the first president of the Akali Dal in Jammu and Kashmir. Incidentally, his political mentor Sheikh Abdullah, who was ousted as the prime minister in 1953, was also incarcerated in the same jail.

~

For the major part of its course, the Chenab doesn't have fjords and, at no point, can it be crossed by walking or swimming through its current. Not only is the water icy cold but its depth is also immeasurable, with deadly, jagged rocks in its belly. Despite some jhulla bridges, the traditional method to cross the river is on inflated animal hides. The hides of buffaloes, horses and sheep were yanked off in one piece. The open ends of these skins, like on the legs and neck were stitched together strongly, and these were then inflated with air. People would mount these 'floating tubes', brave the strong current and make their way to the opposite shore.

Though it is not easy to swim in the river, some experts have mastered the current of the Chenab. In Pul Doda, a group of ace swimmers called Chenab Rescuers has been doing a great service. Sometimes, they are even summoned by the local administration to trace dead bodies of accident victims and those who die by suicide.

At one point of time, Pul Doda became notorious for suicides. People would casually stroll on the bridge, climb up the railing and jump into the unforgiving and unrelenting river. It was simply referred to as a *chalang* [jump or dive]. No one who jumped into the river ever survived. The very word 'chalang' had become spooky, haunting and calamitous. In Doda, children would dread the word and they would seek comfort in the warm embrace of their elders, far away from the threatening river. The word was so horrific that it meant just one consequence: death, mostly without the trace of the body that drowned; was swept, gulped, devoured; and vanished forever.

Due to the stigma attached to suicide, it would become the talk of the town, triggering speculation and scuttlebutt. One day, in the mid-1980s, a young woman from a respectable family of Doda disappeared without any trace. Some people recounted that she was last seen walking on the bridge, which could only mean one thing – chalang. Since she lived a happy life, her family did not believe that she could die by suicide. They looked around for her and even got a search carried in the river. Finding no success in tracing her body, the family finally organized the fortieth day of the 'deceased'. Befitting the tragedy, almost the whole of Doda town turned up for the memorial service.

Much water had flown under the Chenab bridge when the missing woman appeared after 15 years along with her three children. Much to the embarrassment of the family, it turned out that the woman had eloped with her lover. Though belonging to the same religion, due to stark social and financial differences between the two families, it was unlikely that the man would have been accepted by the woman's affluent family. The Chenab has been a raconteur of many stories of unrequited love, but in this case, by concealing a falsehood for so long, the river fructified one.

Today, Pul Doda has become a major tourist destination, with the construction of a promenade along the waterfront and jetties providing joyrides. The Chandrabhaga Lake, which runs for 30 miles, has become a centre for water sports. A new bridge called Ganpat has come up on an alignment not far from the old one. Once upon a time, Ganpat used to have a perennial water spring and the women from the nearby villages would come here to wash blankets, quilt covers and bedsheets. The spring emerged from beneath a big rock that had many beehives clinging to it. Bee is called *gan* in Kashmiri, and therefore, the place is called Ganpat.

While the bridge was under construction, it became infamous for suicides. To prevent people from taking their own lives, the administration raised the height of the railings of the bridge and topped it with barbed wire. Though the number of suicides reduced, it did not stop those determined to die. Desperate souls would seek escape in the Chenab's depths.

Not much of Doda's history is recorded. The plateau where the town thrives once had a lavish plantation of poppies. In Dogri language, *doda* means a poppy pod. Thus, the folklore attributes the etymology of the town to the intoxicating bulbs. Then some historians tell the story of Deeda, a utensil maker from Multan, now a flourishing city in Pakistan's Punjab, who came to Chenab Valley for business.

Impressed by his dexterity in making utensils, the then raja of Kishtwar persuaded him to permanently settle on the plateau. He also offered him land to set up a utensil factory. Deeda migrated to this place along with many skilled workers and started a utensil-making unit. Gradually his business flourished, and the natives also joined in setting up their small businesses near the factory. The place slowly converted into a small township. After the death of Deeda, the place came to be known after his name. With the passage of time Deeda, became Doda.

In his book *A Gazetteer of Kashmir*, C.E. Bates, who visited Doda in 1867, noted:

> Doda town is situated on a small plain area, above the right bank of Chenab River, on the foot of a grassy hill. The old fort is situated on the edge of plain area. It was a muddy building used as prison during Dogra rule.

The fort C.E. Bates talked about was one of the strongest and sturdiest. It was used to stock grain, armaments and defence material. Constructed with bigger bricks to resist the musket fire, the corners had dome-shaped towers to keep a strict watch on the movement of the enemy. The courtyard of the fort had a deep pit, known as 'Cha Bacha', which was used to incarcerate criminals. Gradually, the walls of the fort collapsed, and in 1952, Sheikh Abdullah decided to demolish the fort and build the Government Higher Secondary School for Boys over its ruins. Ghulam Rasool Kilam, a local mason, was entrusted with the job, and he was able to accomplish the task successfully. However, he was not paid any money for his work since Sheikh Abdullah was deposed as the prime minister of Jammu and Kashmir in 1953 and put in jail. When Sheikh Abdullah came back to power in 1977, Kilam approached him for his dues, which were paid to him after twenty-five years.

The illustrious alumni of the school include educationists,

lawyers, police officers and administrators. However, one of its students, Nawaz Ahmed, nicknamed Dama, was one of the earliest to join the ranks of the militants. Being beefy, he had often been bullied by fellow students.

In Doda, the Muslims and Hindus have always lived in harmony. However, in 1992, after the Babri Masjid was demolished, communal tension reached the town. A few days after the demolition, Santosh Thakur, a firebrand activist of the BJP, was killed by terrorists in broad daylight near his house in Nagri locality.

After his schooling in Doda, Thakur completed his graduation in Jammu and studied law at Aligarh Muslim University. He had practised in the District Court of Doda and earned a name for himself, helping the poor fight their cases pro bono. Weeks before his killing, Thakur had participated in *karseva* in Ayodhya and he was collecting money for the building of the temple for Lord Rama. His killing evoked a strong protest, and his funeral was attended by thousands and black flags were hoisted in many places in the town.

There is a belief that Farid-ud-Din Baghdadi's wife in Nagri was a great-grandaunt of Santosh Thakur. The argument looks plausible because Nagri has been a predominantly Hindu settlement. When the militancy started in Doda, a lot of Muslims shifted from villages on the hill and settled here. Today, both mosques and temples dot the skyline of Nagri, from where the Chenab looks like a green ribbon, flowing below the plateau.

Bidding farewell to painful memories, the Chenab reaches the picturesque town of Khilani. Vast flatlands straddle the town, with terraces sloping down to the river on one side, and climbing the mountain on the other. In the last decade or so, Khilani abandoned maize cultivation and shifted to a 'purple revolution' after the introduction of the lavender crop. Hectares of land covered with the purple flowers of the perennial crop merge beautifully with the blue sky and the muddy Chenab.

Historically, the people in Khilani have lived in communal harmony. However, tensions arose in the late 1990s when a church came to Kodapani, a small village, slightly further from Khilani. Ostensibly, Christian missionaries came here to spread modern education and provide health facilities. Soon, they were accused of trying to convert people, especially some Muslim sweepers, raising a furore.

Tension arose again in 2010, when Terry Jones, the pastor of the Christian Dove World Outreach Centre in Florida, announced that he would burn 200 copies of the Holy Quran on the anniversary of the 9/11 attack by Al-Qaeda. The pastor, who is also the author of the book *Islam Is of the Devil* (2010), urged the American Christians to 'stand up' to what he described as a monolithic Muslim threat. Today, the church sells coffee mugs and T-shirts with the title phrase of the book displayed on the memorabilia. On social media, many like-minded Americans render support. The threat of 'International Burn-a-Quran Day' inflamed strong emotions throughout the Muslim world, which hinted at violent retribution. The protests also reached Doda district. The local police had to provide security to the church and a convent school in Batote. The church, with its crucifix, still stands in Kodapani and resonates with hymns in the praise of Jesus during Sunday mass. All around, life goes on, in absolute normalcy.

10

The Vertical District

The Chandrabhaga Lake is a wide and large water body in Assar village, extending till Dharmound in Ramban district. The stagnant water resembles a frozen bowl of basil-green soup. Situated on the left bank of the river, Assar, with its fertile agricultural fields, is called 'the vegetable basket' of the Chenab Valley. Apart from the luxuriant fields of maize and wheat, nearly twenty varieties of vegetables are grown here.

The vegetable production as a commercial crop came to Assar in 1960, when a West Pakistan refugee (WPR) named Mulkh Raj came to the village. He distributed seeds and fertilizers to the farmers and encouraged vegetable production. However, this started the circle of exploitation of the small growers, as Mulkh Raj would become the first commission agent, an intermediary between the farmers of Assar and markets of Jammu.[79]

The system of commission agents became stronger over the years, making the grower poorer and the wholesale merchant and agent richer. The vegetables, if not sold in time, would rot, giving no choice to the farmers but to sell at whatever low price they were offered. 'You will be left with no choice but to throw your vegetables in the Chenab,' the commission agents would warn them. Aware of the exploitation, the farmers of Assar have been demanding for cold storage to escape the sinister clutches of the commission agents and traders who push them into distress sales.

A ring of villages across the Chenab also grow vegetables for commercial purposes. These villages are connected with Assar through a cradle box. In 1988, a great tragedy occurred here when an army aviation helicopter, presumably flying too low, hit the cable of the cradle box. The machine crashed and plunged into the Chenab, taking two pilots along with it. The rescue operation started with the local divers, but they were unable to find even a tiny part of the helicopter, let alone the pilots. The navy divers summoned from Bombay, with all their paraphernalia and expertise, scoured the river depths but returned empty handed. After ten days, they gave up, having searched a great area in the river waters. A month later, the rotting corpse of one of the pilots was recovered from Salal Hydroelectricity Project in Reasi.

Road traffic accidents on the Kishtwar–Batote road have been common. Many a times a whole bus plunges down the river, killing dozens, destroying families and clans. The surety of death is perceived as a foregone conclusion each time a vehicle comes in contact with the water of the Chenab. In December 2022, an Alto car rolled down from the highway and plunged into the Chenab. On the bank of the river, two identity cards, a driving license and a purse was found. The car was retrieved from the river, but there was no trace of any luggage or the occupants of the car. Police investigation identified Manjeet Singh, a small-time contractor from Bhaderwah and his wife and six-year-old daughter as the occupants of the ill-fated vehicle. In no time, the smiling photograph of the young couple with their cute daughter in pigtails found its way on social media. A plethora of heartfelt comments and condolences poured in for the family. Some netizens even cursed the Chenab for having yet again gulped innocent souls.

The police continued to look for the bodies and investigate the case. It was later found that Manjeet Singh was under heavy debt as he had taken a loan of INR 30 lakh from different banks and private lenders. Unable to pay the debts, he staged the accident. Twenty days later, the family was traced in Panchkula, Haryana, where they had been living with changed identities.[80]

The Chenab moves forward from the lake and passes underneath Dharmound. Soon appears the panoramic view of the river flowing by the bowl of Chanderkote on one side and the Chandrabhaga lake on the other. Meanwhile, just behind the river, the pine forests seem to climb up a mountain ensconcing the highway town of Batote in nature's green lap.

There are a large number of Sikhs residing in Batote. The first batch arrived with Sant Rocha Singh. Rocha Singh was born to Brahmin parents in Pakistan. He was barely fourteen years old when his father died, leaving him in the care of his mother and younger brother. The tall and handsome Rocha Singh chanced to meet Guru Gobind Singh in 1705. That meeting changed him forever. He spent the rest of his life in the company of saints. For his dedication, Rocha Singh was taken into the Khalsa fold, and it is presumed that he travelled all over Jammu and Kashmir to spread the message of Sikhism. More Sikhs settled in Batote, escaping the communal frenzy of 1947. A gurudwara in the town, erected in the memory of Sant Rocha Singh, is a place for pilgrimage.

Nestled amidst green hills, Batote is famous for its natural beauty and exotic migratory birds. Due to its salubrious environs, blessed with pleasant weather and fresh air, it is also considered to be a natural health resort.

In the 1930s, the Batote Hospital became a recuperating centre for patients of tuberculosis. The hospital, located amidst a copse of pine trees, was considered to be a perfect spot for rejuvenation.

In 1935, Saadat Hasan Manto was admitted here. Manto, with his paternal roots in Kashmir and maternal lineage in Afghanistan, was born in Ludhiana in 1912 into a family of legal luminaries. In 1934, he joined the Aligarh Muslim University to pursue graduation. However, his education at the university was cut short as he was diagnosed with tuberculosis. He spent three months for his treatment in the Batote sanatorium. After regaining his health in the healing surroundings, Manto returned home. Undoubtedly, the fresh breeze blowing across the pines on the Chenab's banks played its role. There is nothing to prove if his stay in Batote influenced his writing or not, but he eventually became one of the finest writers in the Urdu language and matured into a celebrated playwright, artistic essayist and a story-writer.

On an early morning in September 2019, not far from the sanatorium, gunfire and explosions shattered the peace of Batote. Even during the peak of militancy in the Chenab Valley, Batote had largely remained peaceful. However, being situated on the highway, it has been a transit point for the militants entering surreptitiously into Jammu city or moving towards the Kashmir Valley. Earlier in the day, a group of three terrorists had emerged from the forests on the Doda-Batote highway. Two of them hid behind the trees and took positions while the third came on the road and signalled a vehicle to stop. The driver of the vehicle, displaying great presence of mind, sped away. On the way, he saw an army vehicle and informed them about the armed militant on the roadside. When the army vehicle approached the spot, it came under heavy fire. In a short time, enforcements arrived and the hot pursuit of the terrorists began.

After a few hours, the terrorists were spotted in the lower part of Batote town, hiding near the quarters of the GREF. On seeing a Territorial Army patrol passing by, the militants panicked, threw grenades and escaped further up in a locality of clustered houses. They climbed up the stairs of a randomly chosen house and forcibly entered inside. The house belonged to a local tailor, and the militants took his family hostage.

The security forces cordoned off the house and plugged all exit routes. The terrorists released the women but kept the tailor captive. Frenetic appeals made on a public address system, asking the militants to surrender, failed. A fierce gunfight ensued, and the tailor was freed. After the encounter, three dead bodies with weapons and ammunition were recovered. The house was pockmarked by gunfire and one portion was extensively damaged by the blasts.

The terrorists were identified as Osama Javed and Zahid – both from Kishtwar – and Moin-ul-Islam. Son of a school teacher, Osama belonged to Sonder village in Marwah. Hizbul Mujahideen had assigned him the task of reviving militancy in Kishtwar. He was able to recruit Zahid from his own village and, with the help of some overground workers, established a few hideouts in Kishtwar.

In November 2018, the militants struck right in the middle of Kishtwar town. The Parihar brothers, who ran a stationery shop, closed rather late one night and headed for home on foot. A militant appeared out of the blue and shot them dead at point-blank range.

Ajeet Parihar, the elder brother, was the secretary of the BJP and one of most recognizable faces in the town. For last three decades, he had brazenly condemned militancy and would fiercely lead the protests against Hindu killings. After the Chapnari massacre of 1998, he had made a fiery speech that moved even Home Minister Advani, who had visited Premnagar. The murders of Parihar brothers was followed by a few incidents of weapon snatching from the government forces.

Five months later, two terrorists found their way inside the District Hospital, Kishtwar, and rained bullets on a senior RSS leader Chandarkant Sharma and his personal security officer (PSO). The PSO died on the spot and Sharma was airlifted to Jammu where he succumbed to his injuries. The latter was on duty in the hospital where he worked as a medical assistant. He had always espoused the case of Hindus and opposed militancy. A few months later, another incident of weapon snatching was reported. This time, the terrorists barged into the house of a local politician and snatched the weapon from his PSO.

These incidents baffled the police and the locals alike. It became clear that there was a militant group operating in town that would plan and audaciously carry out attacks and then evaporate into thin air without any trace. After sieving through a large data of Internet traffic and call detail records (CDRs), a few numbers were marked as suspicious. Finally, the investigators zeroed in on a house within Kishtwar town. By the time the policemen were able to discover the hideout – a secret pit dug on the terrace of a house – the terrorists had escaped, leaving behind a few blankets and some ammunition. The interrogation of the owner of the house led to a local boy named Nissar Ahmed. He had ostensibly transported the terrorists in his auto rickshaw during the murders of Parihar brother and Chandarkant Sharma.

After a few more arrests, the name of Moin-ul-Islam came up, who had joined Osama and Zahid a month earlier. Hizbul Mujahideen had specially sent Moin-ul-Islam from Shopian for a suicide mission. He had been tasked to kill the most prominent BJP leader in the town. Due to the high security of the intended victim, a suicide mission was the only way to kill him.

The police crackdown in Kishtwar had rendered Osama and his accomplices helpless; the security forces were closing in on them. Having been on the run for a few weeks, the militants decided to leave Kishtwar and move to Kashmir with the help of Moin-ul-Islam. Though it is not clear how they reached Batote, it is possible that they were helped by someone. It was later learnt that they wanted to hijack a vehicle to move to Kashmir and ended up in the local tailor's house, which became their grave.

From Batote, the highway descends and meets up the Dr Shyama Prasad Mookerjee tunnel in Nashri. At 9 km, it is the longest road tunnel in the country and was thrown open in 2017. Aptly named after Mookerjee, the town is symbolic of integration of Kashmir with the rest of India. Mookerjee, a prominent Jan Sangh leader, was best known for his vigorous opposition to the special privileges given to the state of Jammu and Kashmir.

The vehicles coming from Jammu get their first glimpse of the

Chenab at Nashri. Down below in a gorge, the river crawls so slowly that it almost looks like a frozen worm. A few miles further, from the small town of Peerah, the Baghlihar Dam is clearly visible. The high walls of concrete gravity dam slide down to the riverbed. When the sluices of the dam are lowered, the water gushes down, raising a white cloud of foam, and as one reaches near the dam, the roar of the water drum in the ears.

The BHEP is a run-of-the-river power project, the first owned by the state of Jammu and Kashmir and executed through the state Power Development Corporation. The two-stage 900 MW project was conceived in 1992, and the work commenced in 1999. The project was implemented by Jai Prakash Associates Limited for the civil and hydro-mechanical part, the same company that constructed the Dul–Hasti project in Kishtwar. The contract for electro-mechanical work was taken by a German company, Voith Hydro. Another German company, Lahmeyer International, was the initial project consultant for Power Developent Corporation (PDC).

The project was an engineering challenge because of the fragile and unstable mountains, which required extensive tunnelling. As the timelines got extended and the costs escalated, the project kept running into roadblocks. Then there were issues of labour unrest backed by the left-wing lobby.

Provoked by the trade union leaders, the workers went on strikes, stalling work for weeks. Corruption was rampant and the trade union leaders were bribed heavily. The local police and civil administration were also said to have been complicit in this wrongdoing. It was whispered that many stake-holders in those days had their hands in the deep pockets of the Jaypee Group. There were allegations against the contractors as well, who purportedly denied their workers legal rights and safety norms. Whenever workers died because of accidents at work sites, the police investigations would be a mere eyewash.

Wealth continued to be made on the dead bodies of the poor, and the Chenab readily gulped down the blood of innocents.

The small town of Chanderkote became a hub of activity after the Baghlihar project was commissioned in 1996. Till then, it was a nondescript locale on the highway, having a few households, roadside eateries and automobile workshops. It is the only place in the whole of Chenab Valley having a considerable population of Shias. They speak the Shina language, indicating their migration from Kargil district. Right in the middle of Chanderkote, there is a grandiose *imambara* [a building or a hall where Shias gather for religious ceremonies] which comes to life in the month of Moharram. The mourners gather here and, beating their chests, sing 'nohay' or the lamentations in memory of Husayn-ibn-Ali and his family members who fell during the seize of Karbala. When the Muharram processions on the tenth and fortieth day are taken out in the town, they pass through the main bazaar, and the air reverberates with the sound of bloodied chains striking against naked chests and backs. Perhaps for the first time, the Shia laments mix with the roar of the passing Chenab.

The Baghlihar project changed the destiny of Chanderkote by providing employment to both skilled and unskilled locals. The place underwent gentrification and saw huge construction activity, with many concrete and pre-fabricated structures coming up. Many offices were built, and so were guesthouses, helipads and residential areas for the officers and workers. Under the corporate social responsibility initiative, the Jaypee Group opened a hospital within their campus and a school that provided free education to the local children and those of the labourers and staff engaged in the project.

However, the biggest contribution of the project was the increased road network. The new roads were built to connect the various sites of the project within the vast area. There is a road leading to the ancient Gajpat Fort, located on top of a hill, overlooking the project. The history of the fort is shrouded in mystery, but it is widely believed to have been built in the year 1570, most probably by a vassal of the king of either Bhaderwah or Kishtwar. Nothing remains of the old fort except for a stone wall and an ancient temple of Kali Mata that is approached by a steep climb of a thousand steps.

On one side of the temple complex, there is a dilapidated basement that descends a flight of steps to a pit. This place served as a jail in the old days. Gulab Singh had imprisoned Sultan Khan Chib, the last king of Bhimber, here. Suffice it to remember that the Jammu kingdom had a long struggle with the estate of Bhimber to bring it to subjugation. In 1825, Sultan Khan Chib died in imprisonment and was buried in the local graveyard in Chanderkote, on the left bank of the Chenab. It is said that a Hindu shopkeeper from Ramban, who was a friend of Sultan Khan Chib, had tried to construct a tomb for the dead king. When Gulab Singh came to know about this, he immediately directed the shopkeeper to either stop the work or face banishment from his estate. Therefore, the construction of the memorial could not take place, and today, the grave of Sultan Khan Chib is bereft of any special epitaph. In 1858, Mian Hathu Singh, the governor of Rajouri and half-brother of Maharaja Ranbir Singh, was imprisoned here. Allegedly, he was conspiring to get the Maharaja killed and usurp the power at Jammu durbar. Later, Mian Hathu Singh was shifted to the jail in Doda Fort, where he died. After his arrest in 1953, Sheikh Mohammad Abdullah was also kept in Gajpat jail for a few days before he was shifted to Bhaderwah.

From atop the Gajpat Fort, one can gaze at the Chanderkote bowl and the Chenab flowing in the middle of it, taking a semi-circular bend around the project area and then straightening towards Ramban. On the other side, tinned terraces of houses and shops in Dharmound, Peerah and Nashri either glimmer in the sun or are shrouded by the wandering clouds. Amidst this alluring reverie, Batote plays hide and seek around the pine trees.

Just short of Chanderkote, the Chenab is replenished by Kunfer Nullah that slithers down from the hills on the opposite ridge, flows under a wooden bridge and assimilates into the river. The Chenab surges forward and slowly starts to widen at a place that used to be a major collection centre of wood, when it was transported through water in the old days. Here, a barrier of barbed wire, firmly bound to the poles on the riverbank, was thrown in the river. Without causing any hindrance to the flow of the water, the logs of the wood would get entangled in the wire. The arrangement was locally called *boom* and, thus, the place came to be known by the same name. The timber was then retrieved in boats and piled on the shores before being transported to the depots.

From Boom, the river flows under the Jaiswal Bridge. With the widening work of NH-44 underway, the bridge was converted into a meticulously designed balanced cantilever, double-lane bridge. After passing under the Jaiswal Bridge, the river opens up, having been fettered for at least 40 miles back in Pul Doda due to the Baghlihar project. Here she regains her old freedom and ebulliently pounds against giant black boulders, which have eroded heavily over the years. During monsoons, the waves rise up to tens of metres and, with their muddy water, rush forward in a mood to uproot everything in their path.

On the old alignment of the Jammu–Srinagar road lies the township of Maitra. Before the Jaiswal Bridge, this road crossed the Chenab on a suspension bridge built by Maharaja Ranbir Singh. The town Maitra, which was sparsely populated in the early days, expanded due to the exodus of the villagers from the upper reaches of Ramban hills, haunted by the militants.

On the left bank of the Chenab, Maitra houses the army transit camp. The military convoys plying on the highway break their journey here. 18 November 2001 was a cold day. The transit camp was bustling with soldiers in uniforms. Many of them were enjoying the sunshine, milling about in the open space right in the middle of the campus. Others were inside the dining hall having lunch. Suddenly, the lazy silence was shattered by a loud explosion, followed by the eruption of gunfire. Two suicide attackers, in camouflage dungarees and rucksacks hinged to their backs, had forced their entry inside the camp. In the next half an hour, there was heavy exchange of fire as the blood spilled in the camp. In no time, ten soldiers and three civilians lay dead, and many others were injured. The badly mutilated bodies of two militants could be identified only by their aliases, with the insignia on their Kalashnikovs indicating that the *fidayeen* (suicide attackers) belonged to Lashkar-e-Taiba.[81]

It was a shocking incident because Ramban town had remained largely peaceful, amidst all the turmoil around. The Hindus of Maitra blamed the attack on the Muslims of the locality, who, they alleged, had provided shelter to the militants. The schism between two communities widened further.

Ramban became a police district in the late 1990s. The formation of the police district was necessitated because of the militants swarming the heights in droves. The police officers who were posted here in the initial days would complain that it was a small district, located on two sides of the highway running parallel to the Chenab. Then someone would remind them not to measure the size of the district just by its length but also to look skywards as it rose vertically, almost into the clouds. Therefore, it earned the sobriquet of a vertical district. Indeed, it is one – the mountains slowly rise up and peaks remain perpetually covered with snow. Between the snowy peaks and the smaller mountains, there are sporadic settlements and terraces of cultivable fields, dwarfed by the high mountains. Like other towns in the Chenab Valley, Ramban, too, has its share of spiritual history. On his way to Doda from Gool, Farid-ud-Din Baghdadi was said to have stayed in Ramban for a few days. A small ziyarat dedicated to him still exists in the middle of the town, marking the place of the saint's meditation. The ancient Raghunath temple is the most revered monument in the district. Every July, a pilgrimage to the shrine of Raja Sankhpal originates from here. Sankhpal, the manifestation of a serpent, is a local deity.

Ramban district has a lot of significance because of the highway passing entirely through its length. Since 1947, for a long time, this has been the only road link connecting the Kashmir Valley with the rest of the country. The evolution of this road is evocative of many stories, deeply entrenched in the trade and political history of Kashmir.

After the first Anglo-Sikh war, the Treaty of Amritsar was signed in March 1846. It transferred the ownership rights of people and land between the Ravi and the Indus from the Sikh Empire to Maharaja Gulab Singh. Interestingly, when Gulab Singh went to take the possession of Kashmir, he travelled via the Mughal Road in Poonch. This alternate route was a lesser-known pony track through the inhospitable terrain of the Chenab Valley, which passed through Kishtwar, Bhaderwah and Ramban, and, after crossing the Banihal Pass, entered the valley.

Gulab Singh decided to not only revitalize this route but also to partly realign it on a shorter axis of Udhampur, Batote and Banihal. This way, Ramban prominently came on the alignment of the proposed route. Earlier, the track was meant only for the horses and mules. In certain cases, humans were forced to work as bonded labour, to carry other humans through the hazardous terrain. Though it was not an easy task to chisel a track through the sandstone mountains, the existing path was widened and levelled at many stretches. Till then, Ramban was a small village consisting of a few households and was called Nashband, which means 'closed nose'. All this changed when the route was spruced up and a wooden bridge was laid on the Chenab. With the increase of the traffic of royal caravans, military troops, traders and postal services on this route, Ramban developed into a popular halting station. The merchants from nearby villages established their ventures on the roadside and the town started growing.[82]

Maharaja Ranbir Singh remained determined about improving the track and sanctioned Rs 1 lakh for the project. The Maitra Bridge in Ramban was also strengthened to enable the movement of loaded camels over it. Later, he ordered the replacement of the wooden bridge with a steel suspension bridge. Local engineers were employed for this purpose. However, the bridge was completed by a British engineer, Alexander Atkinson, during the reign of Maharaja Partap Singh. Coming to about 225 ft in length, this impressive bridge remained the only road link with Kashmir for a long time.

Such was the importance of the bridge that it found a mention in a famous Dogri song:

Taare tudaan paiyan kandiyan peya brasala!

[In the higher reaches, it snows and in the lower, it rains!]

The song talks about love in different seasons – when it snows and rains – while insinuating the naughty way of the Gaddi boys.

Aun tuki thakki odeya, ikale ni jayan thara.
Gadiyan de chokru burey, ikle ki ponde maara.

[I have warned you, don't go to the stream alone.
The Gaddi boys are naughty, if you're alone, they will tease you.]

Then the song meanders towards Ramban:

Ramban pul baneya, baneya vaaj garrariyan.
Teri meri preet lagiye, lagiye vaaj rawariyan.

[A bridge has come up in Ramban without the pulleys.
You and I have been matched without a mediator.]

One of the most popular songs, it is played across the Jammu province and parts of Himachal Pradesh, and has been performed in some of the theatres in the United States and European countries. In October 2016, Natrang Jammu, a theatre group from Jammu, performed the song at Trafalgar Square in central London in front of a mammoth international audience.[83]

By the end of the nineteenth century, the road was wide enough for the movement of carts and came to be known as Banihal Cart Road, more popularly, the BC Road. However, it was mainly used as a private route for the royalty and their friends. Any other traveller who desired to use the road had to take special permission from the Maharaja's secretariat.

In 1894, Maharaja Partap Singh appointed Walter Roper Lawrence, a British civil servant, as the first settlement commissioner of Jammu and Kashmir. Lawrence, in his book *The Valley of Kashmir* (1895), expresses regret that the valley was not connected with plains through Banihal Pass, which would have been easier and shorter. It is pertinent to note that by 1890, the Jhelum Valley Cart Road, connecting Rawalpindi and Srinagar, had been constructed, enabling travellers to enter Kashmir in wheeled vehicles for the first time. Later, the same road was used for the tribal invasion in 1947. After the repulsion of the tribal raid and partition of Kashmir, the Jhelum Valley Cart Road was closed and, hence on, restricted only for the exclusive use of the UN vehicles.

By the end of the nineteenth century, the Maharaja, in consultation with the British, was contemplating a rail link between Jammu and Srinagar, aligned with the BC Road. Though the railways did not come up, a basic road started to be laid in 1901, after the Maharaja sanctioned Rs 40 lakh for the project. Lt Col Joshua Duke, who spent most of his last twenty years as a surgeon at a Kashmir residency, recorded in his *Duke's Guide to Kashmir* (1842):

> The road at present in 1901 is in a transition state. The survey for an electric railway was completed in 1900, and in 1901, a cart

road, starting from the north bank of the river Tawi was aligned for a railway and much of the roadway has been completed till Udhampur.

The most difficult part on this route was to conquer the 9,200 ft high Banihal Pass in the Pir Panjal mountains that separated the Vale of Kashmir and the Chenab Valley. The Jammu durbar had requested the services of the British engineers, but they could not be spared. Finally, under the supervision of Engineer Laxman Joo Tikoo, a path was constructed over the Banihal Pass at a cost of Rs 30 lakh, and the first horse-driven carriage crossed over the pass in 1916. Almost thirty-one years later, Maharaja Hari Singh's convoy of forty Rolls-Royces, jeeps, American limousines and a hunting wagon would cross over the same Pass, having lost Kashmir in the wake of tribal raids.

On 2 May 1921, when Maharaja Partap Singh's car drove on the Ramban bridge, it became the first vehicle to have done so. Next year, the road was thrown open to the public. Since the bridge was weak, the passengers would disembark from their vehicles and walk across the bridge to board the vehicles again on the other end. There is a historic photograph of Prime Minister Jawaharlal Nehru crossing the bridge on foot on his way to Srinagar in 1948. Incidentally, four years earlier, the same road and bridge had been used by Muhammad Ali Jinnah for his last visit to Kashmir. After spending about two months in Kashmir, he had left via Jhelum Valley Cart Road. In 2004, the old suspension bridge was declared unsafe, yet the vehicles continue to pass over it, one at a time.

Today, Ramban is the district headquarters and is always bustling with activity. The villagers of the adjoining hills throng the town, which happens to be their major shopping centre.

Situated almost in the middle of the Jammu–Srinagar highway, it continues to be a popular halting spot for the traffic. This situation is likely to change since a two-lane viaduct over the Chenab was thrown open for the traffic in June 2023. The 1.08 km-long viaduct is an engineering marvel, as it curves around the Chenab, it bypasses the Ramban town and the interminable traffic snarls.

Since its journey from the confluence at Tandi, the Chenab is perhaps the widest while flowing past the town of Ramban. The river marches forward, sometimes green, sometimes grey and muddy during monsoons. Passing by the town, it turns tempestuous, alternating between arrogance and humility, pleasing and exasperating, disturbing and assuring. As the river broadens further, it becomes serene and turns soothing and docile.

Four decades ago, this tranquility was disturbed when a tourist taxi plummeted into the water, caused a loud splash and vanished. The driver perhaps failed to negotiate the sharp curve and drove straight off the cliff, as if succumbing to the siren call of the Chenab. There was a honeymoon couple in the taxi, headed for Kashmir. Who were they? Wouldn't they have been in their sixties now, maybe with grandchildren? Were their dead bodies ever recovered? Could their families cremate them with religious rites? I have no answers. Even after making efforts to sift through the old records of Ramban police station, I could not find anything. Forty years is a long time. When I was very young, I had read about the incident in a local newspaper: 'A Taxi Carrying a Honeymoon Couple Plunges into the Chenab.'

11

The Master and His Servant

From Ramban, the Chenab flows forward, wide and tranquil, concealing its immense depth as if in a benevolent and forgiving disguise. For about a mile along its left bank, seasonal crops swirl in the fields. The steps of these fields rise gradually up to the parapets of a road slowly curving up the hill, towards Gool. Meanwhile, from the right bank, NH-44 moves up, whereas the Chenab transmutes into a steep gorge once again. Running parallel to the river, this stretch of the highway is very fragile and prone to landslides and shooting stones, often depositing the debris in the Chenab. The road is also susceptible to traffic accidents. As per local beliefs, the river is thirsty for blood, and many fatal mishaps have been witness to this macabre yearning.

A few miles later, the Chenab takes a massive westward turn and changes its course, as if refusing to go towards Kashmir. Here, the southward Bichelri Nullah joins the river. The nullah originates from Zaban Glacier situated in Sanglaab Valley, close to Banihal Pass. On its journey, Bichelri Nullah is joined by fourteen mountain streams before it empties into the Chenab and loses its identity forever.

The mountains on both sides of the river rise into the sky and are dotted with houses situated at a fair distance from each other. On an overcast day, the dwellings at the highest points get enveloped in the lenticular clouds. Some of these houses, surrounded by terraced fields, are situated at the highest parts of the ridges. With no network of roads, why would anyone choose to live in such isolation and difficulty? Well, it does make sense to not have a cluster of houses in the mountains for the fear of landslides that could take down the whole village. This danger is considerably reduced when the houses are apart and the damage can be minimized.

However, another theory says that during the rule of local principalities, the hapless people would choose to settle in inaccessible areas to evade the troublesome 'arms' of the government: the policeman, forest guard and the revenue clerk. Whenever these officials would visit for tax collection or other official purposes, the inhabitants of these areas would leave their houses and escape to further heights, challenging the government authority. The locals were adept at traversing the local terrain and were always one step ahead of the game, seemingly making the government employees, who invariably hailed from the plains, sulk. Moreover, the terrain was intimidatingly steep; the mules would also struggle to clamber up.

Due to these reasons, the villages perched on glorious heights, swathed in dense forests, became a safe haven for the militants. By the mid-1990s, the militants were present in major parts of Ramban, including Gool Valley.

Like in other areas of the Chenab Valley, Hindus were left fending for themselves here too. The selective murders of Hindus led to symbolic protests and political posturing, but nothing was done to safeguard the community. Much of this militancy was heralded by the Chenab division of HM, which mostly comprised of local cadre. Posters demanding the migration of villagers would appear frequently, and a painful exodus of Hindus began. The abandoned houses of the displaced Hindus were set on fire. Those who decided to stay back for fear of falling into penury lived life on the edge, often huddling together during the nights with the VDCs as their only hope.

One such area that faced the maximum brunt of militancy was the bowl of Sumbar, consisting of about half-a-dozen hamlets inhabited by Hindus, Kashmiri Muslims and Gujjars. Situated at a steep trek of about 8 miles from the roadhead, the village overlooks the Chenab. With the nearest police post and army picket miles away, the place became a safe transit route for militants operating in Gool and Banihal regions.

Sumbar was commonly approached from Dharamkund, a small town on the bank of the Chenab. On the right bank, a huge stock of the purest form of gypsum is spread over a belt nearly 3 km long in the lower contours of the hills.

Amanullah Peer, a local militant from Sumbar, soon rose in the ranks and became the supreme commander of the Chenab division of HM. Belonging to an influential family with good landholding and livestock, Amanullah was from the privileged class of Syeds, who are considered as the direct descendants of the Prophet. He had five uncles, the brothers of his father, two of whom had settled in Pakistan after the Partition.

With relatives in Pakistan, Amanullah made a few visits there on valid documents. On one such visit in the early 1990s, he came under the influence of jihadi organizations, who roped him for the 'freedom struggle' in the Chenab Valley. Allegedly, he met the top leadership of HM in Pakistan, including its supreme commander Salahuddin, who motivated him to join his outfit. He undertook arms training and returned to Sumbar as an armed terrorist.

While the security forces were busy combating terrorism in the Kashmir Valley and parts of Doda district, Amanullah was slowly and silently building his network by recruiting local youth, picking them from poor families. With negligible chances of government employment and lack of education, the youth looked forward to joining the ranks of militancy.

Mohammad Rafiq alias Wasim Khan, popularly known as Billoo Gujjar, would go on to become one of the most important confidants of Amanullah Peer. Born in a poor family, Billoo was employed as a servant in Amanullah's household from a young age. Apart from helping in the household chores, he would also take the cattle out for grazing. Following the footsteps of his master, Billoo joined militancy in his teens and would go on to dominate the hills of Ramban and become one of the most dreaded terrorists in the Chenab Valley. Owing to a childhood accident, he had restricted vision in one eye, making his right eye smaller than the other. It was an easy giveaway, making him avoid public appearances, having an easily recognizable face. The condition was much like that of infamous David Coleman Headley, the conspirator of 26/11 Mumbai attacks who suffered from rare heterochromia iridium, wherein pupils have different colours – brown and blue.

Despite having a reward of INR 5 lakh on his head, Amanullah Peer remained largely elusive and was randomly traced on the radio frequencies as Code 38 or Syed Iqbal Shah. The horrifying ruthlessness with which he handled distractors ensured that there was silence about his whereabouts. It began from his own village Sumbar, which he soon converted into his fiefdom of terror. In April 1994, he killed two Hindu brothers by dubbing them as informers. A year later he killed another Hindu man and his young son, belonging to his own hamlet of Jwari in Sumbar. These killings were a strong message to others to stay clear of the militants and their activities.

In the mid-1990s, when the divisional commander of HM was killed in an operation, Amanullah replaced him to head the outfit in Ramban. He was able to control a vast area of Ramban, extending well into Gool Valley and beyond. In Gool, his terror was not only confined to helpless Hindus; Muslims also faced his wrath at the slightest sign of suspicion. Amanullah elicited a lot of reverence because of his mastery over the Holy Quran and Islamic teachings. Awed by his aura, most of the villagers addressed him as Peer Sahib. They were eager to host him and seek his benedictions. Much folklore was spun around Amanullah's apparent invincibility and the desperation of the armed forces. Information about his whereabouts remained scarce, but he had garnered fame as a sort of Houdini, breaking cordons and managing to escape traps. Villagers whispered about his miraculous power of vanishing from battle scenes and ability to change directions of bullets fired at him. However, in reality, he was a coward and always stayed clear of any kind of direct military confrontation. The cadres religiously carried out his ruthless orders of exterminations. Billoo Gujjar, a true disciple of his master, gained notoriety for his panache in escaping cordons too, and he outlived Amanullah by four years.

From Dharamkund, the Chenab moves along the Gool road. Short of Sangaldan, the river takes a massive turn at Tanger village and moves towards Sawalakote to finally enter Reasi district.

The roadside town of Sangaldan was purely a Muslim town before the Hindus escaping from the militancy in the uphill villages started to settle here. From June to September, the town buzzes with thousands of visitors, especially from south Kashmir, Kargil and far as Punjab. These people come to take a dip in the sulphur springs of Tatapani, located a few miles away. The hot springs are famed for their healing powers, especially in curing dermatitis and arthritis.

It was believed that Amanullah Peer and his accomplices used to secretly visit the springs for a dip. After him, Billoo Gujjar, too, would visit here. This information probably got leaked as the security forces once raided the place. Irked by this, Billoo Gujjar triggered an IED blast near Tatapani in September 2009, killing one Hindu and four Muslims. It was a clear message for the people to refrain from leaking information about his movement.

After a decade of bloodshed, the erstwhile hotspots of militancy in Ramban hills have transformed into bustling areas of economic activity. The harbingers of development include Sangaldan, now an important railway station on the Katra–Banihal line. A 7 km tunnel begins from the town, passes through Sumbar, and ends at Kohli village. In Sumbar, where electricity was a distant dream ten years ago, today, an engineer engaged in railway construction can order a book on Amazon in a moment.

From Sangaldan, the road rounds up to the pristine valley of Gool, situated in the lap of lofty mountains rich with deodar forests and lush meadows. Gool, then known as Karlog, is believed to have been inhabited by the forbears of the Thakurs of Ayodhya. They cut down the dense forests and crafted tracts of cultivable fields. Initially, the area remained Hindu, which is also evident from the decrepit ruins of some religious spots. Gradually, some pastoral nomads – who would otherwise come here in summer for pasture lands – started to settle down and got ownership rights on the land.

At a short distance from Gool is Dang Gam, the heritage site where Ghoda Gali [The Street of Horses] is located. The site has hundreds of stone horses carved out from monoliths. The artistically chiselled riders in traditional clothes are firmly astride the saddles. They wield bows and arrows and have swords dangling at their waists. According to the myth, these sculptures were carved by the Pandavas while in exile. More horse statutes and other versatile stone carvings are found in a few other areas of Gool. However, due to the ignorance of locals and apathy of the government, these historical artefacts are fast disappearing, getting damaged and even stolen.

After Akbar annexed Kashmir, the place was renamed Dangbatal, and the jagir was granted to a Hindu raja whose descendants held it for a long time. As already discussed, Sheikh Farid-ud-Din Baghdadi stayed here while on his way to Doda and took a Hindu wife. Attracted by his message of love, many people converted to Islam at his behest. When General Zorawar Singh was sent to Reasi, he annexed Gool and fixed an annual tribute to be paid to the Jammu durbar.

In 1880, a large number of Kashmiris chose to settle in Dangbatal, escaping the drought in Kashmir. This turned the town into a Kashmiri-speaking, Muslim majority region. Subsequently, the place was renamed as 'Gool', emphasizing its unique topography of roundness. From every side and angle, Gool appears to be *gol* or round in shape.

In the 1990s, Gool lost its tranquil charm and became a hotbed of militancy. It became a meeting point of the infiltrating groups of terrorists from Rajouri and Poonch. These new groups were received by their brethren operating in Gool and were further guided into Doda and the Kashmir Valley.

Stretching 40 miles, the only motorable route from Ramban to Gool was fraught with dangers. The Chenab, flowing by the roadside for at least half of the distance, rendered the road safe from one flank. However, on the mountainside, the terrorists were in an advantageous position – they could easily plant IEDs and ambush vehicles.

In June 1997, a bus from Jammu revved up towards Gool. A little short of Ghoda Gali, on a sharp bend, a man in uniform appeared unexpectedly and signalled the bus to stop. The commuters in the bus mostly comprised the locals of Gool. There were two bubbly young girls accompanying their father, who sat just behind the driver's seat. After the end of ten-day vacation, some government school teachers were also returning to Gool. As the bus stopped, the uniformed man stepped inside brandishing a Kalashnikov, and three more militants, two in olives and the third in a Pathani suit, emerged from behind the pine trees. One of them went towards the driver and pointed a gun at him through the window. The weary travellers, tired after a gruelling journey, were suddenly frantic with worry. The elder of the two girls, Shaista Masood, wrote an article for *The Wire* about this, twenty years later: 'What I Saw After I Watched a Massacre of Innocents in Kashmir':

> I will always remember my father's presence of mind – he reaches over to the driver, who is panicking at the wheel, and puts a hand on his shoulder. He says: '*Daro nahi aap. Bus ko control karo aur side main laga do* [Don't be afraid, control the bus and pull over].'[84]

The terrorist who had entered the bus ordered the Hindus and

Muslims to separate. Finally, half-a-dozen men, including the driver and conductor, and three school teachers identified themselves as Hindus. When they were ordered out of the bus Shaista's father intervened, 'We will all get down. They are our respected teachers and we know them well.' Listening to those words, every passenger got up to get down from the bus.

In the article, Shaista claims that on a nearby cliff, she could see some uniformed men and expected them to intervene. A scuffle ensued inside the bus as more travellers opposed the militants who started hitting them with rifle butts. When a militant tried to harm a teacher, Shaista interceded. Grabbing his rifle, she cried, 'You cannot do this in the name of Kashmir's freedom movement. It's un-Islamic and inhuman.'

Finding unexpected resistance, the wily militants suddenly changed their strategy. 'We don't mean any harm,' they swore on Allah and took away three teachers, ostensibly to discuss a few matters. About 15 m away, all three were shot dead in cold blood. Leaving behind three dead bodies, the bus was ordered to proceed and the militants climbed uphill. The three teachers killed were Kashmiri Pandits – Ravinder Kabu, Sushil Kumar Bhat and Ashok Kumar Raina, the principal of Gool Government Higher Secondary School.

Author and journalist, Rahul Pandita, in his memoir *Our Moon Has Blood Clots* (2013), mentions the gory incident as the slain Sushil Bhat was his close relative. He wrote:

> That night I am alone on the bus to Jammu, in the last seat. They are showing *Khalnayak* on the bus. I am numb with pain. At dawn, we cross the border of Jammu and Kashmir. At the Lakhanpur gate, I buy the *Daily Excelsior*. No, no, no, no. This is not Ravi. Why is there blood on his face? Why is his photo on the front page? So it is Ravi. The previous day, Ravi left Jammu with two other Pandit colleagues for Gool. The summer vacations were over and I'd met him a fortnight ago. 'I am trying

to be transferred to Jammu. Shubham is growing – he needs me,' he had told me. Just before Gool, the bus comes to a halt and armed men enter. They have specific information about three Pandits on board the bus. Ravi knows what this means. He hugs the other two men. They are asked to step out of the bus, which leaves without them. Ravi tries to fight the men. He is hit in the face. All three of them are shot.[85]

The interminable exodus of Kashmiri Pandits in the early 1990s saw a large number of government employees, most of them school teachers, moving away from Kashmir. Since they could not return to the area for work, they were adjusted via a government policy in the schools of Jammu region. The three teachers killed in Gool were part of that scheme.

A high-level team from Delhi visited Gool to probe the gruesome murders. The resistance shown by the passengers was applauded, and some of them were even offered government jobs. However, Shaista claims that her statement was not recorded, probably suspecting her to spill the beans about the presence of security forces in the vicinity, which did not come to their rescue. She also claimed that her father refused the bravery award for his daughters for fear that it might mark them ominously in the diary of the militants. However, these allegations were never proved.

Later on, a theory emerged that this killing was done at the behest of a school student. Apparently, he had been disallowed from appearing in a board examination on some administrative grounds by Principal Raina. The embittered student had left his studies and joined HM. He convinced his commanders to let him exact his revenge. The killing had the tacit approval of Amanullah Peer and was carried out at the behest of his acolyte Billoo Gujjar.

The Ramban–Gool road in those days was largely dilapidated, with heaps of debris by its sides, making it easier to plant IEDs. In 2001, a few miles short of the spot where the school teachers were killed, a BSF gypsy slowed down on a bend, and running over a powerful IED, was blown into pieces. The commandant, S.S. Dhaiya, a brave officer from Rohtak, Haryana, died instantly along with five of his men. The martyred officer had taken a proactive role in carrying out operations against the terrorists and had been successful in eliminating many of them. That fateful day, he was on a routine patrol to dominate the area, having received information about the presence of terrorists on the adjoining hills. The IED was so devastating that the gypsy was tossed into the air and a huge crater, mangled metal, body parts and blood were left behind.

In November 2001, Amanullah Peer tasked his men to kill some VDC members. To conceal their involvement, Pancheri area in Udhampur was chosen for the proposed killings. After a few days, a deadly group consisting of twelve terrorists, including Amanullah Peer and Billoo Gujjar, reached the right bank of the Chenab near Tatapani in Sangaldan. Following the orders of Amanullah, few fellow militants, including Billoo, shaved off their beards and changed into army and police uniforms. The select group crossed the river with the help of ropes and wooden logs and reached Tanger, where they were hosted by an overground worker (OGW) named Mohammad Din.

On the way to Pancheri, the group encountered a survey team of Sawalakote project accompanied by a few policemen. After a brief exchange of fire, the terrorists managed to flee. The police followed their trail and reached the house of Mohammad Din, who pretended ignorance.

Next day, the terrorists reached Chakka Galiote village in Pancheri. They formally introduced themselves as the security personnel of Sawalakote hydroelectricity project and wished to recruit the VDC members for security detail of the project. Four VDC members, along with three other young men, including two Muslims, made an appearance. They were asked to deposit their guns and line up for measurements. In a matter of minutes, the seven men were riddled with bullets. The terrorists fled with the deposited weapons.

A case was registered by the local police and the carnage was condemned by everyone. In 2002, the case was closed since the identity of the terrorists could not be established.

In January 2003, Amanullah Peer's luck finally ran out. The local police had been tipped off regarding his presence in a house in Dedha village. It was not every day that one received information about the 'vanishing dervish'. In the biting cold, a police team started from Gool and silently moved towards Dedha. They had rightly anticipated that in case the militants came to know about the cordon, they would try to escape from the rocky Simb Nullah, passing close to the village. Therefore, another team took position a mile away from the targeted house, hiding behind the boulders of the dried-up stream. At the first light of the day, when the hiding terrorists were challenged and asked to come out of the house, they jumped from the window and ran down the nullah.

With Kalashnikovs tightly clutched in their hands, Amanullah and his three bodyguards fled, only to be ambushed by the police personnel from the Ind post. The battle lasted for barely ten minutes and four dead bodies lay strewn amidst the rocks. By this time, the police party from Gool had also reached the site of the encounter. The policemen moved forward cautiously and their first reaction was of surprise: Who is this old man we have killed? Amanullah Peer lay dead, his jacket and beard soaked with blood, a Kalashnikov by his side, the long antennae wireless set still hinged to his pouch.

The killing of Amanullah Peer was a great setback to HM in the whole of Chenab Valley. Its Chief Salahuddin organized special prayers and condemned the killings. He purportedly said, 'My right hand has been chopped off.' He vowed to avenge the death of his most trusted commander. About 8 miles' uphill climb from Sangaldan, one reaches the sprawling village of Ind, nestled amidst fruit trees and vegetable fields. Predominantly a Hindu village, there are a few Muslim houses on the periphery. Across Simb Nullah flowing parallel to the village, the deeply forested Basantdhar ridge had become a safe territory for militants. Every summer, the Gujjars and Bakerwals would camp at Lapri Top, the highest point on this ridge. They would pitch their tents in vast pasturelands sprinkled with wild lilies and surrounded by deodar trees. Here, the nomads would get in contact with hordes of local militants and others belonging to Pakistan, Afghanistan and Kashmir.

Lapri Top, having tremendous potential for tourism and adventure trips, sadly turned into the equivalent of Tora Bora: the eponymous militant stronghold of Afghanistan. It was said that the militants had established their divisional headquarters at Lapri, with a court, interrogation centre and a signals unit with high-frequency radio sets connected with Pakistan.

An occasional long-range patrol of the army or paramilitary forces could be easily evaded. Either the terrorists received advance information, or the lookouts could easily identify the approaching patrols from their advantageous vantage points. The militants would silently slip into the jungles or shift to the adjoining spurs.

From Lapri Top, the village of Ind is clearly visible: the pinnacle of the ancient Bhim Mandir, located at the lower side of the village, gleaming in the dark. Because of the Hindu population, the village often came under the attack of the militants. However, the brave VDCs and a police post would valiantly respond to these attacks.

The police post was housed in an old building donated by a local Hindu and comprised of a few regular constables and ragtag bands of local SPOs who donned the uniform for a small honorarium. With archaic weapons and elementary training, the biggest asset these policemen possessed was their bravery.

On 15 March 2003, the gibbous Moon hung in the sky and the terrorists descended from various points of Basantdhar and Mahakund Ridges. Oblivious to the sleeping village, they took positions around the police post. The gunfire and blasts that followed were unprecedented and resounded all over the nearby areas. The SPOs manning the posts fought bravely, but they were outnumbered and outsmarted by about two dozen terrorists carrying sophisticated weapons. In the blitzkrieg, eleven people, including nine policemen and two VDC members, lay dead. The terrorists entered the post, kidnapped four Muslim policemen and decamped with weapons and ammunition.

By the time the enforcements reached the spot, the post was pockmarked, half crumbled and smouldering with black smoke. One of the dead bodies of a local SPO, Shadi Lal, was decapitated – the terrorists took his head along. A braveheart, Shadi Lal always remained at the forefront in the fight against militancy. Two of the four kidnapped policemen returned safely; their story was that the militants used them for carrying the looted arms and ammunition. The dead bodies of the other two were recovered from Simb Nullah after two days.

The investigation revealed that the attack was executed jointly by different organizations in the area and was planned and led by Billoo Gujjar as a befitting retaliation to the killing of his master, Amanullah Peer.

In August 2020, the locals fished out a human skull from Simb Nullah. The DNA analysis of the skull proved that it belonged to Shadi Lal, the martyred SPO.

Even after the killing of Amanullah Peer, Billoo Gujjar continued to spread unabated terror. He rose to the rank of divisional commander of HM's Chenab division, with a reward of INR 5 lakh on his head. A spate of bloody killings followed, where many innocent men and women belonging to both communities fell prey to his bullets.

Despite all the efforts of security and intelligence agencies, Billoo Gujjar remained elusive. Such was his terror that one would not report his movement and sighting. However, his womanizing tendencies had come to fore. He had many paramours and frequented a lot of houses. Soon, the news of his wedding to a Kashmiri woman, Mubeena Begum*, from Manglogi–Dalwah village reached the security forces.

---

* Name changed to protect privacy.

Mubeena was born into a poor family that sustained itself on maize crop and cattle. She lost her father at a very young age; it was her mother who was the sole caretaker of the family of four. In the summers, the family would take their livestock to their traditional dhoke in Daram area. In those days, Billoo Gujjar would roam these heights fearlessly, often having his meals in the dhokes of nomadic clans. That is when his eye fell on Mubeena and he became smitten with her beauty. Both got secretly married and had three kids – two sons and a daughter. Mubeena continued to stay in her house in Manglogi because her husband's house in Sumbar was under constant watch of security forces. Billoo would visit her occasionally or call her to earmarked places intimated to her well in advance.

On 5 September 2006, a police component led by a deputy SP (DSP) set off for Dalwah village from Sangaldan. The narrow road snaked up to the targeted village thriving with a full-grown maize crop. The police team left their vehicles at Kantha Morh and walked the rest of the distance of about two miles silently and strategically.

The tip-off seemed to be accurate and specific. Billoo Gujjar had come to meet his wife at her house. Manglogi is a small hamlet in the village Dalwah having a dozen houses surrounded by maize fields.

Mubeena Begum's single-storey mud house was painted white. Situated on the roadside, it had walls of piled up stones on two sides. In a corner, there was a Sintex water tank, and on the other side, a thatched cowshed. The thick foliage and maize crop surrounding the house made it an ideal place to make a surreptitious entry. In the still of the night, the targeted house was quietly cordoned off. Billoo Gujjar, who was probably tucked in his blanket, had a minimal chance of escape. His accomplices were resting in houses about 500 m away on the upper side of Manglogi. The police party quietly observed the house through the blurred images of night vision devices. In a little while, a man of average height with a thick mop of hair and dense, short beard ambled out from the door. A woman, presumably his wife, accompanied him. It was Billoo Gujjar sans his inseparable pouch and Kalashnikov. The duo went to the cowshed where they stood for some time, the man patting the flanks of the cow. Soon, both returned to the house. The police stayed vigilant and patient.

Well past midnight, Billoo Gujjar stepped out of the house, his gun swinging on his arm and a satellite phone tucked inside the pouch. A few metres away from the house, a volley of fire greeted him. Quick to his feet, Billoo leapt inside the maize crop and tried to flee, but the rustling of the leaves exposed his trail. He fired back, randomly and aimlessly. After a brief exchange of gunfire, he lay dead, flat on his face. Surprised at the rattle of the gunfire, his accomplices came running from their hideouts, and taking positions in the maize crop, started firing at the police party. About twenty minutes of gun firing was followed by a lull. The police team was able to retrieve Billoo Gujjar's dead body, but other terrorists fled through the maize crop and melted into the darkness. The killing of one of the longest surviving terrorists was a major success for the security forces, a great relief for the Hindus of the region and a big setback to the Chenab division of HM.

After Billoo's killing, the command of the Chenab division passed on to Manzoor Ahmed alias Furqan Ali. His immediate task was to trace out the informer who had betrayed their leader.

Furqan, along with his associates, connected the dots. They zeroed in on a young man whose house lay a few hundred metres away from Mubeena Begum's house. In the blood feud, where every whisper is heard and every sight scanned, the news of betrayals and friendships, affiliations and animosities, can clearly delineate one's enemies and well-wishers. The murmurs started to point out the informer right away.

After Billoo Gujjar's dead body was retrieved from the maize field, it had to be carried down to Kantha Morh, where the police vehicles waited. The policemen had fetched a cot from the neighbourhood to transport the corpse. Presuming that the cot had come from a friendly house, perhaps it was the giveaway of the informer's identity.

A fortnight after the encounter, Ayesha (name changed), the informer's adopted sister and his uncle's daughter, was kidnapped by the militants while she was coming back from school. The schoolgirl was forced into the maize field and beheaded there. The corpse was desecrated and dismembered brutally. The sack with the limbless torso was discovered two days later. One-and-a-half months later, a group of terrorists led by Furqan appeared in Manglogi village and barged into the informer's house. In a volley of fire, they murdered his sisters, aunt and uncle.

Why did the informer risk his own and his family's safety to pass the information about the most dreaded militant? In fact, it turned out to be a classic revenge story, which had interlocked the destinies of the informer and Billoo Gujjar. The informer's elder brother, Haroon (name changed) had once been an owner of a small grocery shop in the village. The army and paramilitary patrols would occasionally stop at the shop for a snack or a cigarette. Out of courtesy, Haroon would offer them a glass of water or indulge in a small chat. This was misconstrued as intimacy, and Haroon's family went on to pay a heavy price for it.

In 2003, Haroon was abducted from his shop and taken to the forest by Billoo Gujjar. He was hacked to pieces. The man left behind two young daughters and a wailing widow. The younger brother's fury knew no limits and he vowed vendetta – Billoo Gujjar's life for his brother's.

Meanwhile, Mubeena's marriage became common news in Dalwah. In Billoo's pursuit, the informer spent a lot of time at his uncle's house, which was in Mubeena's neighbourhood. He watched her house for endless hours, keeping track of Billoo's visiting times. That day, on a cold September evening, when the maize crop stood at its highest, the informer took his chance, losing everything he had in the aftermath.

Today, there are no militants in Gool, but the scars remain. The informer's uncle's house was secured with a police guard. The sandbag bunkers on the upper floor have started crumbling, telling the sad stories of yesteryears. Mubeena Begum went on to marry a driver from a nearby village. The villagers gossiped that it was Billoo's widow's potential money that tempted the driver into marrying her, and eventually, on discovering no money, the marriage broke. Post the divorce, Mubeena raised her children by herself.

After the killing of Billoo Gujjar, militancy in Ramban district showed a steep decline. In 2007, a dozen militants including seven from Gool surrendered to the authorities. These included Furqan and other close associates of Billoo. Even after the surrender of Furqan, his wife Raja Begum continued to evade arrest. During the times of her husband's spell of terror, she had remained an important conduit for HM. It was learnt that she worked as a courier and a recruiter – sending messages, transporting arms and ammunition, and arranging other logistics for her husband and his accomplices. Eight months later, she was arrested from the court premises of Gool and was later released on bail. The surrendered terrorists served some time in prison and were subsequently bailed out.

However, the past of three surrendered terrorists finally caught up with them after sixteen years. In 2008, unknown terrorists barged into the house of a local cloth merchant of Pancheri, Ashok Khajuria. They killed him and his wife in cold blood. The investigation of the case lingered on for five years till it was handed over to a young assistant SP (ASP) of Udhampur at the directions of the High Court.

The renewed investigation revealed that two militants had knocked on the door of Khajuria's house. They had asked for a piece of cloth to be used as a shroud for the burial of Abdul Latif's mother. She had passed away earlier in the day. Khajuria agreed to sell the shroud on credit, but while entering the details into the credit register – Abdul Latif's name and address – the militants shot him dead at point-blank range. His wife, who had rushed inside hearing the gunshots, was killed too.

The investigators seized the register and picked up all men named Abdul Latif in the vicinity to question them. After a painstaking process, Abdul Latif, a surrendered militant, broke down and confessed to his involvement in the 2001 massacre of Chakka Galiote. However, he pleaded that he was not involved in the killing of Khajuria and his wife. At his behest, two other surrendered militants and an OGW were arrested. Eight other terrorists involved in the massacre, including Amanullah Peer and Billoo Gujjar, were all dead.

12

Fork in the River

The Chenab enters Reasi district from the village Karoonkote situated on its left bank, and flows eastward. The river passes by a number of scattered villages situated on both banks of the river, approached by the zigzagged road network sinuously climbing up and down.

At Dharot, the river reaches a major landmark: an arched railway bridge joining Bakkal and Kauri. At a height of 1,178 ft above sea level and constructed with steel and concrete, this majestic structure is the highest railway bridge in the world. It is about 35 m taller than the Eiffel Tower and five times the height of the Qutuab Minar.[86]

The bridge is an important link between the last leg of the 345 km-long JUSBRL (Jammu–Udhampur–Srinagar–Baramulla) rail link. The railway line was first proposed by Maharaja Partap Singh at the start of the twentieth century, but the project could never start. In 1983, the project of extending the Jammu line till Udhampur was initiated. The most difficult leg of Katra–Banihal started in 2002. During the preliminary survey of the project, the Chenab Valley was chock-a-block with terrorists. The road network was dismal too. After two decades, having missed various deadlines, the railway link is finally nearing completion. The bridge at Kauri is a major landmark in this connectivity.

A joint venture of Indo-European partnership and the flagship project of Konkan Railways Corporation, the bridge is an engineering marvel. It has been designed keeping in mind the difficult terrain, extreme temperatures, high wind pressures and seismic fluctuations measuring 8 on the Richter scale. The bridge has also been made resistant to sabotage, and can withstand high-powered blasts up to 30 kg of explosives.

The Chenab moves forward with a lazy charm now. After traversing through the mountains and gorges, the river seemingly yearns to reach the plains. At Arnas, about 31 km short of Reasi, the Chenab is joined by one of its biggest tributary named Ans. Originating in the glacial heights of Pir Panjal, Ans flows through Koteranka in Rajouri and Mahore before joining the Chenab.

Mahore is one of the most backward and poor areas of Jammu and Kashmir, having witnessed the savage face of militancy starting from early 1990s. Like in the Chenab Valley, earlier, the terrorists who infested these hills were mostly foreigners who gradually roped in the poverty-stricken locals. Here, too, Hindus were caught in the killing zone.

On 17 April 1998, two small villages of Prankote and Dakkikote saw the worst carnage ever. In the middle of the night, long-haired militants in army fatigues forced their entry inside four mud houses belonging to Hindus. The terrorists did not use firearms but slaughtered twenty-six people, slitting their throats with sharp-edged weapons. The dead included women and children. Before fleeing, the militants torched a house from where seven dead bodies were later recovered; they were charred beyond recognition. Though a few army units managed to reach the tragedy-struck area, it took the police an additional day. When two survivors of the massacre were discovered by a police party, they were found to be in a state of complete shock, dumbfounded and expressionless.[87]

Later, the police investigations revealed that the massacre was masterminded by a local militant named Abdul Haque alias Jahangir of the village Thuru in Arnas Tehsil. He was the battalion commander of HM and a close confidant of Billoo Gujjar. Much like Billoo, he was one of the longest-surviving terrorists and the most wanted by the security forces.

Born in 1973, Jahangir was second among his five siblings. After failing his matriculation exam twice, he dropped out from school, and under the influence of a militant from his village, he joined HM, crossed the border from the Rajouri sector and took arms training in POK. On his return, Jahangir became a terror in a large arc of villages in Mahore. After the Prankote massacre, his brutality started to echo sinisterly in the hills. The police reports suggested that he was also involved in the killing of nine people in Jib Baryana, seven in Narla Bambal in Rajouri and sixteen Muslim Bakerwals in Kote Chadwal in Rajouri. Apart from being known as a ruthless killing machine, Jahangir's notoriety doubled because of his womanizing ways.

The massacres of Hindus led to some of the families migrating to safer areas. In order to discourage this exodus, more security forces were inducted in the area, minority pickets were set up and VDCs were increased manifold. However, similar to the Chenab Valley, this did not discourage some Hindus from joining the ranks of the militants.

In 1998, Sham Lal, a Brahmin belonging to a far-flung village of Gandhali Thanole, left his house and joined the ranks of Lashkar-e-Taiba. He was given the codename of Shamsudin. For a few years, he operated in the high reaches of Pir Panjal mountains and then went out of action. It is believed that he is settled in Pakistan and may have converted to Islam. The phenomenon of Hindus joining the militant movement did not have any plausible justification, and was rather astounding.[88]

Some of the Hindu militants operating in Mahore actually belonged to the neighbouring villages of Rajouri district, situated on the same fold of the mountains. A man called Sham Lal (not to be confused with Sham Lal of Gandhali Thanole) from Dhruti village in Kalakote, Rajouri, joined HM and was given the codename of Yousaf. Carrying an award of INR 2 lakh on his head, he operated in the higher reaches of Rajouri and Reasi, and was involved in the killing of four Hindus from his native village. Similarly, Sanjay Kumar – belonging to Kheri Teryath, Kalakote, Rajouri – son of a poor coal miner, dropped out of school in Class VI and joined the ranks of HM militants at the age of thirteen. Codenamed Talwar, he was also involved in the killings of Hindus in the area. His parents always insisted that he was kidnapped by the militants and forcibly made to join their ranks. Krishan Lal, a history-sheeter of Police Station Kalakote of Rajouri district, wreaked a reign of terror in the upper reaches of Rajouri and Reasi. His wife Guddi Devi was enrolled as an SPO, as a lure to get her husband to surrender. She wielded the gun for protecting the defenceless, thus restoring the dignity of the family brought to ignominy by the deeds of Krishan Lal.

Most of these cases of Hindus joining the ranks of the terrorists happened between 1998 and 2002. These militants took Muslim codenames but rarely converted to Islam. As seen in Doda, they were not married to any faith or ideology of jihad but found a way to get out of their own impecunious existence, in the thrall of the power exuded by the gun. After being locally trained and having proven worthy of trust, they were entrusted with Kalashnikovs. Having once joined militancy, these Hindus could not go back. They would sink deeper into the quagmire and any attempt to renege would pave way for destruction of their families. Usually escaping the dragnets of the security forces, these Hindu militants – who had the advantage of being familiar with the terrain – easily obtained food and shelter from Hindu houses. At the peak of this phenomenon, about fourteen Hindu terrorists were operating to the south of Pir Panjal. Gradually, some of them surrendered and others were killed in encounters.

All terrorists who operated in the hills of Reasi were not school dropouts. In February 1999, an ominous ring of a phone echoed in an influential house in Srinagar belonging to a retired chief engineer.

The call from London informed of the 'martyrdom' of Nadeem Khatib, the family's beloved son. Nadeem was educated in Tyndale Biscoe, a leading missionary school in Srinagar. Here, he became friends with Ashfaq Majeed Wani, and the first seeds of rebellion germinated in their minds. Ashfaq Wani was also responsible for imparting training to Firdous Ahmed Baba of Bhaderwah, as mentioned in an earlier chapter.

Khatib went to the United States in 1994 and acquired a commercial pilot's license from a flying school in Georgia. Finding a well-paying job as a flying instructor, he led a comfortable life.[89] However, troubled by the state of the world, the young man started deeply abhorring what he saw as the American exploitation of Islamic countries.

Khatib started to take deep interest in Kashmir and would brood about the situation there. Finally, in 1998, at the age of thirty, he abandoned his luxurious life and proceeded to Pakistan, where he joined the militant outfit Al Badr. After infiltrating India from the Line of Control (LoC), he landed up in Mahore. Perhaps in a transit, he intended to go to Kashmir. Before that, Khatib fell into a cordon at Buthal village and was killed along with his two accomplices.

Six days after the encounter, the phone call from London shocked his parents. They had no inkling of their son having joined militancy; they had been thinking all along that he was well-settled in the United States. In fact, they had been pestering him to get married as he was already engaged to a close relative.

The profile of Nadeem Khatib gave a new colour to the militancy; however, it was an isolated case. Most other terrorists were criminals in the guise of jihadis. Their stories of murder, rape and extortion were common, and they made people obey them only because of the power that emanated from the gun.

In 2008, about one and half years after Billoo Gujjar's killing in Manglogi, security forces cordoned a house in the Kalian village in Arnas Tehsil. Jahangir offered his last resistance before he lay dead ending his decade-long tryst with terror. His widow remarried a Nambardar and his daughters grew up to have normal lives. With the killing of one dreaded terrorist, the terror doesn't end. There were many others on the prowl.

Sometime in 2010, a father brought his daughter, Sakina (name changed) to a police officer posted in Mahore. The girl, hardly fifteen years old, appeared frail and scared. '*Tam das diyan saheb bachi naal bado galat kito hai zalim ne* [May I tell you, Sir, the devil has done terribly wrong with the child],' the hapless father said in Gojri. 'Who was it, Chaudhary Saheb?' the police officer asked politely. 'It was Irfan,' the girl's father whispered, visibly fearful.

Mushtaq Ahmed alias Irfan was one of the longest surviving militants in Mahore. A close consort of Jahangir, they had become synonymous with terror in the upper reaches of Mahore. Irfan was born in the predominantly Kashmiri village of Laar in Gulabgarh and dropped out of school in Class IX. Perched on a high mountain, Laar had no road connectivity or modern means of communication. This made the village very vulnerable to local recruitment. Irfan was one such boy who went on to write the bloodiest chapter of these hills. After getting trained in Pakistan, he also spent some time in Afghanistan fighting alongside Taliban.

Back in Mahore, Irfan carried his terror agenda with impunity. He had a very dark side to his personality, being a paedophile who preyed on young girls. This way, he antagonized many nomadic families whose girls became victims of his lust. Until Sakina's father mustered the courage to approach the police, nobody had dared to take on Irfan, preferring to suffer silently.

Earlier in the summer of that year, Sakina's extended family, along with elders, siblings and cousins, had customarily moved up the hills to Magnad Pathrian. About an eight-hour trek from Mahore, the area of Magnad, lush with meadows, has intermittent rocky gulches on its terrain. Sakina's family had their dhokes near a seasonal stream running down from the higher side of the mountain. These dhokes were transit points as the family would stay here for a few days before climbing the mountain further. Below the snow-capped peaks and above the tree line, the nomadic families passed through the Kali Dhar gully and stepped to Dhamal Hanjipora in south Kashmir. There, in the open expanse, they would pitch their tents and let their cattle graze in the lofty grasslands. In these pristine heights, the only souls were those of peripatetic nomads, gun-wielding terrorists and occasional long-range patrol of security forces.

Sakina loved to hum Gojri songs and playfully take the cattle out for grazing. Then she would help her mother and other women of the clan to cook and feed the family members. That summer in 2010, all this passed well until Irfan, along with fellow militants, emerged from the nearby forests and ran into the clan. With no other choice, the family slaughtered a sheep and cooked food for the terrorists. This continued for a few days, terrorists would come for food and then melt back into the forest. By this time, Irfan's lascivious eye had fallen on Sakina. One day, he led her to a nearby maize field and raped her, forcibly muffling her shrieks. The torture repeated for a few days in a row. Sakina's family could only watch in abject horror. However, Sakina's father was deeply perturbed and vengeful.

Before leaving the meadow, Irfan told Sakina's father that he would meet him at Magnad before the winter sets in and then he directed him to arrange two sturdy horses for him. The helpless father nodded reluctantly. Irfan smiled and then said apologetically, 'If you think I have done anything wrong to your daughter, I will marry her and take her along.' He infuriated the distraught father further.

The fan in the police officer's room whirred slowly as Sakina started to sob. She adjusted her slipping dupatta back to her head and her tiny hair braids done lovingly by her mother got exposed. The susceptibility of Chaudhary and the tears of Sakina moved the police officer. Enraged, he spoke, 'I will not let Irfan see another winter but for that, you will have to tell me in advance when he comes for the horses.'

In a few days, Chaudhary's clan was camping at the Magnad dhokes on their return journey. The cold had already started gnawing at the people and livestock alike. The once verdant meadow was looking pale, waiting to be painted white by the season's first snowfall. Looking at the horses neighing in the distance, Chaudhary knew that Irfan would come to satiate his lust. Horses were important for the terrorists in the hilly terrain, but the marriage proposal with Sakina was a euphemism for her sexual exploitation.

Chaudhary had sent one of his uncles from Mahore to the police officer with the news of the impending arrival of Irfan. A joint team of twenty policemen and para military stealthily trekked up the unfriendly path to Magnad Pathrian.

The combat party took one of the dhokes already emptied for them, where they kept a keen eye outside. On the third day, Irfan, accompanied by another terrorist, came down from Kali Dhar and parked himself 500 m short of the cluster of the dhokes. He sent his accomplice, who was later identified as Abu Hamza, to take a look inside the dhokes to see if anything was suspicious. Hamza randomly checked some dhokes, peering inside, and in one of them saw Sakina cowed in a corner. Hamza did not bother to go to the last dhoke where the men sat alert with their weapons cocked. Chaudhary had already asked the women to cook meat, rice and rotis for the guests. He took the food to Irfan and Hamza with a contented smile on his face.

As the Sun started to dip behind the ridge, Irfan, escorted by Hamza, came for Sakina. It took five minutes of gunfight before the two dead bodies bloodied the dry grass near the dhokes. Irfan – the most wanted terrorist, ruthless killer, child rapist – lay dead, his innards splattered from his torn stomach.

Chaudhary's courage to avenge his daughter saved the honour of many other children. The two dead bodies were tied to cots and were carried down to Mahore on a narrow pathway hugging the mountain. Droplets of blood dripped from the cots on the same earth that Irfan had reddened with the blood of the innocents. The word of Irfan's killing had spread like wildfire and thousands had gathered outside the Mahore police station. They wished to have a glimpse of the dreaded monster. This unflinching resolve and spirit of men and women like Chaudhary, Sakina and the sensitive police officer deserve many salutations.

The killing of Jahangir and Irfan within two years marked the beginning of the end of the horrific saga of terrorism in the inhospitable hills of Reasi. In the subsequent years, the residual militancy was also given a death blow, ushering in a peaceful time. Over the years, the road network under the Pradhan Mantri Gram Sadak Yojana (PMGSY) and other schemes have made many of the mountainous villages motorable, and the reach of mobile phones has rendered the place easily accessible. It also appears that the people of the region – Hindus and Muslims – have unofficially vowed to never let those dark days of militancy ever plague them again.

Ostensibly, this resolution of the people has been unwavering as was witnessed in July 2022. A few Gujjar families had settled down in Tuksan Top, Mahore, for their annual summer jaunt. In a dhoke, Myshkin (name changed) was camping with his family, his livestock fattening on grass in the nearby pastures. One night, when the family was settling down after dinner, two unknown men carrying backpacks knocked at their door. They desired to spend the night there. 'We have gotten late and at this hour we cannot proceed further to our village,' one of the men with a thick beard pleaded. Having smelled something sinister, Myshkin pretended to welcome the strangers and even ordered food to be served to them. Then, on the pretext of tending to the animals, he went out and, having gathered some men, returned to his dhoke. By this time, the two men seemed to have lowered their guard and set aside their rucksacks. The group of men pounced upon the strangers and overpowered them, tying them tightly with ropes. In a few hours, a police party from Mahore police station reached the dhoke and arrested the duo. Their rucksacks were stuffed with two Kalashnikovs, magazines, grenades and a pistol.

One of the arrested terrorists was identified as Talib Hussein Shah, a resident of Draj in Rajouri. Born in a family with a good landholding, Talib dropped out of school and shifted to Katra. Here, he purchased a pony and started earning money by taking pilgrims to the Vaishno Devi shrine. After getting married in 2009, he left Katra and joined his elder brother to work as a carpenter. Soon, he started to dabble in politics and joined a mainstream political party. He became an active member of the party and rapidly rose to hold important positions in the Poonch–Rajouri belt, starting from booth president, to eventually become the publicity secretary of the IT cell of the party.[90,91]

Talib's destiny changed in August 2020, when he received a random call from Pakistan. The caller identified himself as Salman and he started to call Talib regularly albeit from different numbers using VPN. After some time, Salman introduced Talib to two more people based in Pakistan. One was Bilal from Kashmir and other a milk seller originally from Doda. The three remained in touch with Talib. They would lament about Kashmir and share provocative videos and speeches eulogizing jihad. After Talib was radicalized, he was formally inducted into Lashkar-e-Taiba. Having roped in another youth, Shabir, Talib started to play into the hands of his handlers.

On the first task assigned to them, Talib and Shabir treaded through the forest and reached Lamberi situated at a distance of 15 km from the LoC in Rajouri sector. At a marked place, confirmed by the coordinates from Google Maps, both crouched behind a tree and, in the still of the night, waited patiently. After sometime, a drone flew in without blinking and dropped an assault rifle with two magazines. In an hour's time, the same drone made a second sortie and dropped three pistols with six loaded magazines, an underslung grenade launcher (UBGL), and INR 60,000. After collecting the assignment, the duo, after a trek through the forest and taking a bus for the last leg of the journey, reached Draj. Near his house, Talib buried the consignment in a forest. After a few days, he was tasked to kill a Hindu from Draj, who had apparently antagonized someone's electoral interests in the local elections.

The intended victim survived the attack and a first information report (FIR) was registered against unknown persons. After a few days, a Muslim youth was killed by Talib, presumably due to someone's personal enmity against the slain. In the coming months, Talib picked at least three more consignments of drone-dropped weapons, explosives, grenades and money. Deftly handled by Salman, Talib was now deeply trapped in the web of terrorism. In a short time, he carried out at least five low-intensity IED blasts in Koteranka region of Rajouri, injuring a few persons. While the mysterious blasts were being investigated, Talib continued to live a normal life, even carrying out his politics.

In May 2022, Talib was tasked to visit Shopian and take one Faisal Bashir Dar, a resident of Pulwama district, under his fold. Walking through the mountains, he brought Faisal to Rupadi Gully, a pass in Pir Panjal that connects Rajouri with the Kashmir Valley. His accomplice Shabir was present at the spot, having arranged a dhoke for a fortnight's stay. In the meantime, Salman had sent two more youth from Kulgam to Rupadi Gully. Here, they were to be given basic training in handling of weapons and explosives. However, these two chickened out and sneaked away to reach back their homes. Meanwhile, Faisal, who was determined to join Lashkar-e-Taiba, was shifted to Draj. Here, his stay was organized in the dhoke of a local named Sadiq. Talib, Shabir and Sadiq went about their normal lives, planning their moves in coded conversations on their mobiles. They didn't know their phones were under surveillance of the police.

By the time police reached Shabir and Sadiq, Talib had managed to take Faisal out of Draj. They were on the run, desperate to get into Kashmir, from Rupadi Gully towards Tuscan Top and onwards to Kulgam from Kosernag. For the next one and a half months, the duo wandered in the high reaches, their rucksacks hinged to their backs. They ate and lived in dhokes and small ziyarats, inducing fear with their guns or alluring locals through money. Carrying a number of SIM cards, they kept destroying and replacing them. They rode their luck till they dared to knock at Myshkin's dhoke in Tuscan Top. Brave hearts like Myshkin and many from his ilk are the true heroes who have decided not to let militancy take a foothold in these mountains again.[92]

Saluting the bravery of the people living in the hills, the Chenab moves on from Arnas. About 20 miles short of Reasi town, the river takes a southerly course at the village Salal. The first hydroelectricity project in Jammu and Kashmir was commissioned here. Though the project was conceived by British engineers in 1920, it took another five decades for the work to commence. Pakistan had objected when the 690 MW project was initiated back in 1970. The leadership in Pakistan believed that the storage of such voluminous water was a flood risk to their country. Zulfiqar Bhutto, the then prime minister of Pakistan, had said that the project could become an instrument of warfare in the hands of India. Finally, after many rounds of negotiations and considerable changes in the original design, the project was cleared in 1978.

Among many small contractors engaged in the project, one player had started its venture with fifty mules to transport sand. Later, the group won the bids for major projects to become one of the biggest business conglomerates in the country. Finally, the first and second phases of the Salal project were completed in 1987 and 1993, respectively. However, due to the concessions given to Pakistan by reducing the height of the dam and minimizing the water release, the project lost its sustainability and the dam silted up in five years. The project currently runs at a little more than half of its capacity and its future is uncertain.

In the plains of Reasi, the river looks at peace with herself as if setting into her autumn. A few miles further, at Siar Baba, Chenab perfectly complements a spectacular waterfall that cascades down from a height of 400 m. On a sunny day, the waterfall looks like a woman's shimmering, silver-hued saree, contrasting against an azure sky.

An ancient temple of Siar Baba is located next to the waterfall on the hillock. The cave temple with its magnificent architecture is revered by the local Hindus. It is believed that the cave has crores of deities and in the past, many saints of divine powers have meditated inside. There is also a view that the real shrine of Siar Baba is in Kashmir and the one in Reasi is a replica. Presuming that the water and mud of the pond formed by the waterfall has healing powers, a large number of pilgrims from North India come here to take a dip.

On its further course, Reasi town takes the Chenab in its arms. Here, the river widens and is forked into various channels to form small river islands and sandy deltas. Like the river, the town of Reasi – once called Raysal and Bhimgarh – has an indelible footprint in history. One of the oldest towns in Jammu and Kashmir, Reasi was established by Raja Bhim Dev in the eighth century. Bhimgarh refers to a fort built on a hillock, overlooking the town and the Chenab. In 1822, when Maharaja Gulab Singh subjugated the state of Reasi, the fort was bolstered with stone masonry and impregnable walls. How the course of Jammu and Kashmir's history was altered when Zorawar Singh was deputed to the fort, has been discussed earlier.

In 1947, Reasi ceased to be a district and was merged with Udhampur. Taken as an insult, the locals remained resentful, and in 1970s, the whole town united in an agitation for restoration of district status. This movement was spearheaded by a local leader named Rishi Kumar Kaushal. Kick-starting the movement, in a well-attended gathering, he had declared emphatically, 'I will not cut my hair and shave my beard, till the district status to our beloved Reasi is restored.'[93]

Born in 1921, Kaushal became an RSS activist at the age of fifteen. He remained a close associate of Shyama Prasad Mookerjee in his movement against the special status of Jammu and Kashmir, and was imprisoned half-a-dozen times. In the 1950s, Kaushal and his wife pledged that they would sleep on the ground until the post of prime minister in Jammu and Kashmir was not downgraded to chief minister. A popular leader of Reasi, Kaushal was elected as Member of Legislative Assembly (MLA) in 1962, 1972 and 1977 on a Jan Sangh ticket.

The Wazir Commission set up by the government to identify the creation of new districts, in its 1984 report, also recommended for restoration of district status to Reasi. This revived the movement that reached its crescendo in 1986. Civil disobedience movement was started in the same year, which forced the daily life to a standstill for several months. The agitation committee declared Reasi as a district, and a local leader took over the sub divisional magistrate office and declared himself as the district magistrate. Similarly, other offices were also taken over and a new dispensation was put in place. The government ordered a crackdown and the rebellion was soon quelled. For the next many years, the movement remained low-key and a district status for Reasi looked distant even when the hair and beard of Rishi Kumar Kaushal kept greying and growing.

Finally, in 2007, the status of a district was granted to Reasi A big function was organized in the town and Rishi Kumar Kaushal cut his hair and shaved his straggling beard in public. After he died in 2017, his marble statue was installed at a prominent chowk in Reasi town, which was named after him.

The spirit of resilience and rebellion has not been new to Reasi. About 550 years ago in Aghar, a village about 4 miles from Katra town, a boy was born in a Brahmin house. He was named Jitmal and was raised by his aunt Jojan after the death of his parents. The boy became an ardent devotee of Goddess Vaishno Devi and would go to her cave every morning to pray. Clad just in a sarong and carrying a brass tumbler, Jitmal would trek 10 miles to the abode of the Goddess, always barefoot and on empty stomach. Without a break, he followed this routine for twelve years. Pleased with this devotion, one day, the Goddess appeared before him. She asked him to seek anything from her – wealth, power, land or whatever his heart desired. Jitmal, with his folded hands, humbly said, 'What would any wealth mean to a farmer who has got everything in life?' Then he asked for pure drinking water for his village, blessed by Her divine feet. The Goddess asked him to mark seven places in his village and assured that his wish would be fulfilled. 'There are enough springs in the hills, how would I know the water comes from your feet?' Jitmal enquired. 'The water would be preceded by the flow of milk for a few hours and you would know the source of the water.'

Even today, at seven places in and around Aghar, fresh, cold water gushes out. Jitmal asked for a second wish, too, and desired to see the Goddess every day in her physical form. 'You will be blessed with a daughter who shall embody me. Take care of her and you will get to see me every day.' 'But I am not married and I have vowed celibacy, how will I be blessed with a daughter?' Jitmal asked. The Goddess gave him a lotus flower and told him to take it home. The story goes that a small girl emerged from the flower. She was named Bua Kori, and Jitmal raised her lovingly.

However, Jojan did not welcome the child in the house as she expected her seven sons to inherit Jitmal's land. The relations strained between him and his aunt, and it is said that the woman mentally tortured the little girl. It is also said she had once planned to get Jitmal killed by pushing him down the cliff. At this hostile behaviour of Jojan, he donated all the land to her sons and left his village with a pair of oxen, and shifted to a friend's place in Jhiri near Akhnoor in Jammu.

One day, Jitmal visited Mehta Bir Singh, a local feudal lord, and requested him to provide him with a piece of land for tilling. Mehta gave Jitmal a tract of barren land on the condition that he would give him one-fourth of his produce. Due to the ample blessings of Vaishno Devi and hard work of Jitmal, the barren land produced a bumper crop. Hearing about the yield, Mehta Bir Singh came to the farm. Jitmal had gone to the river Chenab to take a bath. In the absence of Jitmal, Mehta asked his men to lift three-fourth of the crop, thus reversing the original agreement.

On his return from the river, Jitmal was livid to see the violation of the agreement. Mehta remained adamant and his men started to forcibly take the grain. Incensed by this injustice, Jitmal jumped onto a heap of grain and shouted, '*Sukki kanak nayi khayan Mehtya, dinna ratt ralayi* [Don't eat raw wheat, oh Mehta, let me mix my blood in it].'

These turned out to be his last words as he took out a dagger and stabbed himself to death, drenching the whole crop with his blood. Mehta, panicking at the turn of the events, ordered that the corpse be hidden inside the hollow of a tree trunk. Later, Bua Kori with the help of her pet dog Kalu was able to locate the dead body of her father. After lighting the pyre, she jumped into it, ringing a sad end to the story of the father and daughter.[94] As per folklore, heavy rains ravaged the crops that year and the blood-soaked grains were washed away. All humans, animals and birds that had partaken of those grains, suffered from various afflictions and misfortunes.

Over the years, Jitmal assumed heroic proportions in local folklore and started being worshipped as Bawa Jitto. In his native village of Aghar, there is a huge temple complex dedicated to him and Bua Kori. The temple has a source of fresh water, which was one of the original seven sources granted as a boon by Vaishno Devi. The temple also preserves Jitmal's brass tumbler and the dagger he used to kill himself. Most of the pilgrims who come on Vaishno Devi pilgrimage pay obeisance at the temple. There is also a tradition of offering plastic dolls and other toys at the temple for little Bua Kori to play with. In June–July, a three-day festival is organized in the temple. On the third day, a traditional wrestling competition takes place. This event is attended by famous wrestlers of North India, and the competition is watched by thousands of people. A large temple has also been established in Jhiri in Jammu to honour Bawa Jitto.

After Reasi attained the status of district, its growth has been quite visible. The pilgrimage tourism has also seen a major upswing. Sacred places like Shiv Khori now find a prominent place in the religious tourism circuit connecting Vaishno Devi and Baba Aghar Jitto.

The etymology of the name is explained thus: *Khori* means cave and it belongs to Shiva; hence, Shiv Khori. About 40 km from Reasi town, the road for the major part of the journey travels by the side of the Chenab to reach Ransoo village. A trek of 3.5 kms, parallel to a streamlet, is required to access the Shiv Khori.

According to the legend, a demon named Bhasmasur meditated for a long time to please Lord Shiva. Shiva appeared before the demon and granted him a boon. It turned out to be a sinister wish, according to which the demon was endowed with the power to turn anyone into ash (*bhasma*) by placing his hand on their head. Lord Shiva queried who the demon intended to kill. 'It is your head I wish to place my hand on!' Bhasmasur laughed. Realizing the vicious intent of the demon, Lord Shiva, along with his family escaped from the demon. When Shiva stopped at the place where the cave is now located, he realised that the demon had been following him. The two fought but Shiva decided not to kill the demon. He hurled his trident fiercely, which penetrated the mountain and created the narrow cave. Shiva along with Goddess Parvati, Kartikeya, Ganesha and Nandi entered the cave. The demon with his huge size could not follow them inside the cave.

Lord Vishnu was watching the drama unfold. He took the guise of Mohini, the beautiful courtesan and lured the demon into a scintillating dance. Bhasmasur got so enthralled with the beauty and dance of Mohini that he started following every dance step as dictated by her. Amidst her languid moves, Mohini gracefully placed her hand on her head. As soon as Bhasmasur replicated the move and put his hand on his head, he turned into ash.[95]

The cave remained hidden for a long time and was discovered serendipitously about fifty years back. Once, a Muslim shepherd followed his straying goat and ended up in the cave. He found a group of seers meditating. While ordering the shepherd and the goat out of the cave, the seers warned him not to tell anyone about their presence. However, the shepherd could not keep it a secret and blabbered to the whole village of Ransoo. He immediately died after that, perhaps cursed by the sages.

The cave is quite wide at its mouth but gradually narrows further in. In the sanctum sanctorum, there is a 4 ft. shivling and natural formations of Goddess Parvati, Lord Ganesha, Lord Kartikeya, Nandi, Hanuman and Lord Vishnu. The roof of the cave is etched with snake formations in the rock, through which water trickles on the phallus. It is believed that the cave is endless and goes all the way to Amaranth, where the ice lingam of Shiva reigns supreme. As per folklore, many sages across ages have attempted to cross over but never returned.

A little away from the Katra–Reasi road, the Chenab flows by a different axis of villages to finally change its course westward and enter Jammu, the last district it would traverse in India. In Bhabbar village, on the banks of the Chenab, an ancient gurudwara of Banda Singh Bahadur is situated.

Banda Singh Bahadur was born in 1670 in Rajouri as Lachman Dev. One day, while hunting, he accidentally wounded a pregnant doe, resulting in two foetuses tumbling out of her womb. In front of his eyes, he could see the doe dying, writhing in great pain. The grief overpowered him so much that in remorse, he left his home at the age of fifteen and became an ascetic. He wandered from place to place for many years and finally settled down in a small cottage on the banks of the river Godavari in Nanded, Maharashtra. Here, he was rechristened as Madho Das Bairagi; he learned the tantric rituals that were a blend of Hinduism and paganism.

In 1708, Guru Gobind Singh visited the cottage of Madho Das, who was busy meditating on the banks of the Godavari at that time.

Madho Das refused to meet the Guru and sent two tantric spirits to convey his message. However, due to Guru Gobind Singh's immense spiritual powers, the spirits returned helplessly. Finally, Madho Das ventured forth to meet the Guru.

After hearing about Madho's grief at the sight of the blood of the doe, the Guru ordered a goat to be sacrificed so that Madho Das could distinguish between the blood of the humans and animals. At that time, Guru Gobind Singh was fighting the tyranny of the Mughals. After a long debate, he impressed upon Madho Das the need to stand up against the cruelty being inflicted by the Muslim rulers. Madho Das became a disciple of the Guru, who baptized him into Sikhism. He bestowed on him the name Gurbaksh Singh; later, he became popular as Banda Bahadur: The Brave One. The two stayed together at the cottage for one month before Banda Bahadur proceeded on his military campaign. Guru Gobind Singh gave him five arrows and a band of twenty Sikh soldiers for his future battles.

For the next eight years, Banda Bahadur fought bravely against the Mughals and vanquished them at various places. He captured the city of Samana, southwest of Patiala. At that time, Samana had a coin mint and the treasury fell in the hand of the Sikhs. Now they were financially stable and militarily stronger. As a result, the Sikhs controlled the territory between Sutlej and Yamuna, including Sirhind and Sadhaura. Banda Bahadur developed the village of Mukhlisgarh as his capital and named it Lohgarh or the 'fortress of steel'. In the captured areas, he abolished zamindari system and ordered that land be restored to the tillers. After establishing himself firmly in Punjab, Banda Bahadur turned his attention towards the hill principalities that were traditionally opposed to the Sikhs. These principalities were subjugated without much resistance and the raja of Chamba, Udai Singh, was so pleased with the warrior-saint that he gave his daughter in marriage to him. She took on the name of Susheel Kaur. After learning warfare and horsemanship, she supposedly fought battles alongside her husband. They were blessed with a son, who was named Ajai Singh.

In 1713, Banda Bahadur reached Reasi along with his family and an army of 1,000 Sikhs. He decided to settle near Bhabbar, on the banks of the river Chenab. Once, while meditating under a berry tree, Banda Bahadur retrieved a long wooden log from the Chenab. He raised it as a flagpole for the sacred Nishan Sahib: the exalted ensign. Nishan Sahib is a triangular yellow flag made of cotton or silk, imprinted with an emblem, tassels adding to its beauty. The emblem depicts a double-edged sword called *khanda* embossed in a circle flanked by two single-edged swords or *kirpans*. During this time, he took Said Kaur, the daughter of a nawab of Wazirabad (now in Pakistan), as his second wife.

In the absence of Banda Bahadur, Mughal Emperor Farrukh Siyar, on ascending the throne of Delhi, renewed his fight against the Sikhs. He organized all his imperial forces to retain the lost territories. One by one, the forts of Sikhs were subjugated. These included Sirhind and Lohgarh. The Mughals started to persecute the Sikhs, especially in the Gurdaspur region, and anyone with a beard and a turban was put to the sword. After two years of sainthood in Bhabbar, the warrior in Banda Bahadur was reborn. Answering the call of religion and motherland, he left his pregnant wife Said Kaur and a young son for the call of duty. Susheel Kaur and Ajai Singh accompanied him on his new campaign. For the next year, he was able to win some of the territories back before he was driven to Gurdas Nangal near Gurdaspur. Here, a siege was laid to his fort and supplies were cut. The Sikhs fought valiantly for eight months before they started succumbing to hunger and thirst. The Mughals finally stormed the garrison and captured Banda Bahadur along with his wife and son. About 740 of his most loyal soldiers were also captured.

The Mughals made their captives parade in the streets of Delhi, as if displaying their trophies. The streets leading to the Red Fort were filled with eager crowds. Some agents and soldiers of East India Company watched the 'spectacle' from the sidelines. Ganda Singh, a historian and academician, wrote in his book, *Life of Banda Singh Bahadur* (1935):

> Banda Singh and the other Sikh prisoners were conducted, in a procession, to the city of Delhi. First of all, came the heads of two thousand executed Sikhs, stuffed with straw and mounted on bamboos, their long hair streaming in the air like a veil. Along with them was carried, at the end of a pole, the dead body of a cat to show that every living creature of the Gurdas Nangal down to the quadruples like the dogs and cats had been destroyed. Banda Singh came next, sitting in an iron cage, placed upon an elephant, and dressed, out of mockery, in a gold embroidered red turban and a heavy robe of scarlet brocade, embroidered with pomegranate flowers in gold. Behind him stood, with a drawn sword in hand, a mail-clad officer from amongst the Turani Mughals of Amin Khan.
>
> After his elephant came the other Sikh prisoners, seven hundred and forty in number, tied two and two upon saddle less camels. Upon their heads were placed high fantastic fool's caps of ridiculous shape, made of sheep skin and adorned with glass beads. One of their hands was pinned to the neck between two pieces of wood which were held together by iron pins. Some of the principal men, who rode nearest to their chief's elephant, were dressed in sheep-skins, the woolly side turned outward so that the spectators might compare them to bears. At the end of the procession rode the three triumphant Mughal nobles.

After having watched the procession of death, most of the people retreated to their shops and other businesses. Their entertainment followed for weeks. Every day, hundred Sikhs were brought out of the fort and publicly executed in front of a cheering crowd. The Sikhs were also given an option of renunciation of their faith and conversion to Islam, but they refused these proposals at the cost of their lives. Susheel Kaur and her son were shifted to the royal harem. She was cajoled and coaxed to convert to Islam and marry a Muslim man. On her refusal, the dignified woman was mentally and physically tortured.

Finally, her son was snatched away and taken to his father. Banda Bahadur was ordered to kill his own son, which he refused. The child was savagely murdered in front of his father. His tender chest was ripped asunder barbarously with a dagger, and the bloodied heart pulled out and stuffed inside Banda Bahadur's mouth. The valiant leader's eyes were gouged out, his skin was shredded with piers and he was chopped into pieces. One of the greatest warriors against the Mughal rule was killed after horrendous and unbelievable torture.[96]

Bibi Susheel Kaur was informed about the brutal murders of her husband and child. She was threatened with rape and the prospect of being sold to a whorehouse. The courageous woman chose to kill herself with a knife than surrender to the Mughals.

Dera Banda Singh Bahadur Gurudwara on the banks of the Chenab is a most pious place. His house, consisting of three rooms, has been well preserved. One room was used by his family, while the Guru Granth Sahib was reverentially placed in another. The third room was where Banda Bahadur used to meditate. The gurudwara, over the years, has expanded in its size and grandeur. It houses the artefacts of the saint – a turban, sword, three arrows and a drum set. Within the gurudwara premises, the berry tree under which Banda Bahadur meditated and the Nishan Saheb continue to enthral the devotees. On Baisakhi, a great fair is organized at the gurudwara. The flag and the cloth wrapping on Nishan Sahib are refurbished. Water from the Chenab is used to fill a pot and also to cleanse the utensils.

This tradition has been carried on for 300 years, immortalizing the memory of Banda Bahadur and the Chenab.

13

The Timber Trail

The beauty of the Chenab Valley undoubtedly owes itself to the mighty river that flows through it, which is further enhanced by the middle and high mountain ranges of the Himalayas. These ranges shelter the river while replenishing her with numerous streams and waterfalls. The mountains cast spellbinding shadows on the meadows, flatlands and the river surface. The added splendour stems from the swathes of green forests hugging them. These forests are also the source for fuel, fodder, medicinal herbs and, above all, timber. Above the vegetation line, the peaks of the mountains rise up in the skies, cloaked in snow, throughout the year. This tapestry of colours, with the blue skies, white peaks, green forests and the dark-coloured waters of the Chenab, presents a captivating landscape. While one travels along the river, the enchanting fragrance of wood and verdure wafts in the air, adding to sensory delight. This is accompanied by the symphony of the bleating sheep and the flutes of the shepherds tending them.

The value of the trees was not unbeknownst to the people of India. The concern for conservation and forest ecology finds a mention in the ancient Hindu texts. Kautilya in Arthshastra recommends fines and stringent punishments for illegal tree felling. In Jammu and Kashmir, about 500 years ago, the aphorism of Nund Rishi reveals the urgency for protection of forests: *Ann poshi teli yeli van poshi* [Food is subservient to forests]. However, this did not deter the plunder of the woods. The people who dwelled in and around the forests were the first claimants of the forest wealth. Some *jagirdar*s [landowners] who had tracts of forests in their estates tried to impose taxes on either individuals or villages. Since this was done in a perfunctory manner, it did not bring any systematic change. Gradually, the contractors came into the picture and they became the conduit between the state and the people. After fulfilling their duties of paying the fixed revenue to the state, these contractors monopolized the trade to their advantage. Sometimes the loot was more organized, as seen during the floods of 1893 in Kashmir. After the water receded, for two months, the forests were opened to the villagers. They could collect free timber for repairing their ravaged assets. The villagers went about felling trees unabashedly, in excess of their requirement. Moreover, many other villages that were not affected by the floods also joined in the grand heist.

However, the systematic plunder of the forests started in the wake of the second phase of Industrial Revolution in the middle of the nineteenth century. This was also the time when the British were consolidating their control over India. A large number of public buildings, barracks, bridges and godowns were being constructed, entailing increased requirement of timber. In 1853, when the first train chugged from Bombay to Thane, it opened new vistas for exploitation of forests. The railway network increased rapidly in the country, and requirement of wood for both carriages and sleepers expanded drastically.

In Jammu and Kashmir, the demand for timber also increased with the advent of the boat industry. With the opening of the Jhelum Valley Cart Road, a large number of European tourists came to explore Kashmir. Enchanted by the beauty of the valley, many of them applied for purchasing land, looking to stay for longer durations. Maharaja Ranbir Singh outrightly denied all permission. In response, they turned to the waterways and came up with the concept of 'floating camps'.

In 1898, Swami Vivekananda, along with his Western followers, visited Kashmir for the second time. During his stay, he made excursions to various shrines, ruins of old temples, palaces and other historical sites. Impressed by the spiritualism and beauty of Kashmir, Swami Vivekananda wished to establish a Sanskrit college and give young people training in non-dualism. Maharaja Pratap Singh treated him with utmost respect and many of his officials paid him a visit in the houseboat he was staying in. During the course of these discussions, Swami Vivekananda requested for a tract of land, which was readily agreed upon by the Maharaja. However, the British resident refused to formalize the land grant for unknown reasons. The succeeding Dogra rulers also remained adamant and did not let any outsiders buy land. With non-availability of land, water was the only option left.[97]

The best example in this regard is of R. Foster and the Clermont houseboats – a group of seven houseboats moored in Nassembagh or 'The Garden of the Morning Breeze', on the western shores of the Dal Lake. The passage to the houseboats is through a large garden of variegated flowers, shaded by a row of mighty chinars, believed to be 400 years old.

R. Foster, an English shipping tycoon from Clermont Hall, Norfolk, visited Kashmir in late nineteenth century. Having fallen in love with the region, he desired to visit every year. Foster requested the government to allocate him land, where he planned to build his own vacation home. The government, while denying his application, advised Foster to purchase a houseboat instead, mentioning that it was willing to provide a place for mooring it. Foster went on to purchase the same houseboat in which he had stayed for the first time as a tourist. During his stay in the valley, he met Ghulam Muhammad Butt, a local Kashmiri. Impressed by Butt's honesty, he developed a liking for him, and soon the relationship turned into close friendship. In 1947, when the British left India, Foster also had to leave. The ultimatum delivered to Butt was along these lines: 'Either you should take care of the Clermont or I shall burn down everything.' Butt accepted the offer and became the caretaker of the chain of houseboats. The houseboats were eventually transferred to the Butts, and now the third generation of the family are the owners.[98]

The Clermont has been witness to some of the most significant events of Kashmir history. In 1953, one of the houseboats hosted a crucial meeting between Sheikh Mohammad Abdullah and American diplomat and presidential candidate Adlai Stevenson. Before leaving the houseboat, Stevenson wrote in the guest book: 'An enchanted interlude that mended body and mind and that I shall never forget – thanks to Mr G M Butt.'

The year 1953 was a watershed moment in the history of Jammu and Kashmir, and the aforementioned meeting must have taken place few months before the arrest of Sheikh Abdullah in August 1953. After his arrest, he was lodged in Gajpat Fort, perched on a hill in Ramban and later shifted to the Bhaderwah jail. A decade later, when the Moi-e-Muqqadas – a relic widely believed by Muslims to be the hair of Prophet Muhammad – was reported to have gone missing from the Hazratbal shrine, the whole of Kashmir was in the streets, protesting violently. Being at a short distance from the revered shrine, the Clermont must have been in the thick of this mass agitation. Sheikh Abdullah was released in 1975, and he went on to head the government of Jammu and Kashmir again. When the charismatic leader passed away in 1984, he was buried on the shore of the Dal Lake, not very far from the Clermont.

The Clermont became famous not only for its exquisite aesthetics and enviable luxury, but was also renowned for the host of celebrities who stayed here. In the visitors' register there are heart-warming notes by Yehudi Menuhin, Dilip Kumar, P.G. Wodehouse, Joan Fontaine, the family of Lord Mountbatten among others. In 1966, George Harrison stayed here for one month, taking sitar lessons from Pandit Ravi Shankar. One can only imagine the enchanting sight of Harrison strumming his Spanish guitar in accompaniment with Ravi Shankar's sitar, creating musical fusion, embellished by the silence of the placid lake and the breeze rustling the chinars.

George Harrison's remark dated 11 October 1966 in the guest book reads:

> To Mr. Butt – with thanks
>
> A very peaceful stay at Clermont, special thanks to Rehman who served us exceptionally well! Wife and I whelmed by all.
>
> Good wishes for future
>
> George Harrison

No definite period has been ascribed to the introduction of houseboats in Kashmir. Some historians believe that since the valley was created from a giant lake, a large number of waterways were formed. These were navigated by the locals using boats. *Hanji*s or boatmen have existed for years, living in houseboats, mostly along the Jhelum. Then there were the Darpad Doongas, or cargo vessels with open sides, which were used to accommodate the colonial officers and tourists' way back in the early part of the nineteenth century. If the stories are to be believed, a British Army officer, General James Dunlop, went on a doonga ride once – and ended up designing wooden walls for the vessel. That was how the houseboats came into existence![99]

Another version traces the houseboats to a shopkeeper named Pandit Nariandas, who catered to the needs of foreigners. One day, his shop was gutted in a fire, leaving him devastated. Rising from the ruins of his burnt property, Nariandas retrieved some of his inventory and moved to a Hanjis doonga and moored it at a suitable place. Due to the unique concept of floating merchandise, his profits swelled. He began to improve his shop by replacing its matted walls and roof with planks and shingles. This was the first houseboat afloat.

Nariandas was approached by a European who proposed to buy his boat for a good price. The clever shopkeeper agreed to the deal and realized that boat making was a lucrative concept. So he became a houseboat builder. People nicknamed him as Naav Narayan, literally Boat Narayan, and the first houseboat he built was named *Kashmir Princess*. In 1906, Francis Younghusband wrote that the idea of a 'floating house' first came from a sport-loving Englishman named M.T. Kennard between 1883 and 1888. For a long time, till the name 'houseboat' caught on, Kashmiris used to call these boats 'the boat of Kennard'. Younghusband further writes that by 1906 there were hundreds of houseboats skimming on the waters of lakes.[100]

Due to unbridled pillage of the rich forests, Maharaja Ranbir Singh felt the need to exercise tenacious control over their management. In 1857, he created Mahel-i-Navara or the forest exploitation unit, which functioned under the state revenue department. This was for the first time that the forestry staff was specifically earmarked. However, the purpose of the staff was not conservation but mainly to collect revenue from the contractors who were engaged in haphazard forest work.

In 1883, the forest department was formally organized, and rules and regulations for the control of forests were passed by the government by the name Ain-i-Janglat or the constitution of forests. Eight years later, J.C. McDonnell, an officer of the Indian Forest Service, was appointed as the first conservator of forests. He created a functional department, marked out the forest areas and made a plan for controlling the relentless felling of the forests. Rules for demarcation of forests were notified in 1914, which finally culminated into the Jammu and Kashmir Forest Act, coming into force in 1930.

During the initial days of the forest department, most of the sale work was done by the departmental agency. Later on, the standing trees were purchased by contractors on royalty basis. Soon this method was given up and main compartments of forests were now sold on three to five years lease. This was the beginning of the powerful lobby of forest lessees. The vast resources of natural forests came under the hammering of a gavel. It was like shopping for various ornaments in a jewellery shop. And what was the jewellery on display? It was the 'green gold'. After the beginning of the formal auctions along with the 'shoppers' a few 'bandits' also trooped in and resorted to daylight robberies. They carried back their steal bags brimming with unimaginable wealth.[101]

The lower hills of the Chenab Valley are rich with chir and kaayur, i.e. pine trees – an evergreen conifer tree of the genus *Pinus*. With its dense foliage of long-needled leaves, the pines shade the arc of land under them even though they are generally Sun-loving and relatively shade-intolerant. The spreading branches of a young pine tree form a pyramidal shape; it gradually flattens with age and spreads out like a Japanese umbrella. In summers, some of the needles dry up, turn auburn and fall down to form heaps around the trees. Since pines are rich in resin, these dried-up needles are highly inflammable, and a little spark quickly spreads into a colossal forest fire. Although the dangers of a forest fire cannot be overemphasized, it is an essential phenomenon for balancing the cycles of nature.

Apart from being an ornamental accessory, pine wood is used for light furniture, doorframes, firewood, turpentine and resin. The branches of pine are also used in the kangris or the Kashmiri fire pots. A popular Kashmiri saying endorses this: *Kaashur yaar guv kaayur naar* [The burning charcoal of the pine timber is a friend of the Kashmiri]. During the good old days, when kids from urban areas happened to be in the hills for a family outing or a school picnic, they would love to collect the pine cones – locally called *satiyan* – strewn all over the forests. Some of the collected cones were painted in different hues and showcased as decorative pieces in the living rooms of middle-class homes.

As the mountains climb up, the pine trees start to disappear and the mighty deodars or divdhors (cedars) start to emerge in all their beauty. Though a high-altitude tree, deodars also grow in low-altitude valleys. Another evergreen conifer tree, deodar stands elegantly, like an alert sentinel with its strong branches and a trunk of enormous girth. *Cedrus deodara*, the botanical name of the tree, is derived from *devadaru*, which means 'timber of the gods'. No wonder the tree is sacred to Hindus; it is also often mentioned in ancient Indian religious texts. Hindus believe that forests full of deodars are the abodes of ancient sages who were devotees of Lord Shiva.

These trees grow as high as 50 m and, with their drooping foliage and conical crowns, give a great ornamental value. The wood of deodar is highly valued for its strength, durability and rot-resistance. Because of these properties, it has always been in great demand for building material, furniture, houseboats, bridges, doors and railway sleepers. In the Chenab Valley, Himachal Pradesh and Uttarakhand, most of the temples are made of deodar wood. The inner wood of the tree has aromatic properties and is used to make incense, perfumed oil, anti-fungal antidotes, room fresheners and insect repellents to be used on the hooves of horses, cattle and camels. In Indian films, the hero and heroine have often romanced around these trees, running among them, hiding behind them, singing and dancing. The tree is also symbolic of eternal love, indicated by the quintessential carvings of a heart on their trunks, not only in the movies but also in real life.

Deodar has a great tendency to grow as a pure crop, but it should not be taken as a rule because some other conifers as well as broad-leaved species also grow alongside it. Coniferous associates of deodar include the blue pine, spruce, kail and fir. In fact, fir and kail can grow at higher altitudes where deodar cannot withstand the low temperature. These trees stand stoically, braving the snow, sub-zero temperatures and strong winds.

Like humans, trees, too, have a prescribed life, and eventually, the most stubborn of them die, falling with a thud. The bigger the fallen tree, the more the earth shakes. And there are trees that die prematurely succumbing to some disease or get uprooted due to the vagaries of weather or an earthquake. However, the biggest threat to these trees arises from the human axe. The felled trees, enormous in size and weight, were destined to be carried away. The

Chenab inadvertently facilitated this nefarious heist. This inevitable combination of the river and the forest has been testament to man's unquenchable avarice.

When the sale of timber got institutionalized through the system of auction, Indian bidders encroached into the monopoly of the British. One of the first to delve into the timber trade in Jammu and Kashmir was Rai Bahadur Jodhamal Kuthalia. Born in Haroli in present-day Himachal Pradesh, Jodhamal's family was most opulent and held a large estate. Carrying forward the philanthropic ways of his ancestors, Jodhamal donated 100 acres of land to the estate of Kangra for the purpose of construction of a 400-bed tuberculosis sanatorium. Throughout his life, he evinced great interest in public institutions and humanitarian work. In order to alleviate the sufferings of the common people, he made generous contributions for education, scholarships, health and civic amenities. In the 1930s, he got the official houses of the DC and SP, Hoshiarpur, built. Perhaps it was one of the earliest cases of corporate social responsibility.

Jodhamal invested heavily in the deodar-rich forests of the Pangi Valley and harvested a golden crop. Due to the inaccessibility of the valley and its treacherous terrain, not many forest lessees had the wherewithal to venture there. Not only was Jodhamal able to penetrate into the forests, but he also tamed the Chenab.

From the Pangi Valley, Jodhamal followed the course of the river and came to the Chenab Valley. He continued to earn a good name in Jammu and Kashmir for honest business and gave employment to hundreds. In order to facilitate his business, he widened and repaired the track from Killar to Paddar and laid out rope bridges over the Chenab. Along this path, he also built caravanserais and resthouses. Though it was done to ease the mobility of his workers and ponies, the general public, too, benefitted from it. Later, when Jodhamal expanded his timber business in the Chenab Valley, the refurbished track, almost overlapping with the Ram Rasta, was extended till Kishtwar.

This wood business would not have been possible without the Chenab. Since times immemorial, water has been a transportation medium of wood through timber rafting or log driving. In timber rafting, logs were bound together to form a raft, which was then propelled with oars to ride the current of the river. This practice was common in most parts of the world including North America and Europe. In Germany, for example, the wood extracted from the Black Forest was conveyed mostly by timber rafting. On the other hand, in log driving, the timber was hurled into the river and its course would transport the logs. This method was applied in fast-flowing rivers like the Chenab. However, with the advent of roads, railroads and sea vessels, this practice waned.

Following the footsteps of Jodhamal, Dan Singh Bist from Nainital in today's Uttarakhand also came over to Jammu and won many contracts for the extraction and supply of timber. I happened to see one of his applications, addressed to the director general, Supply and Development, Karachi, for grant of supply of deodar sleepers' first-class quantity of cft. Dan Singh Bist did business in Jammu and Kashmir for a number of years. One of his three wives was Nepalese and a daughter born to them studied in a missionary school in Tangmarg. Later on, she happened to marry a local Rajput, whose family held important positions in the Maharaja's durbar. Her son turned out to be my classmate in primary classes at school and became a close friend. This friendship lasts till date, strong like the river Chenab. Following the success of early timber merchants, many other firms started to bid for contracts in Jammu and Kashmir. Firms like Spading-Dinga Singh, owned by two Sikhs from Punjab, Ghani Joo and Company from Kashmir, and few others made good profits. But the difficulties involved in transportation of timber through rivers eradicated most other companies.

In Jammu, Sheikh Mohammad Amin made huge strides in the timber trade. With his sheer hard work, Amin became one of the richest men in Jammu. In the mid-1950s his opulence and lifestyle had become the talk of town. He built himself a palatial mansion on a hill overlooking the river Tawi. Being from weaver's caste, the locality came to be known as Julakha Mohalla or the Weavers' Colony. After the Maharaja, whose fleet included Rolls-Royces and Chevrolets, as well as a few other people from aristocracy, Amin was one among the first to own a car in Jammu. After buying the car, he could not figure out how to get it to his house. Julakha Mohalla was an old-style cluster interconnected with narrow alleys. Left with no choice, Amin ordered a road to be built by cutting the mountain that lay at the foot of his house. The circular road of Jammu that circuits the Muslim-dominated localities of Julakha Mohalla, Khatikan Talab and Gujjar Nagar today had come up so that Sheikh Amin's car could be parked in his house.

Amidst the flow of wine and the gyrations of nautch girls, on many evenings, Amin's abode would turn into a pleasure house of musicals and Urdu poetry. His indulgence came as an opportunity for his employees – the Sarafs and the Mahajans. They basically worked as clerks to maintain the accounts of wood extracted and sold. Taking advantage of their master's indulgence in hedonism, they would manipulate the records and steal some timber through their henchmen. As long as the money kept arriving in droves, Amin did not bother to check the embezzlement, happening right under his nose.

The systematic steal of his money did not affect Amin's extravagance. In the late 1960s, when his son got married, it was news not only in the sleepy town of Jammu but also in the city of Bombay that never slept. He chartered a plane to take his family and friends for the wedding, since his son was getting married to the sister of Feroze Khan and Sanjay Khan, the leading actors of Bollywood at that point in time. This was at a time when going to Bombay was a privilege of a few, and flying in a plane, of fewer.

The Mahajans and Sarafs who were not even invited to the wedding took full advantage of the erratic ways of their master. They soon became small contractors of timber and gradually expanded their business. Coinciding with the depleting fortunes of Amin, they would go on to become some of the richest men in Jammu. While they diverged into different businesses and made mansions for themselves, the imposing house of Sheikh Amin fell into neglect after his death. Today, the dilapidated building stands amidst erratic growth of shrubs, with its paint peeling off.

In my childhood, watching logs of wood getting tossed into the Chenab, startled and amused me in equal measures. My inquisitiveness was sorted out after I happened to have an animated conversation with Uncle Piku. Both Uncle Piku's daughter – who works as a doctor in Dubai – and I address him as 'Piku'. He suffers from chronic constipation and I take care of him, his daughter told me jocularly. The name struck in our conversations. *Piku* is a Hindi comedy film and loosely based on a 1980 Bengali short film *Pikoo* by Satyajit Ray. In the movie, Amitabh Bachchan plays an old widower, a hypochondriac with chronic constipation who traces every problem to his bowel movements. Though often exasperated by her father's condition, Deepika Paduokone – who plays Piku, his daughter – loves her father and takes good care of him.

Piku's daughter would frequently fly down from Dubai to look after her father. Their partially constructed house in Srinagar sprawls over two acres and is nestled in the middle of Zabarwan Hills. Standing by the flowerbeds at the edge of the lawn, one gets a clear view of the famous Tulip Garden and the Dal Lake. Further on the left side, the Royal Springs Golf Course – one of the most beautiful eighteen-hole putting delights – looks like a postcard. That evening, when Piku educated me about the timber trail, his daughter was busy plucking cherries from the trees a little further from the lawn.

Piku inherited the wood business from his father, who started as a labour contractor. His task was to provide workforce to the established forest lessees. Though he would make good money in the business, his ambition lay in becoming a lessee himself. In order to muster the capital to buy a compartment of forest, he collaborated with Ganga Ram, another local businessman. Ganga Ram was also keen to get into wood business, being well versed with the forests and its potential wealth. He was into catechu business, which is a thorny deciduous shrub, used as an ingredient to give red colour and a typical flavour to chewing betel leaf.

After joining hands, Ganga Ram and Piku's father floated a timber firm and organized enough capital to win auctions of forest compartments in the Chenab Valley. The business was furthered by Piku and Ganga Ram's son.

Initially, Piku would mostly bid for the high-quality deodars of Nagsena forests, a few kilometres ahead of Atholi in Paddar. In fact, he got obsessed with the Nagsena forests and would normally outwit the other bidders and go to any extent to win the auction.

The forest was named after Nagsena, a monk, thinker and philosopher who lived two centuries before Christ. He was born in a Brahmin family in Kajangal village of Kishtwar district. After learning the Vedas at a very young age, his quest for spiritual learning increased. To quench this thirst, he joined the Buddhist fold that took him to Patliputra or modern-day Patna, the capital city of the state of Bihar. Here he studied all three canonical texts of Trpitaka [Three Baskets].

Prior to this period, when the Mauryan Empire was at a decline, marauding tribes from Central Asia invaded India. Finally, Indo-Bactrians succeeded in establishing sway over a major part of northern India. The most prominent Indo-Greek king of the time, Menander, extended his kingdom up to the Ganga–Yamuna doab and established his capital at Sagala, modern-day Sialkot in Pakistan. A polymath, Menander mastered the knowledge of many philosophical schools developed at that time in India. He openly challenged contemporary intellectuals to philosophical debates and always won. Purportedly, Menander famously declared, 'The whole of land has become devoid of scholars and there is no one who can dare face me.' Finally, the Buddhist scholars cajoled Nagsena to take on Menander in order to decimate his ego. In order to take the challenge, Nagsena reached Sagala, where an assembly was convened in the palace of King Meander. The discourse carried on for days, and finally Menander accepted defeat at the hands of Nagsena. He then converted to Buddhism and became Milinda. The entire discourse was later compiled in the form of a book called *Milindapanho* (The Questions of Milinda), thereby becoming a major semi-canonical text of Buddhism. Written in Pali language, Milindapanho is the only text that talks about Nagsena, and some of the places mentioned in the book are believed to be in the present-day Nagsena Tehsil of Kishtwar district.[102]

Presumably, Piku did not know much about Buddhism; his own philosophy centred on hedonism. He started raking in money and, as a true connoisseur of fine things, acquired many luxuries – finest scotch, Rolex watches, designer suits, Mont Blanc pens and a Mercedes Benz numbered 786. Piku became obsessed with the revered number of Islam, 786, which is believed to be a numeric form of the Arabic phrase '*Bismillah al-Rahman al-Rahim*', which literally translates into 'In the name of God, the most Gracious and most Merciful'. In an intriguing case of faith, Piku would first purchase the number and then the vehicle, while other people did it the opposite way. It became a style statement for Piku. Back in school, when most of us came on cycles or school buses, Piku's daughter drove a green Willys jeep having a black tarpaulin top, with registration number 786.

'How does the forest department put a price on a compartment, and how do the lessees determine a profit there?' I asked Piku, rather ingenuously. 'It is a tedious process, you see. The forest guard is supposed to know each tree as if it's his own child, and like a good parent, he is expected to know the health of his children, though this is a big family he is taking care of,' Piku replied philosophically. He was right. A forest guard was supposed to frequently patrol the forests and conservation areas under his jurisdiction. He was supposed to be well versed with each contour and corner of the jungle, the pathways and the trees therein. He was also responsible for preventing illegal hunting, poaching of wildlife, smuggling of forest produce and deforestation.

The auction of the forest compartments and the subsequent harvesting were preceded with a lengthy process of tariffing. It is a term used in forestry for counting, selecting, measuring and marking trees to predict the volume of timber that will be produced by felling. The forest officials, along with the forest guard, were responsible for tariffing, and they would make spot visits and check the health of each tree. The old and diseased trees were then earmarked to be felled. Though different methods like paint, tape and cuts are used, in Jammu and Kashmir, a hammer was used to mark the tree at two different spots, one above the other, on the trunk. The hammer would stamp a number to each tree. The trees were classified by measuring the trunk diameter at breast height, usually a standard of 4.5 ft above the ground. The results were then converted into a volume of timber for that species of tree using a tariff table, and thus, the auction price for a particular part of jungle was worked out.

'How did you know that it was a fair price set for a jungle by the forest department?' I probed further. 'Oh! You mean the stumpage. Before bidding, we would go and check the trees, and determine the value or volume of a tree. The trees to be felled were hammered by the department and then we would calculate our profit before bidding,' Piku explained.

It was a fair system, and the forest department would put a right price for a compartment so that everyone could be happy and make a profit. The clandestine element of the timber business was triggered when the healthy trees were felled, the ones which were not hammered. In this game, the lessees, the forest guards and the whole department were a party. This is from where the big money came. Forest lessees became rich and so did the forest officers and the guards.

After winning the bid for a compartment, the lessees would set up their transitory work sites and residential camps by constructing wooden cubicles or thatched huts, or pitching waterproof tents.

These camps were well secured from the wildlife. Bears were scared away with fire, and shepherd dogs were kept for forewarning about predators. Then there were few gunmen with licensed weapons to ward off more serious threats.

The whole process of cutting, chiselling and transportation of the wood entailed a lot of hard work. The lessees and their managers would stay in the jungle for months to supervise the operations. The labourers would work all day in the forests, hewing the trees. Then dozens of men would carry the fallen trees to the sawmill setup inside the camp. Next, the carpenters stepped in their saw machines, debarking and bucking the trunks and branches into sleepers or planks. These were then stamped with the indelible mark of the company. Each timber firm had its own mark, which helped to sort out the ownership of the timber at the log boom.

Next, the logs were to be shifted downhill, which was a laborious task due to the heaviness of the wood and lack of roads. If the distance from the camp to the roadhead was short, the logs were manually pushed downhill, especially the ones in cylindrical shape that could be easily rolled over. Due to the steepness of the mountains and lack of tracks in the forests of the Chenab Valley, animals were not used to haul the wood. For bigger lessees like Piku, a larger system was required to shift the enormous amount of timber his license permitted to be hewed. For this purpose, a gravity-driven cableway was set up with a wire-rope knotted to the wooden poles at regular intervals. At least four to five sleepers were placed on the wire-rope and they would roll over and reach the designated spot. Here, the men were deployed for the collection of the logs that were then yarded on the bank of the Chenab.

'Wasn't it boring out there in the forest?' I asked. 'It was work and I am a lumberjack, you see! Just like you go to office and sort out the bad guys, I sort out the wood,' Piku answered and then fell into inexplicable silence. With no electricity, there was no scope for much of entertainment. 'There was no radio signal in the hills and I could not follow cricket commentary and BBC news,' Piku expressed regret. To fight the loneliness and for recreation, he did not forget to carry a carton of fine scotch and a 'Made in Japan' tape recorder with him. Those dark nights lit up with kerosene lanterns resonated with the ghazals of Ghulam Ali and hits of Lata Mangeshkar in accompaniment of the jungle symphony.

The lumbering season would ideally start in April and continue throughout the summer. By early September, the chill of winters would slowly start to register and the work was normally wound up. Now was the time to set the timber on sail. Starting September, piled-up wood transported from the wire-rope would eventually be thrust into the Chenab. One after the other, each sleeper rode its own luck, bobbing and dancing over the current of the river, surging ahead, not looking back even once. During this time, the water in the river was far less due to the freezing of the river in Lahaul-Spiti and other cold regions. During the peak season, the river over a stretch of hundreds of miles, would carry tens of thousands of wooden logs on its current, almost looking like a river of wood. Staying for so long in the ice-cold water, the wood gets seasoned – its strength and durability is increased, making it very suitable for use in building material and heavy furniture.

On the downstream journey, dozens of men called log drivers were tasked to ensure unhindered journey of the timber. Expert swimmers, these men were mostly hired from Kullu Valley. They would run along the river and keep a watch on the floating timber. Most of the jam points, where the logs were likely to get obstructed, were identified in advance. Though there were not many obstructions in the Chenab, at certain spots, the logs would invariably meet boulders or drift to the riverbanks. It was the job of the log drivers to free the logs and ensure their hassle-free sail.

Another important task of the log drivers entailed keeping the timber smugglers at bay. Timber thefts were not uncommon, and notorious smugglers were a menace. Some of them had been doing this for decades, passing on the skill to the next generation. The smugglers navigated the waters using inflated animal hides and blatantly stole the logs. In their perspective, it was the 'outsider lessees' who were stealing the timber! As locals, they believed that the first right over the forest and river was theirs. 'Despite all our efforts, at least 20 percent of the wood did not reach the depot,' Piku sighed.

There were various collection centres for the wood. These places had a 'log boom' or 'log fence' immersed in the water, which worked as a barrier across navigable stretch of water to contain the floating logs. The boom was nothing but a barrier of barbed wire thrown into the river, which was firmly wound to poles on the banks of the river. Without causing any hindrance to the flow of the water, the logs of the wood would get entangled in the wire. The timber would then be retrieved in boats and piled on the shores to be transported to the depots.

In the initial days, one of the largest collection centres was in Thathri. The etymology of the name comes from the Kashmiri word *thath*, which means heap of wood, referring to the wood retrieved from the Chenab. During the days of the timber trail, the people from Thathri and nearby villages earned their money by collecting wood from the river. The wood was either locally sold for fuel or transported to Jammu both by government and private agencies. However, this practice stopped after the construction of the Dul–Hasti project. 'Yes, the project was a great setback, and even I had to leave the forests of Nagsena and move towards Ramban forests,' Piku said, with a tinge of sadness.

Before Independence, the method of water transportation was the most prevalent. The timber would flow from as far as the Pangi Valley, and travelling through the Chenab Valley and plains of Jammu, it would get collected at various places like Sialkot, Wazirabad, Gujrat and Gujranwala in the present Punjab province of Pakistan. These places had booming sports and furniture industries that thrived on harmonious trading relations between Hindus and Muslims. While suppliers of the wood were both Hindus and Muslims, the artisans and craftsmen were mostly Muslims. Similarly, the buyers of the finished products were mainly Hindus, who would then retail or sell these products in different parts of the country. All this changed after Partition due to the religious displacement of the people and their businesses. The trading relations which existed for hundreds of years were snapped in just one night. Akhnoor, the last Indian town on the Chenab, became the biggest collection point where a large log boom was set in.

The stoppage of the timber trade brought to a halt the established businesses on both sides of the border. After some time, the influential lobby through diplomatic channels was able to get the trade opened. Now, selected timber merchants from Pakistan could trade with Indian wood suppliers. These deals were mostly brokered by middlemen based in Pathankot. The Pakistani merchants would visit India using valid documents and buy timber through the middlemen. The wood was then transported to Pakistan in trucks through the Wagah Border, near Amritsar. In the new arrangement, the price of the timber shot up exorbitantly, and in the process, the forest lessees and the middlemen became richer.

'It was fair business, mutually beneficial and the Pakistani merchants were honest in their dealing,' Piku reminisced about the good old days. As the relations between the two countries deteriorated, the aforesaid arrangement also came to a stop and the timber trade between the two countries was stopped forever. Moreover, when the Salal project came to Reasi district, the timber trail also came to a halt. 'Anyway, it had to come to an end someday, *jaise kissi ki nazar lag gayi* [as if someone's curse fell on it],' Piku said with melancholy. His eyes wandered in a void as he recollected the golden time of timber trail.

By the late 1960s, the opulence of the forest lessees came under government scrutiny. Ghulam Mohammad Sadiq, who remained the chief minister of Jammu and Kashmir till 1971, was the first to propose total government control on the forests and to end the roles of the lessees. As a first step towards the nationalization of forests, Government Lumbering Undertaking (GLU) was created in 1973.

Seeing their monopoly slowing slipping away, the forest lessees grew deeply resentful and restive. Sheikh Abdullah, who became the chief minister in 1975, pushed the idea further and was determined to take the forests completely under the government control.

There is an interesting anecdote about how a group of lessees pooled in a huge sum of money for a bribe in order to stall the new policy. When they approached a top government functionary with a suitcase stuffed with money, he got very angry. Apparently, he wanted the cash in an imported suitcase and not in the Indian one. Responding to the crisis, one of the lessees dashed to Kathmandu, from where he managed to buy a foreign-made suitcase. However, the lessees lost both their money and the imported suitcase when the State Forest Corporation Act, 1978, was promulgated in 1979.

The erstwhile GLU was replaced by the Jammu and Kashmir State Forest Corporation (SFC), which inherited its assets and liabilities. The GLU employees who used to carry out extraction and sale of timber through forest lessees got merged with the SFC. This corporation was conceptualized to undertake removal and disposal of trees through open auctions. The supply of timber to the consumers would be undertaken at concessional rates through fair price depots.

The establishment of the SFC was unable to create efficiency or transparency in the system. The corporation got mired in allegations of corruption, favouritism, nepotism and financial misappropriation. The original mandate of the corporation remained confined to collection of dry, deceased, wind-fallen, top broken or snow-fallen trees. The corruption had basically shifted from private lessees to government officials. Sometimes, when the audit of the stocked wood was ordered, mysterious fires would erupt in the depots and any evidence of malpractices or embezzlements would go up in smoke. The problems of the forest department were further compounded with the advent of militancy in the Chenab Valley. When the militants entered deep inside the forests, they took complete control of their surroundings. In this changed scenario, forest guards were amongst the first victims who fell to militant bullets. These guards who took motherly care of each and every tree in the forest were now unable to enter their own home.

The militants ruled the jungles and they offered free access to certain people while others were debarred from entering it. This also led to mass scale illegal felling of trees. The militants not only facilitated this loot by favouring some of the forest contractors but also got a major share of the money. In other words, the local 'Area Commander' of the militant outfit was now the new conservator of forests. Some officers of the security forces and local police were also accused of getting their fingers in the pie. Truckloads of walnut furniture found way to mainland India to adorn the houses of many government officers.

The forest lessees faded into history but the timber smuggling went on unabated. Today, the most famous private school in Jammu is the Jodhamal Public School, named after Rai Bahadur Jodhamal who continues to spread his mission of education. The Mahajans and Sarafs diversified into various others businesses from the capital accumulated from the timber of the Chenab Valley and they continue to flourish. Sheikh Amin's septuagenarian daughter based in London, has been trying hard to sell her terraced house in Julakha Mohalla but is not finding any takers for the once glorified address.

At Jia Pota Ghat in Akhnoor, a group of expert swimmers sit on the banks of the Chenab, their eyes glued to the flow of the river, in hope of an occasional piece of wood drifting on its surface. Some trees that naturally get uprooted can be occasionally seen making a foray in the river as an ode to the old times of the timber trail. These young men, at the slightest hint of a substantial piece of wood, dive into the river to retrieve it. It is either used for fuel or sold in the open market for a meagre amount.

After long hours of learning, the Sun had dipped on the horizon, the incendiary sky reflecting on the serene waters of the Dal Lake. Gusts of breeze blew from the rich forests on the surrounding hills, and the first lights of the Palace of Fairies were getting lit as we wound up our conversation. 'You know, about twenty years back on an evening like this, a friend of mine after a long chat and cups of *kehwa*, took leave from me as it was time for him to offer his prayers,' Piku said, taking refuge in sweet nostalgia. 'And this classmate of yours tells him, "Uncle I know it's time for your namaz; your friend here has also been biding his time so that he could open his bottle."' Apparently, the taunting innuendo had stirred an emotional nerve in Piku and that evening he did not open just one bottle, but about twenty of them – Blue Label, Royal Salute, Laphroaig, Remy Martin – one after another, and poured them down the washing basin. 'Since that day, which was twenty years ago, till today, as we sit here, I have not consumed a single drop of alcohol,' Piku bid me goodbye on a sober note. I drove back down the Zabarwan Hill with the scent of wood, pondering on the glory days of timber logging, with a wicker basket full of freshly plucked cherries.

14
The Light of the Eyes

The Chenab enters Jammu district at Maira Mandrian tehsil of Akhnoor. About 30 km northwest of Jammu, the town of Akhnoor is situated on the right bank of the river. It is towered by a ring of mountains of the Shivalik and Kalidhar ranges in the east and north, respectively. Archaeological footprints at various places in and around Akhnoor have established that the place was a strong bastion of the Indus Valley Civilization. In 1977, the excavations in Manda – about 10 km from Akhnoor – unearthed black-slipped ware, red ware, bangles, triangular tiles of terracotta, jars and potshards with Harappan markings. Therefore, Manda was mapped as the northernmost site of Harappa civilization.[103]

Continuing its tryst with history, a few kilometres away, on the outskirts of Akhnoor, a monastic Buddhist site was excavated at Ambaran. Situated on the right bank of the Chenab, an eight-spoke stupa, of high-quality baked bricks, surrounded by stone pathways and meditation chambers was excavated. Some historians believe that Akhnoor was an important transit station for the itinerant monks, who were constant companions of the caravans of traders ferrying goods from the Indian mainland to Kashmir and further afield to Central Asia.[104] Historians further propagate that the site was abandoned around seventh century due to flash floods in the Chenab. Anyway, we can imagine how delightful a scene it would have been with the red-robed monks housed at the site, their chants blending with the song of the river.

After Ambaran, many other discoveries related to Buddhism were made in the close vicinity, on either side of the Chenab. His Holiness the Dalai Lama visited these Buddhist sites in 2012 and authenticated the relics. The Chenab, having made another rendezvous with Lord Buddha, might have silently admired these sites. Travelling through the Bhot lands of Lahaul-Spiti and the Pangi Valley, the river had last seen the Buddha at Gulabgarh in Paddar. Perched on a small hillock, Akhnoor was presumably named by Emperor Jahangir. Once, returning from Kashmir, the Emperor's eyes became infected and a saint advised him to visit a place close to the Chenab. With the effect of the breeze wafting from the river, Jahangir's eyes fully recovered and he named the town 'Ankhon ka Noor' or light of the eyes. Eventually, the place came to be known as Akhnoor. A similar story is attributed to one of the queens of Jahangir. Having a vision problem, the said queen was treated by a Hindu priest. She was given a herbal remedy and asked to wash her eyes in the waters of the Chenab. She followed the treatment and was cured of the ailment.[105]

Today, Akhnoor is an important town, straddling the highway connecting Jammu and Poonch. It is mostly inhabited by Hindus who indulge in small businesses and agriculture. However, before Partition, a substantial population of Muslims lived here. Frederic Drew wrote in *The Jummoo and Kashmir Territories* (1875):

> The inhabitants of Akhnur are much mixed; a portion of them are of the same various castes as about Jammu; but there are a large number besides of Muhammadans, who bear the name of Kashmiri, and, doubtless, were originally of that nation. Unlike, however, Kashmiri settlers in other parts, who usually retain their distinct language, ways, and look, these have lost their native tongue and speak only Punjabi, and, in appearance and character, though very different from Dogras, they are not recognizably Kashmiri.

As the communal clouds started to hover over north India, the migration of Muslims from Jammu started as early as April 1947. However, the bulk of Muslim exodus from Akhnoor happened after the tribal invasion in Kashmir. The resultant communal riots in Jammu spilled over to Akhnoor. Many Hindus and Muslims went missing, presumably tossed into the Chenab. A large number of Hindus and Sikhs especially from the Sialkot district had also migrated and settled in different areas of Jammu including Akhnoor. Apart from the ease of the distance, these people chose Jammu because of linguistic and cultural affinity and the fact that they felt safe in a state which was ruled by a Hindu maharaja. These displaced people came to be known as West Pakistan Refugees (WPR).

For the next seven decades, the WPRs were treated as second-class citizens and remained deprived of many fundamental rights. Entitled to vote only in parliamentary elections, they remained ineligible to contest and vote in the state assembly and local bodies. Because they did not possess the state subject – a document meant only for those born in Jammu and Kashmir – they could not buy immovable property in the state or apply for government jobs. Due to these reasons, the WPRs remained restricted to agricultural labour, small businesses or private employment. Seventy years of struggle bore fruit in 2019, when the special status of the state was abrogated and the WPRs became equal citizens. In November 2020, when the WPRs voted for the first time in District Development Board elections, the mood was of jubilation and political empowerment.

The 74 km-long border of low hills, undulating terrain and rivers has subjected the people of Akhnoor to the dangers of minefields, shelling and the battles fought in this sector.

In August 1965, Pakistan launched Operation Gibraltar in Kashmir. The regulars of Pakistan Army, in the guise of locals, entered Kashmir intending to support and provoke the Kashmiris into an uprising against India. The name of the operation was inspired from the Muslim conquest of Spain and Portugal, which was launched from the port of Gibraltar, the British overseas territory. The plan was to be coupled with Operation Grand Slam, which consisted of an attack from the western front and diabolical cutting off the Akhnoor Bridge over the Chenab. The then president of Pakistan, Ayub Khan, had pointed out the bridge on the map and had famously said, 'It is going to be the "jugular" for India.'

It is said that the first bridge over the Chenab in the Akhnoor region was laid out by Afghan King Ahmad Shah Abdali during one of his raids. Between 1748 and 1767, Abdali invaded the northern territories of India at least eight times. Although there is not much historical evidence available for Abdali's journey through Akhnoor, he established the Afghan rule in Kashmir in 1752. For the next sixty-seven years, the local Kashmiris – both Hindus and Muslims – were brutally oppressed by the Afghans. In 1932, a single-lane, steel-bridge was laid over the Chenab, connecting Akhnoor with Jammu.

In the wake of a strong military response by India to the invasion, the operations Gibraltar and Grand Slam were abandoned midway by Pakistan. The war of 1965 turned out to be another disaster for Pakistan shattering its dream of annexing Kashmir. The bridge over the Chenab remained strong and sturdy. However, it succumbed to nature's fury in September 1992 as it was washed away by a sudden flood in the river. The army engineers laid out the pontoon bridge within days and traffic was restored. The steel bridge was erected again and was thrown open to traffic in April 1994.

In April 2008, Prime Minister Manmohan Singh inaugurated a two-lane cantilever bridge, located a few kilometres from the old steel bridge. The bridge, constructed at a height where the inundated Chenab waters cannot reach, lead to a new conundrum: It became a spot for dying by suicides. To act as a deterrent, a high wire mesh was installed on both sides of the bridge. Despite preventive measures, the suicides continued unabated.

In 2012, a probationary sub-inspector, Sushil Khajuria, went missing from his residence in Jammu. He was last seen by an army sentry posted at a checkpost, a few metres short of the bridge. He had parked his car, a Santro, near the sentry post and stepped down on a muddy track leading to the bank of the Chenab.

Sensing something suspicious about the abandoned car, the army informed the police. Some tell-tale signs suggested that the police officer might have been consumed by the Chenab. A team of expert divers was pressed into service, which searched downstream, without any success. A few days later, Pakistan rangers flashed a message on the hotline and informed about the recovery of a decomposed dead body. The cadaver was handed over to the Indian authorities and keys of the Santro were recovered from the pocket of the deceased.

In the 1971 war, while Indian forces were busy with the liberation of East Pakistan, on the western front, Pakistan invaded Chamb with the old motive of moving towards Akhnoor and cutting down the approach on the north of the Chenab.

A large area of Chamb is scattered on a ridgeline. It had a mixed population of Hindus, Sikhs and Muslims. In the south, the Chamb sector was strategically advantageous for Pakistan. Being open and plain, it made an ideal battleground for tank warfare. On the other hand, the area towards India is hilly and funnel-shaped, rendering the movement of troops difficult. There was a fierce tank battle and air raids, forcing the people of the town to flee to safety, leaving behind their single-storeyed stucco houses, making it a shattered ghost town scorched by fighting and the elephant grass on its ridgeline in flames. While fleeing for their lives, the villagers left behind aging relatives, livestock and heavy wares. The people assumed that they would eventually return, as had happened in the past.[106]

Gary J. Bass, in his book *The Blood Telegram* (2013), wrote about the battle of Chamb:

> In Kashmir, Pakistan attacked fiercely in the Chamb sector. The combat there was the worst of the war. Pakistan had massed terrifying firepower: some two hundred heavy guns as well as the medium ones, which rained down sixty thousand rounds on the Indians in under two days. Soon the hillsides were burned black. The Pakistanis would start deafening artillery barrages late in the afternoon and keep firing until long after midnight, eerily lighting up the night. The ground shook. The Indian soldiers had a sick sense of doom. The incoming shells cratered the battlefield, propelling solid rock and soil high into the air. They smashed sandbagged concrete bunkers. When they hit a trench, they blasted up a grotesque rain of mud and human limbs. A nearby shallow river reddened.

The shallow river in question here is the Manawar Tawi, one of the important tributaries of the Chenab. It starts as a small rivulet originating at Ratan Pir Ridge in Pir Panjal. Flowing down the middle mountains, the river soon gathers substantial amount of water from the snow and rain-fed streams, and transforms into a prominent river. The river flows along the Rajouri–Jammu highway for the major part. Later, it meanders near the LoC, almost becoming a geographical divide between India and Pakistan.

Amidst fierce fighting, Pakistan was able to capture Chamb and territories to the west of Manawar Tawi, forcing the Indian troops to retreat to the east of the river. The Indian Army blew up the only bridge on Manawar Tawi at Mandiala crossing and was able to halt the advancement of Pakistani troops.

Meanwhile, India captured a narrow strip of territory in the Sialkot district of Pakistan, which juts into the area south of Akhnoor and is surrounded by Indian territory on three sides. This dagger-shaped feature of 170 sq. km is an islet with its base in the Tawi River in Jammu. It zeroes in down to the north till it comes to Kachi Mand Nullah, where it is the narrowest. Then it opens up towards the Chenab to form the head, with the 'beak' pointing towards the Akhnoor Bridge. Pakistan calls it a dagger piercing straight into India's heart. The feature is strategically important because it provides the shortest access to the Akhnoor Bridge and was an integral part of Operation Grand Slam in 1965. For India, it is the 'chicken-neck area', implying that is the vulnerable neck of Pakistan, which can be twisted anytime.[107]

India won the war of 1971 but lost the battle of Chamb and 39,000 acres of land. About 5,000 families were uprooted from this area, and they came to be known as displaced persons (DPs) and were settled in various parts of Jammu. Pakistan renamed Chamb as Iftikharabad, after Major General Iftikhar Khan Janjua of their army, who led the division to capture Chamb. However, when he entered to savour the victory in a ghostly town strewn with destroyed tanks and dead bodies of soldiers of both countries, his helicopter crashed. He succumbed to his injuries a few days later. The town has a granite memorial in his honour.

After the surrender of the Pakistan Army in the eastern sector, the Indian Army declared a unilateral ceasefire on 17 December 1971, bringing an end to a thirteen-day war and the birth of a new country, Bangladesh. Indian Prime Minister Indira Gandhi and her Pakistani counterpart Zulfiqar Bhutto met in the picturesque Shimla, the capital of the hill state of Himachal Pradesh, in 1972 and signed the Shimla Agreement. The two countries decided to convert the Ceasefire Line to the Line of Control (LoC). Pakistan was allowed to retain Chamb, and India kept the territories gained in other sectors, including those in the Ladakh region.

On his sojourn to the Shimla summit, Prime Minister Bhutto was accompanied by his daughter Benazir Bhutto, who later became the first woman prime minister of Pakistan. Born in a wealthy and aristocratic family, Benazir did her schooling from the elite institutes of Pakistan. During the war of 1965, she, along with fellow students, took air raid practices. When she came to India, she was an undergraduate student at Harvard University. Benazir was seen as a symbol of both modern Pakistan and women's liberation.

Though she was an eager participant in the anti-Vietnam War campaign at Harvard, she fully endorsed her father's doctrine of Kashmir becoming part of Pakistan one day. In Shimla, in the days of no social media or paparazzi, she became a toast of the Indian press and was widely photographed in her stylish Pakistani suits and bellbottoms. While her father was busy with bilateral talks, she took time out to take leisurely strolls on the Mall Road and visited local shops but did not buy anything. A newspaper ran a headline 'Peerless, penniless' (the word *benazir* means peerless). She even attended a special screening of the Meena Kumari–Raj Kumar starrer *Pakeezah* at the Ritz theatre. At the Convent of Jesus and Mary school in the city, she met some of her old teachers who had moved from Pakistan to India. That time, she had famously said, 'I was born in independent Pakistan. Therefore, I am free of the complexes and prejudices which had torn Indians and Pakistanis apart in the bloody trauma of Partition.'[108]

The Shimla Agreement came as a ray of hope for peace in the Indian subcontinent, just like Benazir Bhutto came into the life of a young police officer posted in Akhnoor during those days. A bachelor, he was so smitten with her that he penned a mushy love letter to her, proposing marriage. Apparently, he stuffed the letter inside a glass bottle, corked it tightly and tossed it in the Chenab. He was expecting the waters to carry his heart's message to Pakistan. Neither did the Shimla agreement bring everlasting peace nor did the infatuated police officer receive any response. At some point in history, all three – Indira Gandhi, Zulfiqar Ali Bhutto and Benazir Bhutto – would die violent deaths to change the course of history.

Due to mutual mistrust between the two countries, even during the peace times, the border in Akhnoor has remained mostly hostile. However, despite this adversity, illicit activities on both sides work in a perfect bonhomie. Right after Partition, the border became notorious for its porosity, enabling easy passage to and fro. There have always been gangs of cattle-lifters, gold smugglers, narcotic dealers and espionage modules on both sides. On the Indian side, many villages were infamous for bootlegging. Mostly situated on the banks of the Chenab, these villages had many families traditionally involved in bootlegging. Giant cauldrons were placed near the Chenab and illicit liquor was brewed. When there was a police raid, it was easy to escape, running along the river.

This locally brewed liquor was utilized for daily consumption, but a large quantity was smuggled across the border. For this purpose, sometimes small boats were used, but the common method was through tyre tubes. The tubes were filled with liquor, firmly sealed and then let loose on the river. On the other side, the smugglers would retrieve these tubes, and the racket continued.

After the erection of the fence, the smuggling activities have decreased, but the most lucrative drug trade continues unabated. Most of the narcotic smugglers on both sides lived close to the fence and had access to their agricultural lands along the border. In certain cases, the whole family was involved in the trade in one way or the other as seen in Sarfu Ram's family.

Born in poverty, Sarfu Ram developed contacts across the border in the early 1990s, and thus began his foray into the world of narcotics. With his knowledge of the area – its each contour, riverine, grassland and swamp – Sarfu became an expert border-crosser. The security agencies would also use his expertise and facilitate his crossing for collection of intelligence. He was arrested a few times but was always let off. Finally, his luck ran out and he was convicted and sentenced to six years of imprisonment. In the jail, he came in contact with other criminals, enabling him to spread his network to Punjab, Haryana and Delhi. From jail, he continued his trade through his son, who, too, was later arrested.

After his release, Sarfu Ram was arrested again in August 2011. After a few days, he was found hanging in the lockup. It was alleged that he had used his trousers as a noose and had hanged himself on the iron bar of the window. Even after his demise, Sarfu Ram's family carried on with the nefarious business. A few months later, the police retrieved eight packets of high-quality brown sugar from their home, and arrested Sarfu Ram's wife, sister-in-law and nephew.

Due to its strategic location, Akhnoor is an important military station with a large presence of army establishments. When there was no fence on the border, Pakistan would push armed militants through certain stretches with regularity. These infiltrating groups would mostly pass through the forested escarpments and then get onto the hills of Rajouri district and fan out further into the Chenab Valley and Kashmir.

However, a suicide attack on an army establishment in 2003 raised many questions. Some believed that the group had freshly infiltrated from Akhnoor, while the others opined that the terrorists had come on a truck from Rajouri side.

That July morning, as Akhnoor was readying to wake to a new dawn, the chimes of temple bells were silenced by loud explosions and gunfire. Three terrorists stormed the Tanda army camp on the outskirts of Akhnoor town. The gunfight continued for three hours leaving two junior commissioned officers (JCOs) and four soldiers dead.

After a prolonged lull in firing, the area was thoroughly searched and declared cleared. In the afternoon, the top brass visited the spot for inspection. Suddenly, a terrorist emerged from the bushes and lobbed two grenades. A brigadier was killed and seven officers, including the top generals, received minor splinter injuries.

After the search was over, dead bodies of three terrorists were recovered, along with weapons and grenades. One of them in khaki uniform had epaulettes of the Pakistan Army. It could not be authentically determined if the fidayeen came from Rajouri or was a part of a freshly infiltrated group. Nevertheless, it is not impossible for a group to infiltrate from Akhnoor sector and strike the same day, as was evident in January 2017. Taking advantage of the winter fog, a heavily armed terrorist group intruded 2 km inside the Indian territory and attacked a GREF camp, killing three casual labourers. The terrorists also set on fire a few barracks, offices and vehicles parked inside the camp. After the attack, a massive search was launched to trace the terrorists, but they just vanished into thin air without leaving any trail. It was speculated that after the attack, they managed to exfiltrate under the thick cover of fog.

For ages, the majority of the population of Jammu plains on both sides of the Chenab have been dependent on agriculture. However, the irrigation largely depended on the rains and few wells. Therefore, the requirement of canals, with water diverted from the Chenab and the Tawi, became an absolute necessity. In 1873, Maharaja Ranbir Singh sanctioned the Shahi Canal, which originated from the left bank of the Chenab in Akhnoor. The excavation work was done for the major part of the route. But the project failed due to wrong levelling and was abandoned midway.

A few years later, the project was revived as Rajpura Canal and digging reached till Hazoori Bagh – the Maharaja's garden in Jammu city, now lost in the deluge of rapid urbanization. But when the water from the Chenab was diverted into the canal, it did not flow regularly, leading to another devastating failure. In 1903, Maharaja Pratap Singh, with the involvement of English engineers, got a fresh survey done and started the project with renewed effort. To recognize the efforts of Maharaja Ranbir Singh, the canal was named after him. Ranbir Canal would go on to become the lifeline of Jammu.

Today, the Ranbir Canal flows alongside the Jammu–Akhnoor road with its embankments elevated from the level of the road. On its west, dense inhabitations have sprouted in the foothills of lower Shivalik. These low mountains, thriving with wild shrubs and acacia forests, once used to be the stronghold of Mian Dido and his fighters. On the east of the canal, about 10 miles away, runs the international border, secured by the fence.

Among hundreds of villages along the border, situated amidst large tracts of farmlands, Jhiri is famous for its 500-year-old temple. The temple is dedicated to Bawa Jitto, who gave up his life, protesting against the atrocities of influential landlords. Every autumn, a nine-day grand festival is organized in Jhiri, which is attended by lakhs of people. Many of these devotees offer plastic dolls at the temple for Bua Kori to play with. Jhiri fair is considered to be the second most attended fair in India after the famous Pushkar fair. The festival is marked by folk ballads, wrestling competitions, local dances and sugarcane cultivators selling their yield.

From Akhnoor till Jammu, the canal crosses sixteen seasonal streams travelling towards Pakistan. In summers, when these streams are dry, Pakistan intermittently pushes terrorists through these gulches.

On 27 August 2008, the middle-class neighbourhood of Chinore to the west of Jammu city woke to blasts and heavy gunfire. During the intervening night, three heavily armed terrorists had infiltrated not far from the Baba Jitto temple in Jhiri. After hijacking a vehicle, they reached Chinore.

A kilometre short of the house where the encounter took place, a dead body riddled with bullets was recovered. It was identified to be of an off-duty head constable of the army who was supposed to join his new place of posting in a week's time. On that fateful day, he had taken his father's auto rickshaw to reach the family's welding shop in Chinore. He happened to cross the path of terrorists and was shot dead. Another civilian, a retired army man, had reached home after fetching milk when he heard the gunshots. He ran out of the house and, on seeing the terrorists in police uniform, asked for their identity cards. He was shot dead in cold blood. Similarly, Sandeep Singh had come out of his house to visit a nearby ashram when he fell to a stray bullet. Apparently, his mother had had a heavy foreboding and did her best to dissuade him from stepping out. She even tried to lock him, but Sandeep answered the call of death.

The militants also sprayed bullets on a passing motorcycle ridden by two brothers. Shabeel Hussain got hit by a volley of bullets and died instantly, while his brother was able to scamper to safety. As the police and army teams reached the spot, the terrorists barged into a house and took a woman and her four minor children as hostages. After ten hours, amidst intermittent firing and loud explosions, the security forces were able to rescue the hostages and kill the three nameless terrorists sponsored by Pakistan. The civilians were cremated in the community crematoriums not far from the Ranbir Canal.

In Jammu, the Ranbir Canal has cobbled pathways on its banks, which are flanked by tall trees, with benches placed at regular intervals. At this stretch, every year, the canal hosts the famous Baisakhi fair. The day marks the foundation of the Khalsa order of the Sikh religion. It also announces onset of the harvest season. The pilgrims arrive to take a holy dip in the canal waters and to pray in the Shiv Dham temple on its bank.

In the olden days, the fair was one of the biggest events in Jammu city and was celebrated with a lot of pomp and gaiety. However, its popularity and significance has dwindled in recent times. Once famous for palm readers, ventriloquists, bioscopes and puppetry, the fair has transmogrified into modern forms of entertainment, namely, trampolines, joyrides and tattoo art. The only thing that remains the same is the dip in the ice-cold water.

At a short distance from the Tawi River, the canal is bifurcated into two channels, and Rajendra Park has been laid down between them. The park is named after Brigadier Rajinder Singh Jamwal, who is also referred to as the Saviour of Kashmir. He briefly headed the state forces under Maharaja Hari Singh. With a force of just 200 soldiers, he bravely fought the tribal invasion of 1947 in Uri, Baramulla, before laying down his life. Outlined with tall trees, the park has manicured lawns, beds of exotic flowers and concrete canopies.

The canal crosses the Tawi through a subterranean masonry super passage. Before that, a waterfall was engineered where a small hydroelectricity installation was built in 1909, which supplied 1,250 horsepower (hp) of electricity to the Jammu city. Seven years earlier, Mohra Dam had been built on the left bank of the Jhelum in Baramulla. In 1947, when the tribals had raided the Mohra project, the lights went down in Srinagar durbar when Maharaja Hari Singh was busy distributing Dussehra gifts to his ministers.

From the Tawi, the canal peregrinates further for 33 km, irrigating the land in Samba and R.S. Pura Tehsils. It terminates finally at village Deoli, which earlier marked the state boundary with the British-ruled Punjab.

The Ranbir Canal, with its sixteen distributaries, was truly a game changer; the Chenab water it brought was rich with alluvial silt, and made the lands to the east of the Chenab very fertile. As the canal came into being, it also improved the road network. The canal was also made navigable with small boats plying between Akhnoor and Jammu. The rural agricultural economy found a new impetus in the canal's large catchment area. Farmers now moved away from millets and other low value crops, and switched over to sugarcane and paddy. The famous basmati rice – *basmati* meaning fragrant – owes its patent status to the Ranbir Canal.

The fields on the other side of the border also become fragrant with basmati rice. Historically, basmati rice has been cultivated on both sides of the border in the vast Indo-Gangetic Plains. In Pakistan, it is produced between the Ravi and the Chenab, in a fertile region called the Kalar basin. India exports 70 percent rice to Iran, Middle East and Europe. The rest of the exports are handled by Pakistan. One of the leading Indian export brands, India Gate, is based in Noida. Incidentally, the brand was founded in 1889 in Lyallpur, present-day Pakistan, by the present owner's great-grandfather.[109]

However, the two countries have not even spared rice to spar over. For a long time, India has been trying to get a patent for 'basmati'. This has irked Pakistan so much that it prefers to call its variety of basmati as 'colonel' or kainat. In July 2018, India applied for Protected Geographical Indication status for basmati rice before the European Union. This status grants intellectual property rights for products linked to a geographical area, which would give it sole ownership and protected market. Pakistan objected, arguing that it would adversely affect its export business.

After flowing beneath the new bridge at Akhnoor, the Chenab slowly starts to widen. The broadest stretch is at Jia Pota Ghat. A commemorative tablet, depicting the coronation of Gulab Singh by Maharaja Ranjit Singh in 1822, is embossed on a red sandstone wall at Jia Pota. On the plate, Maharaja Ranjit Singh is embossed sitting on a higher chair while he applies tilak on the forehead of Gulab Singh, seated on a lower chair. It is believed that the original Jia Pota tree under which the ceremony took place was uprooted in the flood of 1957. However, in 1999, a park was developed near the site and a large number of Jia Pota trees were planted, which are flourishing today.

The river is the quietest and most tranquil here. As per folklore, a meditating sage was disturbed by the relentless roaring of the Chenab. Irked, he swam to the middle of the flow and tapped the water surface with his sacred tongs, silencing the river into submission.

The ghat is also famous for the temple of Baba Kahi, where his *soungal*s or symbolic chains are kept on a platform. According to the legend, Kahi Devta was the most illustrious son of Vasuki Naag of Bhaderwah, and was responsible for bringing the Chandrabhaga River to the arid land of Akhnoor. For this effort, he was crowned the king of Akhnoor. It is also believed that in the sweltering summers – when the river water rises and touches the soungals of Kahi Devta – the monsoons bless the parched land of Jammu.

Jia Pota Ghat has been witnessing the river's flow, along with the unfolding history, for ages. Its 800 m-long promenade has been tiled, and a long pavilion of red sandstone with arches runs along half the length of the ghat. Next to the ghat is a cave that has links with the legendary Pandavas. Purportedly, in the last year of their exile, the Pandavas often mediated in the cave. It is believed to lead to Amarnath in Kashmir, and nobody is allowed to go beyond a particular point.

The double-storeyed Akhnoor Fort is located to the east of the town, right above the Jia Pota Ghat. The work of the fort was started by Mian Tej Singh, who had an estate in Jammu, and was completed during his son Alam Singh's rule in 1802. Built with baked bricks of different sizes, the fort has lofty walls, enclosing a square of over 200 yards, with one entrance on the riverside and the other on the town side. The fort is strategically located, and it is believed that it had been a major trading bastion at some point in history, where the exchange of goods from plains to adjoining hill regions was undertaken. Frederic Drew wrote:

> The passage across (of river Chenab) the ferry-boat comes to be a serious matter, scores of people, who have been waiting hours for the opportunity; rush in on her coming to the bank, and with the cattle, ponies, and camels that have been forced on board over the bulwarks, soon fill her to overcrowding. When she puts off, weighed down and unmanageable as she is, the force of the current carries her a good half mile away in the crossing the few hundred yards [sic]. Then, emptied of her freight, the boat is laboriously tracked up again for another trip. Two such journeys each way is as much as can be done in the day's work.

Every Sankranti, when the Sun transits from one zodiac to another, a huge rush of women gather on the ghat. A majority of them cross the river on boats from the left bank. The boatmen are offered money, clothes, food grains and fruits as alms. It is believed that these offerings ensure safe and smooth passage across the mythical river in the afterlife. Similarly, offerings are made to Yamaraja, the god of death, and his vahana, the male buffalo.

Very close to the ghat, there is Gurudwara Tapo Sthan. It has been built in the memory of a devout Sikh namely Sant Baba Sunder Singh of Alibeg, a large village now in the Bhimber district of POK. Before Partition, Alibeg was known as Kirtan Ghar because of a local gurudwara and a Khalsa Middle School, being run by Sant Baba Sunder Singh. During Partition, a large number of Hindus and Sikhs migrated from here, leaving the school and gurudwara abandoned. Gurdwara Tapo Sthan was built in 1997 to commemorate the contribution of Sant Sunder Singh for his philanthropic ways.

It is also said that at the location of the gurudwara, Baba Sunder Singh had meditated. Behind the gurudwara, rises the pinnacle of Parsuhram Temple, which is another place frequented by devotees.

The red of the Jia Pota colonnade, the white of the gurudwara, its fluttering, yellow Nishan Sahib flag, the cream and saffron of the Parsuhram temple and the clay-bricked fort atop the hill with the green of the Chenab in the foreground create a special mélange of colours, tradition and history.

The Chenab bids farewell to Akhnoor and moves towards Pakistan. Here, the river is at its widest, with multiple channels forming numerous river islands. The thirty-six villages of Pargwal Block not only face the fury of the river but, being bound by the Pakistan border in the west, have also been assailed with distinctive problems since the days of Partition. When the river swells in the monsoons, the 27,000-odd inhabitants and their cattle invariably end up marooned. Moreover, when tensions flare up at the border, the local populace comes under the direct attack of shelling with nowhere to hide or escape except for a few underground bunkers, which are mostly ill-equipped.

The island is administratively aligned with the town of Khour, where most of the government offices are situated. Physically, Khour is on the opposite side, but is approachable by a circuitous track of 60 km. Therefore, the most vociferous demand of the people of Pargwal has been the construction of a bridge over the Chenab, which would ameliorate most of their problems. Despite earnest efforts of the government, construction of the bridge has been mired in local politics. There are also innumerable objections raised by the Indian Army that is understandably wary about a bridge so close to the border with Pakistan. Finally, the foundation stone of the bridge, spanning 1,640 m, was laid in 2014. Gradually, the piers of the bridge are rising from the Chenab, starting at Hamirpur Kona in Pargwal and connecting to Indri Patan in the Khour tehsil. Not far from Indri Pattan, there is another village on the bank of the Chenab called Hamirpur Sidda.

In 1912, a baby girl was born in a modest Muslim house of small farmers with a tradition of music and dancing. On her birth, a mysterious spiritualist Roti Ram from Akhnoor called her 'Mallika-e-Muazamma' – the great empress – and prophesized that she will reign someday. Mallika was a much beloved child. A childless aunt of hers named her Pukhraj or topaz, and so the baby was given two names – she became Mallika Pukhraj.

Since Mallika's mother insisted on her getting educated, she learnt Urdu and Persian from a distant uncle. At a very young age, her mother shifted to a house in a by-lane of Kanak Mandi not far from Urdu Bazaar in Jammu. In those days, Urdu Bazaar was one of the busiest streets in Jammu, dotted with shops of milkmen, perfumers, kebab-sellers, beetle-leaf kiosks and bakeries. However, the street was notorious for its pleasure houses and was also called *bazaar-e-husn* – the market of beauty – since the women's quarter housed courtesans, dancers and prostitutes. It is not known whether the music emanating from these pleasure houses affected the young Mallika Pukhraj. But it was soon discovered that she possessed a melodious voice. Her mother took her to Delhi, where she stayed for two years. She got training in vocal music from Ustad Ali Baksh Kasuri, father of Ustad Ghulam Ali Khan, and in dance from Mamman Khan and, later, Lachhu Maharaj. At the age of eleven, when she sang at the coronation of Maharaja Hari Singh, the whole durbar was mesmerized. The Maharaja was so overwhelmed that he appointed her as a court singer. She stayed at the durbar for nine years and always got parental protection from the Maharaja.[110] Being one of the few women employed on a salary in the Dogra durbar, and that too as a Muslim courtesan, she was often inflicted with slanderous accusations that she had an unhealthy influence on the Maharaja, or even that she was plotting to kill him. These palace intrigues ultimately led to her ouster from the durbar.[111]

Outside the durbar, Mallika continued to make a name for herself as a singer of ghazals, thumri and dadra, as well as Pahari and Dogri folksongs. She continued to perform in private concerts, along with radio and playback singing in Bombay films. Mallika met many suitors in Lahore. Finally, in 1944, she married Syed Shabbir Hussain Shah, a middle-rung government officer who had fallen in love with her silvery voice. After Partition, she settled down in Lahore, where she remained till the end. Her inimitable repertoire was a blend of poetry and music, and her renditions of Hafeez Jallandhri, Mirza Ghalib and Faiz Ahmad Faiz made her one of the most popular musicians of the time.

Mallika Pukhraj tells her story in her memoir *Song Sung True*, which was published in India by Zubaan Books in 2004. In the same year, she passed away in Lahore, leaving behind her mellifluous music that still resonates on both sides of the border. Her legacy is being taken forward by the youngest of her six children – Tahira Syed – who is one of the most prominent singers in Pakistan.

Hamirpur Kona is the last Indian village on the border, with its agricultural land extending till the fence. The Pakistani tower posts, with white and green crescent flags fluttering atop, are easily visible from the village. One can also see an occasional gun-wielding

Pakistani ranger in a Pathan suit, peering through binoculars towards the Indian side. Hamirpur Kona often comes under heavy machine-gun fire and falls in the arc of mortar shells. However, the woes of the villagers were overwritten by an immortal love story in the shape of a badly sculpted statue that used to stand a few furlongs outside the village.

The vanished sculpture depicted a woman with a curvaceous body embracing a man who lovingly holds her hand. Eyes closed, they look intoxicated with love, exalted by each other's company and comforted by the sensuality of each other's touch. The beautiful woman, with a pitcher by her side, and the man, with an elegantly tied bandana on his forehead and twirled moustache, are the eternal lovers of folklore – Sohni and Mahiwal, the protagonists of the most tragic love story of Punjab and Sindh region. The statue perched on a platform and shaded by a cemented canopy became a mausoleum of love. The locals attribute the famous tragic love story of Sohni and Mahiwal to the village.

In August 2022, on a lazy Sunday, I made a private visit to Pargwal along with two friends. We travelled into the countryside where the fields were flush with the wheat crop, watered by a network of small channels that drew water from a canal replenished by the Chenab. We passed by Bawa Jitto temple, which, at that time of the year, was mostly isolated. The small markets enroute brimmed with tea stalls and groceries, shops selling goods from fertilizer to mobile phone accessories.

To celebrate seventy-five years of independence, under the Har Ghar Tiranga [Tricolour atop Every House] campaign, almost all houses, shops and stores had the Indian flag fluttering from their rooftops. We drove past the simple people of the border belt, largely Hindus, diligently going about their daily lives; the local transport was abuzz on the tarred roads and the old men sat under trees.

As we started to approach the border, the army pickets, camouflaged with nettings, became discernible. We passed through the narrow alleys of Hamirpur Kona, flanked by a cluster of pucca houses and small groceries. Many of these houses belong to retired and serving army men. The tradition of joining the army and other uniformed forces remains strong here, the patriotism perhaps stemming from the horrors of Partition and the wars fought by the nation. On the outskirts of the village, we were stopped by a Sikh soldier who manned a barricade. My friend respectfully stopped the SUV and said, 'Jai Hind, *paaji.*' The Sikh soldier peeped inside the vehicle, adjusted the Insas rifle on his soldier, raised the barricade and waved to us, saying, '*Lang aayo* [Come over].'

After driving on a muddy track for a few hundred metres, a group of men could be seen sitting under a shed. At a short distance, the Chenab was flowing in all tranquillity.

We got down from the vehicle and clicked some photographs: of the river, the crop swirling in the fields and the Pakistani posts with their green-and-white flags. We chatted with the men playing cards; some of whom were old and had crooked teeth. A customary conversation veered towards politics and how Pakistan needed to be a taught a lesson for sponsoring terrorism on Indian soil. 'Wasn't there a Sohni–Mahiwal memorial nearby?' I enquired. '*Tayada matlab shayad mandir kane hai* [I think you mean the temple], a middle-aged man responded. '*O the unda si, us tapu tei, lekin aad bahai leiya uno* [It used to be on that island but the deluge consumed it],' he continued, pointing towards an island amidst two braids of the river. For the inhabitants of Hamirpur Kona, the memorial of Sohni–Mahiwal was nothing less than a temple. However, in 2016, a strong flood on the Chenab swept away the statue of Sohni–Mahiwal, as if rehashing their tragic story once again.

We turned and drove back to the other side of Hamirpur Kona. There was a flurry of activity since it was the southern end of the under-construction bridge over the Chenab. The cylindrical piers stood erect in the water, one after another. By the time we stood beside the river, the sky was laden with threatening clouds, perfectly coalescing with the dark-coloured waters of the Chenab underneath. I breathed in the river and absorbed its chatter and bubble, observing its sinuous charge, garrulous and steady, whimpering and chuckling, threatening and soothing. I moved forward, squatted at the edge of the river and ran my hand on its layers; the water felt icy cold, some of it perhaps surviving from the two glacial lakes of Baralacha La. I cupped some water and threw it over my head, wetting my hair. Temporarily, albeit in a poetic manner, I had become part of the Chenab, and some essence of me perhaps moved forward with the river towards Pakistan. Natalie Diaz, in 'Postcolonial Love Poem', says poignantly: 'Water remembers everything it travels over and through. If you have been in water, part of you remains there still.'

As we drove back after a memorable visit, we travelled alongside Sua Number 1. It is a narrow channel drawn from the Chenab that forms part of the robust canal system in this area. A few times, militants sponsored by Pakistan have travelled along this route to attack Indian installations in the hinterland, as seen during the pre-dawn Chinore attack in August 2008.

15

The New Passport

Alertly watched by the gun-toting soldiers from the observation posts of India and Pakistan, the Chenab quietly enters into the broad alluvial lowlands of Pakistan. After living its life with Indian identity – Asikini, Chandrabhaga, the dark-coloured waters – the river acquires here a new passport and nationality. It whizzes merrily through Sialkot district without any melodrama or hype. The water is babbling and burbling, soaking in the new countryside, absorbing within itself the sonorous prayer calls from the mosques and the rhythm of qawalis from Sufi shrines. At Behlolpur village of the adjoining district of Gujrat, the Tawi and the Manawar Tawi join the Chenab.

The city of Sialkot – mentioned as Sagala in Greek records – has had its place in history. On his Indian campaign, Alexander is said to have conquered the city and razed it to warn the nearby cities that might resist his invasion. The city was rebuilt by Menander, and it became the capital of the Indo-Greek kingdom. After extensively debating with the monk Nagsena of Kishtwar, King Menander embraced Buddhism and Sialkot became a great centre of Buddhist learning. During the course of history, the region saw many upheavals as it was raided plundered, ruled and then lost by many kings and dynasties.

In modern times, Sialkot has been the land of great intellectualism and trade. One of Pakistan's most illustrious sons, Muhammad Iqbal

– a philosopher, scholar, poet and politician – was born in Sialkot in 1877 to a Kashmiri family. Iqbal's revolutionary poetry in Urdu and Persian is considered as the greatest in the twentieth century. Considered as one of the founders of the Pakistan Movement, his political thought influenced a generation of educated Muslims. Being an ardent supporter of Jinnah and his politics, Iqbal always propagated the unity of Muslims. In the poem 'Jawab-e-Shikwa' [Answer to the Complaint], Iqbal laments:

Harm-e-paak bhi Allah bhi Quran bhi aik,
Kuch bari baat thi hote jo, Musalmaan bhi aik!

[And one your Ka'ba, one your God, and one your great Quran;
Yet, still, divided each from each, lives every Musalmaan.]

In the hustle-bustle of the city, the house of the great poet – Iqbal Manzil – stands as a testimony to his legend. It has been turned into a museum and is visited by thousands of people. Many of his personal belongings, including the study table, are preserved inside the museum.

Apart from intellectual bearings, Sialkot became one of the most prominent industrial and export hubs of Pakistan. The city has been known for its paper making, leatherwork and metal industry. However, in the colonial era, the city became a prominent centre for manufacturing of sports goods. Initially, the easy availability of high-quality timber promoted the making of cricket bats, polo and hockey sticks. Much of this wood came from the forests of Jammu and Kashmir, transported on the current of the Chenab. Initially, the finished goods were meant for the bored British soldiers posted in North-West Frontier Province. Gradually, the industry grew and the supplies fanned out to other parts of British India.

In due course, the business shifted to football. Spread over 200 factories and 2,000 stitching centres, production of hand-sewn footballs became the biggest sport industry in Sialkot. After cutting and moulding of the leather, the patching and sewing of the balls was mostly done by the women. Hunkering down in dingy places, scores of them would stich footballs amidst gossip and chatter. These women were paid paltry sums for each ball sewn; sometimes, their monthly salaries were lesser than the eventual price a single football would fetch in European and American markets. Most of the times, the women were allowed to carry work home, where they would balance their domestic duties with football sewing.

The legend of how the football industry came to Sialkot dates to more than a hundred years ago, when a local cobbler was purportedly asked to repair a football brought to him by a British officer. The said cobbler learned how to stich footballs and went on to make a fortune peddling them to British soldiers. This brought a revolution as many football production units opened up. Generally, the footballs were manufactured by the city's Muslim craftsmen and marketed by Hindu and Sikh middlemen. Today, Sialkot produces 60 per cent of the world's footballs and is labelled as the football manufacturing capital of the world. The sporting giants like Nike, Adidas, Puma and Reebok all get their supply of footballs from Sialkot before their famous logos are embossed on them.[112]

And when a football game is afoot besides a destroyed Ukrainian tank in Bakhmut or the silver sands of Mar Bella Beach in Barcelona, under the shadow of Ho Chi Minh statue in Saigon or in a street enclosed by walls splattered with Goddess Durga graffiti in Kolkata, there is a good chance that the ball was sewn in Sialkot. From the crime-infested slums of São Paulo in Brazil and side alleys of Rotterdam in the Netherlands to the war-ravaged ruins of Basra in Iraq and Moshood Abiola National Stadium, Abuja, Nigeria, whenever a football is kicked, chested, headed or handled, there is a Sialkot connect to it. From celebrated football leagues like Bundesliga and UEFA Cup to Calcio Fiorentino of Italy and recreational games in Bangladesh jails, from second-tier football clubs of Addis Ababa to city squares in Seoul, South Korea, from 'Atlas Lions' of Morocco to the kids donning Luka Modrić jerseys in

Zagreb, Croatia, the Sialkot football dances between the feet and the head. A prominent Sialkot-based company called Forward Sports has been supplying balls for FIFA World Cups since 2014. In the eightieth minute of the 2022 Qatar World Cup final, when Kylian Mbappe equalized with a ferocious volley, it was an Adidas Al Rihla from Sialkot that was netted in the Argentina goal.

However, before becoming the football manufacturing capital of the world, the well-established sports industry of Sialkot underwent a colossal upheaval during Partition. Overnight, many Hindu and Sikh manufacturers and traders packed their wares and started anew in Jalandhar, which would later go on to become the sports manufacturing hub on the Indian side. This indefatigable spirit of survival and rebellion of the people, perhaps arising from the poetry of Iqbal, was further consolidated by the work of Faiz Ahmad Faiz.

In 1911, Faiz was born in an influential family of Kala Qader area of Sialkot. The village is situated near the India–Pakistan border. He would go on to become one of the most influential Urdu/Persian writers and poets of his time. A man of many talents, Faiz worked as a teacher, army officer, journalist, trade unionist and broadcaster. For his communist politics, Faiz was jailed; he spent four years in prison. However, it was his poetry that had a great impact on the literary landscape of both India and Pakistan. His verses are celebrated on popular outlets like Coke Studio. His poem, 'Hum Dekhenge' (We Shall See) became an anthem of resistance and defiance. Faiz composed the poem in 1979 as a protest against the oppressive reign of Zia-ul-Haq. In India, the poem was invoked by student protests in various universities in the last few years. The powerful words challenge the mightiest of regimes and authority:

Hum dekhenge, hum dekhenge, lazim hai ki hum bhi dekhenge
Hum dekhenge, hum dekhenge, woh din ki jis ka vaada hai
Jo lauh-e-azal mein likha hai, hum dekhenge, hum bhi dekhenge
Jab zulm-o-sitam ke koh-e-garan, rooyi ki tarah ud jayenge, hum dekhenge

Hum mehkumon ke paon tale, yeh dharti dhar dhar dharkegi
Aur ahl-e-hakam ke sar oopar, jab bijli kar kar karkegi

[We shall see, we shall see, it is inevitable (that) we too shall see
We will see, we will see, the day that has been promised
That is written in the book of destiny, we will see, we too shall see
When the mountains of oppression and cruelty will float away like carded wool, we will see
Underneath our feet, we the governed, the ground will echo like a thumping heartbeat and the sky over the heads of the rulers will echo with the sound of thunder.]

Unfortunately, there is no symbol of remembrance related to Faiz in Sialkot. Unlike the case of Iqbal, there is not a single street, building or library named after Faiz. One reason could be that after his father's death, the haveli in which Faiz grew up was sold off to repay debts. This severed the family's immediate connection to the city. In his ancestral village of Kala Qader, now renamed as Faiz Nagar, a dingy lane leads to a house with a door that stands out for its strikingly elaborate woodwork. A plaque announces it as the abode of Faiz's father. The house was once part of a larger compound-style haveli. Now it is sandwiched between comparatively recent constructions: those that bear none of the aesthetics of old mansions or the earthy poetics of mud-baked houses. Surely, such kind of dwellings must have dotted the landscape when Faiz would have visited the home in his youthful days![113]

Beyond the rivers, there has been a historic link between Sialkot and Jammu from time immemorial. In the early nineteenth century, when Sikh misls were subjugating the Muslim principalities all over the north, many people from Sialkot ran away and took shelter in Jammu. Similarly, in the pre-Partition days, a large number of people from Jammu would look for employment in Sialkot, allured by its prosperity.

This connection was further solidified due to the efforts of Maharaja Pratap Singh, who got 27 miles of railroad laid between Sialkot and Jammu in 1890. According to the 1935 railways timetable, four trains ran between Sialkot and Jammu. This ninety-minute journey not only strengthened the trade and cultural ties but also brought common people together on so many levels. In the 1940s, a group of young men in Sialkot could board the train, watch a movie in Jammu and return home the same day. All this changed after the partition of the country. Notwithstanding the standstill agreement signed by the Maharaja, train operations between Sialkot and Jammu were abruptly suspended in October 1947, and were never resumed again.

Among the four prominent stations on the suspended line, Suchetgarh is right on the border. On the other side, one can clearly see Pakistani outposts, the minarets of mosques, ostentatiously decorated public transport and farmers engaged in the basmati paddy fields. The old building of Suchetgarh railway station is now occupied by a company of the BSF. Though the rails have been uprooted, one can still walk on the stoned pavement that used to be the platform and reach the BSF company commander's office now housed in the office of the station master. A green-and-white milestone announces nostalgically: Lahore–141 km, Sialkot–11 km.

In 2001, when Jammu Cantonment Railway Station at Bikram Chowk was converted into an art centre, all the tell-tale signs of the erstwhile railway line between Sialkot and Jammu were obliterated. Not only the railways but also the lights of Sialkot, once visible from the vantage points of Jammu at night, are now obfuscated due to the pollution.

After assimilating the Tawi and the Manawar Tawi at Behlolpur, the Chenab is regulated at Marala Headworks – one of the four barrages on the river. The other three are: Khanki Headworks located in Gujranwala district, Qadirabad Headworks in Mandi Bahauddin district and Trimmu Barrage in Jhang district. The Khanki Headworks – from where the Lower Chenab Canal originates is the oldest barrage on the Chenab and was built in 1892 by British engineers. On the other hand, Marala started as a weir in 1912 and was converted into a barrage in 1968. Two major water channels originating here – Upper Chenab Canal and Marala–Ravi Link Canal – along with the Lower Chenab Canal, feed the branch canals. The intricate maze of canals, forming one of the largest irrigation systems of the world, run like arteries – giving life to almost the whole of Punjab.

A large portion of fields nourished by these canals belong to rich landlords and are tilled by the landless. The high-walled mansions of the former coexist in perfect congruity with the latter's modest dwellings. In towns and villages, the five prayers of the day billow from the loudspeakers of the masjids, imploring the faithful to the call of the almighty. In the morning, many small children would run to the schools, the satchels swinging on their shoulders. Many of them would get enrolled in madrasas run by various religious organizations. The young boys in their skullcaps would sit facing Mecca and bob their heads back and forth in perfect rhythm while memorizing the Holy Quran. Then the long-bearded maulvis, accompanied by jihad entrepreneurs, would come for talent spotting. Some of the boys belonging to poverty-stricken families would be picked up and enrolled in Islamic seminaries and training camps run by the Contractors of Death, belonging to proscribed outfits. After their indoctrination and training, donning badges of religious duty and dreaming of seventy-two virgins in paradise, these terrorists would infiltrate the Indian territory, guided by their maps and global positioning system (GPS) devices. Then they would settle in the forests on the hills, and hide in safehouses and kill innocents. Many of these terrorists would sneak into the Chenab Valley, line up innocent people and kill them in cold blood in the name of the holy war. Most of them would not return, ending up in nameless graves at unknown places.

On its onward journey, the Chenab flows through the twin cities of Gujrat and Wazirabad, situated on either side of the river. Wazirabad was founded in the seventeenth century by Wazir Khan, the grand vizier of the Mughals and court physician of Shah Jahan. During the Mughal reign, a large number of mansions, caravanserais, mosques and wells were built here. It also came to prominence as a major trading centre. After the decline of the Mughals, the city fell into the hands of Sikhs. Today, some of the ancient, dilapidated buildings with quaint brickwork, arches and domes still exist, caught in the labyrinth of narrow alleys and congested squares.

The city continues to be an industrial hub, with its tanneries, joineries, pressure cooker units, flour mills and lock factories. More importantly, Wazirabad is known as the City of Cutlery for its cutlery industry, the products of which are exported world over. The cutlery industry emanated from the presence of a large number of blacksmiths in the town. During World War II, the industry got a major fillip since knives, swords, bayonets, scabbards, sheaths and daggers were produced on a large scale for the Allied Forces. The industry suffered after Partition, but with the support of the government, it bounced back.[114]

Wazirabad is an important rail junction, with Sialkot and Faisalabad lines of the Pakistan Western Railway branching off and crossing the Chenab at the Alexandra Bridge. The 2,830 m-long bridge was completed in 1876 and was inaugurated by the Prince of Wales. When the first train chugged between Wazirabad and Gujrat – 20 miles away – it was lauded as an engineering marvel only to be surpassed by the Lansdowne Bridge, thirteen years later.

The Lansdowne Bridge, locally called Ayub Bridge, spanned the river Indus at Sukkur and was the largest cantilever bridge of the times. After the completion of the bridge, when it came for the trial run, the railway authorities fell into a tizzy. The length of the bridge and the gurgling waters underneath made the train drivers very jittery to undertake the first run. When the government announced a cash prize for the perilous task, Jamalo Sheedi Baloch, a resident of Sukkur, came forward. Jamalo was a death-row prisoner languishing in a prison close to the newly constructed bridge. Not interested in cash prize, Jamalo took advantage of the situation and signed an agreement with the British administration – that he would be spared from execution if he successfully drove the train over the bridge. On the inauguration day, hundreds of locals, including Jamalo's family, stood on the sidelines with bated breath. When the train slowly chugged across the bridge, with Jamalo as the driver, his family rose to jubilation: '*Leko khati ayo khair saan, ho Jamalo, wah wah Jamalo* [Oh great Jamal, you have become victorious without facing any loss].' The song remains popular to this day and its many versions are sung all over the world.[115]

The Alexandria Bridge had no songs associated with it, but it was an important marvel bridging people across the Chenab. On the other side of the bridge from Wazirabad lies the city of Gujrat: located between the Jhelum and the Chenab. Under the Mughals, the city witnessed much progress. Akbar built the Gujrat Fort and allowed the Gujjars to settle in the area, providing the peripatetic people, a permanent home. Thus, the town came to be known as Gujrat.

Gujrat is best known for the immortal love story of Sohni and Mahiwal. Though many villages and towns along the Chenab have claimed ownership of the story, historians have pointed out the irrefutable connection of the lovers with Gujrat. During the Mughal rule, Gujarat had a prominent position on the trade route between Bukhara in Uzbekistan and Delhi. Apart from the caravanserais, horse stables and pleasure houses, the place boasted of many trade outlets especially of earthenware.

Sohni was the daughter of Toolah, a potter of a nearby village, and was renowned for her beauty. While Toolah worked hard on the potter's wheel, giving life to pitchers, pots, tumblers and other figurines, it was Sohni's artistic hand that created beautiful designs of flowers, creepers and brilliant motifs on them. Then the painted ware was put on sale in their shop: the same spot where Rampayari Mahal was constructed on the bank of the Chenab. In a glorious illustration of serendipity, Rampayari Mahal, too, echoes of a passionate love story. The extravagant palace was built by Rai Bahadur Sunder Das Chopra for his second wife Rampayari, whom he loved madly.

As per the folklore, Izzat Baig, a rich and handsome trader from Bukhara, happened to camp in Gujrat for business. While on a casual stroll through the bazaar, he happened to see Sohni in her father's shop and was completely besotted by her poise and beauty. Baig started to regularly visit the shop, hoping for a glimpse of Sohni. He would always buy one piece of earthenware to justify his presence. In the silent language of love, spoken mainly through the eyes, Sohni lost her heart to him. Izzat Baig did not return to Bukhara and instead, took a menial job at Toolah's house to stay close to his love. He would take the buffaloes out for grazing and came to be known as Mahiwal or the buffalo herder.

As always, the secrecy of the love affair could not sustain for long. Within the potter community, it was considered blasphemous that a girl should wed outside the clan. Therefore, Sohni was hastily married off to a man from her community, who lived in the nearby village of Hamirpur. Drenched in deep sorrow, Mahiwal renounced the world and became a hermit. Eventually, he moved to a small cottage across the Chenab, opposite the village of Sohni's in-laws.

He would beckon her, gnawed by immense pain, as illustrated in a Punjabi song:

Par Channa de dise kulli yaar di.

[Right there across the Chenab is my beloved's hut.]

Sohni refused to consummate her marriage. Instead, she found her lover and started to meet him clandestinely. Each night, when others in the house would sleep, she would tiptoe out, with a pitcher clinging to her waist. With the aid of the inverted pitcher, Sohni would swim across the river to meet Mahiwal and return before dawn. The pining lover would wait for her with a fire lit outside his hut, cooking fish caught from the river.

Ghariya, ghariya aa ve ghariya
Raat haneri nadi thathan mardi.

[Come on, clay pot, let's keep going
The night is deathly dark, the river waves surge right around us.]

The whiff of the scandal spread and the lovers' rendezvous became grist of the gossip mill. One day, Sohni's sister-in-law discovered the place where she would hide her pitcher. She informed her mother, and both decided to replace Sohni's pitcher with an unbaked one. The song reveals that Sohni was aware about the consequences of using an unbaked pot in the strong current of the Chenab:

Kacchi meri mitti
Kaccha mera naam ni
Haan main nakaam ni
O main nakaam ni
Kacchiyaan da honda kaccha anjaam ni
Eh gal aam ni

[I am made of only clay, unbaked
It's only my fate that I'll melt away in the waters
I have failed, I have
Yes, I have failed
Things which are unsound, like me, will have a fate like mine too- uncertain.
And this is usual. It is what it is.]

Pained by pangs of separation, Sohni remained adamant and almost pleaded to the pitcher to keep her afloat, knowing well that she would die:

Haan laike khil ve
Aaj Mahiwal nu main jana mil we
Yaar nu milegi aaj laash yaar di.

> [So help transport me there must go meet Mahiwal this night at any cost tonight, a lover will be greeted with the corpse of his beloved.]

The Moon hung in the sky, its shadow floating on the gentle ripples of the Chenab. Sohni stepped into the river, firmly holding the pot in her hands. As she reached the midstream, her pitcher started crumbling, dissolving in the water. Mahiwal, who watched the waves carrying away his beloved to the depths, dived into the river to save her. But he, too, drowned. The lovers were consumed by the Chenab, reuniting them in death.

The story of Sohni–Mahiwal became a legend that still echoes on both sides of the border in the form of innumerable ballads, poems and songs. There have been many movies made about the lovers in languages like Sindhi, Punjabi, Urdu and Hindi. The story about Sohni's love was also documented in Sufi strains: where *Ishq Majazi* – love for the mortal – is considered a shortcut to *Ishq Haqiqi* – love for the immortal.

The love story has also attracted painters of Punjab, on either side of the divide, for centuries. The first known painting of Sohni came in the eighteenth century from the brush of a Pahari painter named Nainsukh Sen. The gifted artist depicted Sohni bare chested, with her wet hair cascading down her shoulders and falling on her breasts as she smilingly swims across the Chenab. The most popular Sohni–Mahiwal painting came in the 1950s, from the brush of

Sobha Singh, who had set up a studio near Palampur in Himachal Pradesh after Partition. The painting shows Sohni holding a pitcher in her left hand, with her drenched garment clinging to the contours of her body as she is taken in a semi-embrace by Mahiwal, both holding their heads high, sitting on the bank of the Chenab. The two lovers look alluring and ecstatic, as if kindled by the warmth of their love. This painting is the most recognizable face of the love story. Its cheap replicas are still found hanging in many middle-class homes, shops and stationery stores, and even painted behind trucks and other public transport.

The original painting is a prized possession of Dr Karan Singh and is in the collection of the Dogra Palace. Modern artists like Satish Gujral, Manjit Bawa and Arpana Caur have created their own versions from the legend of Sohni and Mahiwal. Arpana Caur, for example, in a series of paintings, has portrayed Sohni as a very courageous and strong woman who, according to her, 'swam while others slept'. She uses the pitcher as a motif, a sort of metaphor for Sohni. A painting by a renowned Pakistani artist, Ustad Allah Bakhsh, shows a distressed Mahiwal receiving the corpse of his beloved. The painting now enjoys a place of pride in the Lahore Museum.

Amidst all the hostility between the two countries, Sohni and Mahiwal continue to spread love transcending borders. So does music in a similar way. Some of the blacksmiths who settled in Wazirabad and Gujrat started using their tongs for a different purpose. Alam and Arif Lohar – father-and-son duo created devotional Sufi music. In 2006, Arif Lohar hit the popularity charts after his song 'Jugni' was broadcasted on the Pakistani music platform, Coke Studio. The song is a sixteenth-century composition by Hazrat Sultan Bahu, who was born in Shorkot, a small town on the banks of the Chenab in Jhang district. He wandered all over Punjab and spread his message through scholarly writings and poetry in Persian and Punjabi. Sultan Bahu's shrine was built in Shorkot, but when the Chenab changed its course, it was shifted to Garh Maharaja, 17 km away. People who were witness to his exhumation claimed that the body remained intact, despite the passage of many years.

Even before the advent of Coke Studio, 'Jugni' had become everlasting, resonating on both sides of the border for hundreds of years. The lyrics encapsulate the divine union of human beings with god through the medium of love:

Alif Allah Chambay di booti
Tey meray murshid mann vich layi hoo
Ho na fuss baat da paani dey key
Har ragaay harjai hoo
Ho jug jug jeevay murshid sohna
Hatay jiss ay booti lai ho.

[My master has planted the fragrant seed of love in my heart
Which flourished with modesty, piety and acceptance of his existence
My beloved is present in every throbbing pulse
My beloved is ever-present
The one who blew life into me.]

The Coke Studio version of the song attained immense popularity in India, blaring in discotheques, wedding parties and recreational gatherings. Arif's father, Amir Lohar, could not get such fame, but he spread the love all over the villages and townships, singing Sufi songs aided by the music of a tong.

Leaving the lovers and tongs behind, the Chenab flows forward and enters Gujranwala district. One of the largest cities of Pakistan, Gujranwala was founded in the eighteenth century and is a relatively modern city. The city derives its name from a village, Serai Gujran or the 'inn of Gujjars'. In the eighteenth century, the city served as the capital of Sukerchakia misl of the Sikhs and its most powerful scion, Ranjit Singh, was born here. He established the great Sikh Empire in 1792 and, seven years later, shifted the capital to Lahore. After the city was annexed by the British in 1848, a large number of Christian missionaries settled here, building schools and churches.

Since the Sikh rule, Gujranwala has had a great culture of wrestling. Among many reputed wrestlers of the time, Rahim Baksh Sultaniwala was one of the greatest. Rahim was born in a family of wrestlers, originally hailing from Kashmir. In 1820s, the family had shifted to the plains and finally settled down in Gujranwala. Weighing almost 300 pounds and standing 7 ft tall, Rahim was a veritable giant. To strike fear into his opponents, he would enter the wresting arena covered from head to toe in vermillion, appearing like a fearsome red demon. Rahim remained undefeated throughout his wrestling career, but his most formidable rivalry remained with Ghulam Mohammad Baksh. Yes, the same wrestler whose name is splattered all over Lahaul-Spiti and Ladakh: 'Don't be a Gama in the Land of Lama'!

Since Rahim towered over Gama – who was just 5 ft 7 in tall – everyone assumed that Rahim would win. However, Gama Pehalwan was not easily pinned down. They met four times, the first three bouts ending in draws. Their much anticipated fourth bout took place in Allahabad in 1910. After two and a half hours of a thrilling, grappling duel, Rahim broke his ribcage and had to concede the fight, resulting in a rare defeat for him. The tradition of wrestling continues in Gujranwala and today there are a number of Akharas – the hallowed pit where the sport is played – spread all over the region. Therefore, Gujranwala is also called *pehalwano ka shehar* [city of wrestlers].

Apart from the moves of the wrestlers, Gujranwala is also rich with the fragrance of immortal poetry, inked by the quills of the saints and poets.

The name of Amrita Pritam nee Kaur shimmers at the top of this list. Amrita was born in 1919, the year of the Jallianwalla Bagh massacre. Her father was a poet and a scholar who edited a literary journal. When Amrita was eleven years old, her schoolteacher mother died. Her father shifted to Lahore where she stayed till Partition. Affected by her mother's death, the lonely child began writing at an early age. Pritam, though starting off as a romantic poet, became part of the Progressive Writers' Movement (PWA) and started delving into social causes and feminism. After shifting to Delhi in 1947, Amrita's repertoire grew vastly: she wrote hundreds of books of poetry, fiction, essays, biographies and anthologies of Punjabi folksongs. A large part of body of her work has been translated into multiple languages. However, her tour de force, which immortalized her, was: '*Ajj aakhan Waris Shah nu* [Today, I invoke Waris Shah]', in which she encapsulated the horrors of Partition. In her heart-wrenching lament, a paragraph goes thus:

Aaj aakhan Waris Shah nu, kito qabran vicho bol
Te aaj kittabe ishaq da, koi agla warka khol
Ek royi si dhi Punjab di, tu likh likh maare wain
Aaj lakhan dhiyan rondiya, tenu Waris Shah nu khen
Ve dard mandaan diya dardiya, utth tak apna Punjab
Aaj bailey lashan bichiyan, te lahu di bhari Chenab
Kissi ne panjan paaniya wich, diti zehar rala.

[Today, I invoke Waris Shah; speak from your grave
And turn today, the book of love's next affectionate page
Once, a daughter of Punjab cried; you wrote a wailing saga
Today, a million daughters cry out to you, Waris Shah
Rise! O narrator of the grieving! Look at your Punjab
Today, fields are lined with corpses, and blood fills the Chenab
Someone has mixed poison in the five rivers' flow
Their deadly water is now, irrigating our lands galore!]

Waris Shah, the poet whom Amrita invokes, was an eighteenth-century Punjabi Sufi poet born in Jandiala Sher Khan, about 50 km from Gujranwala. For his body of work and contribution to Punjabi literature, Waris Shah is called the Shakespeare of Punjab. Not much is known about his early life, but his parents died when he was very young. After acquiring education, Waris Shah shifted to a small village, Malka Hans, where he lived an austere life in a small room next to a mosque. Here he composed his seminal work – the love story of Heer–Ranjha. It is said that when Waris Shah informed his master about the creation, he reprimanded him for writing a love story. He was even locked up in a room for a day. Next day, when he started narrating the story, his master's eyes welled up with tears due to the sheer magic of the composition.

The historians believe that Damodar Gulati was the first to narrate the tale, claiming to be its eyewitness. It is also believed that the story originated in Persia and that 'Heer' has been derived from the Greek goddess Hera. Others say that the story is a kind of reworking of the Radha Krishna myth. While there may have been earlier versions, Waris Shah's re-narration of the qissa, interspersed with the language, customs and anthropological details of the time, survives to this day.

It was also believed that the story came from Punjab, which was the abode of the Ranjha clan. Mauju Chaudhry, an influential landowner of the village, had four sons. Being the youngest and his father's favourite, Ranjha lived a luxurious life, playing melodious tunes on his flute while his brothers toiled on the land. Following his father's death, there was a dispute over the division of land and Ranjha left home in disgust. He arrived at Jhang, where one day he accidently met Heer Sial on the bank of the Chenab. From the first encounter, mesmerized by the melodies from Ranjha's flute, Heer and her friends started foraying into the nearby forests, hoping to encounter the flutist.

Heer and Ranjha fell in love and started meeting regularly in the forest. Heer introduced Ranjha to her father, who hired him for herding his cattle. Eventually, the lovers were seen by Heer's crippled uncle, Kaidu, who was affronted by a Sial girl's alliance with a lowly Ranjha. Married off forcibly to Saida of the Kheras clan in the village of Rangpur, Heer rebelled, refusing to wear new clothes or bridal jewellery, and declining food and water. She found a friend and confidante in her sister-in-law Sehti, who like her, was herself in love with Murad Bakhsh, a camel herder. The women conspired with Murad Bakhsh to escape from the village.

After hearing about Heer's marriage, Ranjha was so heartbroken that he shifted to Tilla Jogian, situated on Potohar plateau in the Salt Range of Punjab province. The place was a centre of asceticism, and a large number of Hindu Jogis, or mendicants, resided here. These Jogis were also called *kanphata*s because of their ear piercings. Ranjha also pierced his ears and tonsured his head. He renounced the material world and became a Jogi. With a bowl in his hand, he travelled from village to village, house to house, seeking alms. One day, he reached Rangpur and saw Heer. Their love was rekindled. Ranjha settled on a nearby hillock where Heer started to meet him again.

Meanwhile, Sehti and Heer had hatched a plan to elope with their lovers. As per the plan, Sehti bit Heer on her foot and spread the word that she had been bitten by a snake. Heer's in-laws sought the services of fakirs and hakims who unsuccessfully tried to cure her. Finally, Ranjha the Jogi was summoned. He ostensibly had a thousand spells in his flute that could cure her. That night Murad helped the lovers escape on camels. The Kheras pursued the star-crossed lovers and discovered them sleeping at an isolated spot. They took Heer away after assaulting Ranjha.

Ranjha sought justice from the local king, who ordered Heer to be restored to the Kheras. On hearing the judgment, the lovers invoked curses on the city of Jhang, owing to which it caught fire. The astrologers advised the king to conciliate the lovers. Heer returned to her parent's house and they finally decided to bestow her hand on Ranjha. However, on the day of her marriage, Kaidu offered Heer a sweetmeat laced with poison and she died instantly. When the news of Heer's death reached Ranjha, he quietly slipped into a room and knelt down to pray. Hours later, when someone entered to check on him, Ranjha was found dead. In their deaths, Heer and Ranjha's love story became immortal.[116]

Notwithstanding the power of the love story, in certain villages of Pakistan, the recitation of Waris Shah's Heer is prohibited. People believe that the verses could have bad influence on the young girls and they too could elope like Heer.

It is quite befitting that the story of the Chenab, which began with two celestial lovers called Chandra and Bhaga, is now ending with corporeal lovers. After all, isn't the Chenab *ashiqan da dariya*, the river of lovers?

Further away from Jhang, the Chenab bifurcates, passing by the towns of Rabwah and Chinote. Both the towns are perched on the Kirana hills or the Black Mountain. As one descends the hills, much of the surrounding area consists of alluvial plains interspersed with rocky outcroppings of slate and sandstone. The etymology of Chinote can be traced to two words: 'Chin' meaning 'Moon' and 'Ote' implying 'from behind'. In other words, the Moon rising from behind a mountain reflects on the placid waters of the Chenab, hence the place came to be known as Chinote. Another folklore is about a Mauryan princeses named Chandan, who, during a hunting trip, became enamoured by the place. She ordered a settlement to be established here and the area came to be known after her: Chandaniot. With the passage of time the name transfigured to 'Chinote'.

Chinote has flourishing trade practices but it is most famous for its woodwork. Given its proximity to the Chenab, ample timber was transported downriver from Jammu and Kashmir. The accumulated timber ended up in numerous joineries, sawmills and furniture factories. In the medieval times, the artisans of Chinote were renowned for their exquisite skills. Shah Jahan had employed these talented men in large numbers for the construction of the Taj Mahal.

Rabwah, which in Arabic means 'elevated place' is situated on a hill, on the other side of the riverbank. This hill stands like a trusted sentinel against the floods that are likely from the Chenab. Rabwah is considered one of the most isolated and mysterious cities of Pakistan. It exclusively houses the Ahmadiyya community, also known as the Qadiyan and Mirzais.

In 1834, Maharaja Ranjit Singh gave Qadiyan and five adjoining villages in the present-day Gurdaspur district to Mirza Ghulam Murtaza. It was a quid pro quo deal, a reward for Mirza's support in Kashmir and parts of hill kingdoms where the Sikhs had been engaged in military campaigns. In 1889, Murtaza Mirza's son Mirza Ghulam Ahmad established the Ahmadiyya movement and designated himself as the *mahdi* of the sect. Thus, Qadiyan became a major centre of Ahmadiyyas.

Finding themselves on the wrong side of the religious partition, the whole of Ahmadiyya community migrated to Pakistan. A decade later, the Pakistan government leased out about a thousand hectares of land in Chak Dhaggian to the Ahmadiyya community on payment of 12,000 Pakistani rupees. The formal inauguration of the settlement was done after prayers and a sacrifice of five goats. Chak Dhaggian was renamed as Rabwah. Temporary camps soon converted into mud and concrete houses.

It was not long before the activities and beliefs of the sect came in direct conflict with orthodox Islam. In 1974, through a constitutional amendment, the Ahmadiyyas were declared as non-Muslims. In 1984, the community was further ostracized by the promulgation of Ordinance XX by then-president Zia-ul-Haq. The ordinance forbids the Ahmadiyyas from adopting any Islamic practices, building mosques, quoting from the Holy Quran or taking honorific titles associated with Islam. Today, one doesn't see minarets of masjids rising in the sky space of Rabwah, and an eerie silence wraps itself around the city since there is a ban on the customary *azan* – the muezzin's call for prayers.

After the ordinance, there was a spate of violence against the Ahmadiyyas. Unable to handle the persecution, the then caliph migrated to the United Kingdom. He shifted the headquarters first to London, and later, to Tilford, Surrey. In 1998, the Provincial

Assembly of Punjab passed a resolution and changed the name of Rabwah to Nawan Qadiyan or the New Qadiyan. Next year, the name was changed to Chenab Nagar as an ode to the river. Today, the Ahmadiyyas have their close-knit community in at least 210 countries of the world, including regions like South Asia, West Africa, East Africa and Indonesia. However, the largest population still lives in Chenab Nagar, overlooking the river that has flowed past many different sects and beliefs, in her everlasting journey to the sea.

Passing through the sacred necropolis of saints who spread messages of compassion and brotherhood, as well as lovers who sacrificed their lives, the Chenab absorbs their influence on her essence as well. Luminescent in her acquired divinity, the river is now venerated as Pir Chenab. Having imbibed Buddhist chants, the blowing of conch shells, the laments of Shias, the Gurbani of the Gurudwaras, the radical beliefs of the Ahmadiyyas, the *kafis** of Sufis, the gospel prayers of the churches and the azan from the mosques, the river encompasses all that *ruhaniyat* or divinity and metamorphoses into a pir: an ascetic, a mendicant, elevated to sacredness.

The land alongside the river is rich with vegetation. Mango orchards, banyan trees and other fruit-laden trees are abundant in these parts. The trees inside and around the *ziyarats* have attained a special divinity of their own. When gullible people beseech their dead saints or *murshid*s buried in these mausoleums, they start to believe in their miraculous powers of granting boons. These trees become 'trees of wishes', as the devotees tie tiny pieces of threads to their boughs and twigs. Each thread denotes a wish sought – progeny for childless couples, prosperity for the destitute, divine benediction during examinations and job interviews, a visa to Dubai or protection from other bad omens. There might be beleaguered mothers who implore their murshids for the well-being of their

* A classical form of Sufi music

sons being hunted by security forces in Kashmir and the hills of the Chenab Valley, '*Ya Allah! Mere mujahid di hifazat farma!* [Oh God! Keep my holy warrior under your protection!]' There is no evidence as to how many of these wishes get fulfilled, but not many militants come back home.

On the banks of the Chenab, the small village of Midh Ranjha in Sargodha district has the largest and oldest banyan tree in Pakistan. It is said that the tree was planted about 600 years ago by Peer Murtaza Shah and his disciple Baba Roday Shah. From the host tree, the adventitious prop roots sprouting from the branches sink deep into the earth, forming accessory trunks, allowing the tree to spread outwards indefinitely. Today, the tree covers an area of about three acres. It is believed that harm shall befall anyone who damages the tree, which has led to its unabated growth and permanence. There is even an esoteric belief of Lord Krishna having composed the Bhagwat Gita originally under a banyan tree. Again, it was under a banyan tree that Siddhartha meditated and attained enlightenment. In the process, the tree came to be known as the Bodhi, the tree of enlightenment. When Siddhartha was deep in meditation and a demon, Devaputra Mara, came to distract him, it was the guardian spirit of the tree that emerged for his protection.[117]

Under the enormous shade of the tree, about twenty graves are visible. These include the graves of Peer Murtaza Shah and Baba Roday Shah, slowly being engulfed by the roots of the tree. Today, when the koels trill from the foliage, the tree roots encroach into the neighbourhood homes. The villagers have now started to cut the additional trunks to bring a stop to its further growth.

In Jhang district, the river is quiet, as if in the winter of her life, losing all her initial vitality. Throughout history, Jhang has been visited by conquerors, invaders, saints and travellers. The Greeks, Turks, Mongols, Mughals, Sikhs and British – all had their fingers in the pie of history. Ibn Batuta, the Moroccan traveller, who hurtled through these areas in the fourteenth century, has mentioned Jhang in his travelogue. In Punjabi, *jhang* means bushes or shrubs; therefore, it is plausible that the name is derived from the forests that once surrounded the area. Amidst all the resting places of saints spread over Jhang district, there also lies the modest dwelling of a favourite son of the soil named Mohammad Abdus Salam, who was one of the most celebrated members of the Ahmadiyya community.

A theoretical physicist, Abdus Salam shared the 1979 Nobel Prize in Physics with two other physicists. He was awarded the prize for his contribution to the electroweak unification theory. In 1974, when the Parliament of Pakistan, unanimously passed a bill declaring members of Ahmadiyya community as non-Muslims, Abdus Salam left the country in protest. He passed away in Oxford, England, in 1996. He was buried in Bahishti Maqbara, a cemetery established by the Ahmadiyya community in Rabwah. The epitaph on his tomb initially read: *First Muslim Nobel Laureate*. The Pakistan government removed the reference to 'Muslim' and left only his name on the headstone.

Notwithstanding all the warfare, sainthood and physics, Jhang is most remembered for the immortal love story of Heer–Ranjha. On the outskirts, not far from the bank of the Chenab, a narrow street flanked by small shops leads uphill to the tomb of the lovers. Most of these shops sell bangles, threads, booklets of Peer Waris Shah and plaster-of-Paris statues of Heer and Ranjha. The tomb, crowned by a green dome, is constructed on a mound and the land descending on its three sides is replete with graves. Sometimes the lovers visiting the shrine take a stroll through these graves, shyly muttering sweet nothings. On the external walls of the shrine, numerous names of young lovers and their passionate messages are engraved. Inside the shrine, there are two old banyan trees in the courtyard, denoting the two lovers. The distance between them is symbolic of their unconsummated love. Under the shadows cast by the trees, numerous lit and unlit earthen lamps are placed to seek boons. The boughs of the trees are bound with threads by lovers facing problems in getting married. Girls looking to get married tie bangles here, and childless women offer cradles. On special days, the local artists, aided with their one-stringed instruments and wizened harmoniums, mournfully play the elegies written by Shah Hussain and Waris Shah.

Inside the sanctum sanctorum, Heer and Ranjha lie in eternal sleep, interred in a cot-shaped common grave. The grave is adorned with colourful chadors bordered with golden trimmings. Some say only Heer is buried here, once again separated from her lover. The dome in the mausoleum, sheltering the hallowed grave, doesn't have a roofing. The locals believe that rain does not enter the chamber, a miracle attributed to the lovers. The effort to repair the roof was undertaken thrice but inexplicably ended up failing. Apparently, the curse of the lovers, against the hard world that conspired against their union, is still playing out.

Wide and enormous, Chenab is all set to welcome other rivers and engulf them inside her own dark-coloured waters. Jhelum comes first, which has had its own journey, rising from Verinag at the foothill of Pir Panjal in south Kashmir. Traversing through the valley, the Jhelum enters POK through a deep narrow gorge. It meets Neelum River, its largest tributary, at Domel, Muzaffarabad. The Neelum enters Pakistan Punjab from Jhelum district and, flowing through the plains, takes a southwest turn to assimilate into Chenab at Trimmu. Here, a barrage was constructed downstream of the confluence. The barrage was built by English engineers in 1939 to channel the water into the canals for irrigation and also as a measure for flood control.

On her further course, Ahmadpur Sial, a small town to the south of district Jhang, witnesses the confluence of the Ravi and Chenab. The Ravi rises in the Himalayas in Himachal Pradesh. After flowing past Chamba, she turns southwest at the boundary of Jammu and

Kashmir and then gushes by for about 50 miles inside west Punjab. She passes by Lahore and turns westwards near Kamalia in Toba Tek Singh district and empties into Chenab at Ahmadpur Sial. The town Toba Tek Singh was named after a kind-hearted Sikh, Tek Singh. Legend has it that Singh served water and provided shelter to the weary travellers passing by a *toba* or a small pond. The place eventually came to be called Toba Tek Singh. Later, a satirical story, 'Toba Tek Singh' by Sadat Hassan Manto, became a sweeping statement on the apathy of two countries towards the victims of Partition.

On her forward journey, the Chenab glides by the town of Layyah. One of the oldest inhabited areas in Pakistan, Layyah is a sandy land between the Indus and Chenab. Layyah derives its name from a wild shrub of fuel wood, commonly known as *layyan* or lie, which is grown in half of the district. The other half is Thal desert with a sparse vegetation consisting of thorny bushes.

One of the longest rivers in the world, the mighty Indus stretches over 3,200 km, and is the source of India's name. The great Indus Valley Civilization thrived around its fertile riverbanks. The river rises in west Tibet's Mount Kailash, at the confluence of Sengge Zangbo, also known as the Lion's Mouth, which is a perennial spring, and the river Gar Tsangpo. Then it turns northwards through Ladakh, where the river Zanskar joins the Indus with its own untrammelled flow, and meanders through Baltistan and Gilgit.

Replenished by the glacial waters of the Shyok, Shigar, Suru and Gilgit rivers, the Indus traverses through the Lower Himalayas, Karakoram Range and Hindu Kush mountains. Then it moves as far as the Kohistan region of Khyber Pakhtunkhwa province, where the colossal glaciers on the slopes of Karakoram Range, the Kohistan Highlands, enhance it with fresh water. The river now skirts around the northern and western sides of Nanga Parbat massif, swirling through deep gorges, widening at will. After emerging from the highlands, the Indus flows as a rapid mountain river between the Swat River and Hazara district until it reaches the reservoir of

Tarbela Dam. The Kabul River joins the Indus just above Attock. Finally, it cuts across the Salt Range near Kalabagh to enter the Punjab plains, flowing lethargically in braided formations. Before flowing past Mianwali, Rajanpur, Dera Ghazi Khan, Jhang and Layyah, it edges closer to Chenab, preparing for the ultimate union.

On a different course, Chenab continues on the last leg of her journey. When the river meets Satluj, 17 km north of Uch, it is an ineffable intermingling, where who consumes whom is unknown, but Chenab ends up losing her identity, only to find prominence as Akesines in Greek texts. The other Hellenized forms of the river – Sandrophagos, Sandabaga and Cantabara – also find frequent mention.

During his Indian conquest, Alexander founded the Alexandria town at the confluence of river Akesines and Indus. The historians resort to hyperbolic exuberance while talking about the vastness of the river; almost three miles wide, and how difficult it was to tame its boisterous waters. However, Alexander was able to erect an impressive citadel on the banks of the mighty Akesines. With the passage of time, the citadel, along with the city of Alexandria, passed into history and the rivers also changed their courses. In modern-day Pakistan, the town of Uch Sharif stands on the buried remains of the ancient Greek city. Located on an elevation, the place started to be called *Uch* in local parlance, which means high or raised. The place became a refuge for Muslim religious scholars fleeing persecution in the twelfth century. In the present day, the town remains a famous tourist and pilgrimage centre, renowned for its beautiful shrines dedicated to Sufi mystics.

Suddenly, all the stories the Chenab carried from Baralacha La perish in the waters: the tragedies of soldiers, rashly driven vehicles, helicopters crashing against the cable of a cradle box, the occasional chalang from Gajpat Bridge, Range Officer Todd and his loving dog, the honeymooners' taxi, Sub-inspector Sushil Khajuria, the victims of crime, Sohni–Mahiwal and the smorgasbord of unending characters, caught in the Chenab's menacing flow.

The mystic Satluj, referred as 'Satudri' in the 'Nadi Stuti' hymn, is another river to reckon with. Longest of the five rivers of Punjab, it rises in Lake Rakshastal in Tibet. Then it flows under the Tibetan name Langgen Zangbo or the Elephant River and enters Himachal Pradesh through Shipki La, a pass between India and China. The Satluj enters Punjab, and near Harike, the district of Tarn Taran, Beas drains into it. Onwards, the Sutlej enters Pakistan about 15 km east of Bhedian Kalan, Kasur district of Punjab, and flows through Bahawalpur district, it meets the Chenab at Uch Sharif, forming the Panjnad River, or the Five Rivers.

The Panjnad flows 44 miles southwest to its junction with the Indus near Mithankot in Rajanpur district. The confluence of the Panjnad and the Indus is overlooked by the impressive mausoleum of Khawaja Ghulam Fareed, the famous Sufi poet of Saraiki dialect of Punjabi. He was born in 1885 in Mithankot and, after being orphaned at a very young age, was brought up by his elder brother. Ghulam Fareed memorized the Quran at the age of eight. On hearing about the child prodigy, the nawab of Bahawalpur took him under his wing as a protégé, providing him religious education in his own palace. Purportedly, Ghulam Fareed left for the Cholistan Desert after the demise of his brother and settled there for eighteen years. The wilderness of the desert and his own solitude reflected in his work, which evokes melancholic beauty. Befittingly, the Chenab, with her last heartbeats lost forever in the Panjnad and the Indus, bids farewell in the milieu of Sufi musings.

Taking the five rivers of Punjab in its embrace, the Indus flows through a gorge near Sukkur and into the fertile plains of Sindh, passing by Jacobabad, Hyderabad and Mohenjo-Daro in Larkana district. The river forms a large delta to the south of Thatta near Karachi, finally terminating in the blue waters of the Arabian Sea.

Afterword

On a languorous afternoon on 22 April 2025, the news started to trickle in. Soon, television channels were agog in varying decibels, breaking the various versions of the terror attack. Think about Pahalgam (The Valley of Shepherds) and the first images that come to mind are the silver waters of the Lidder River cleaving through the valley, anglers waiting patiently for their share of trout and dense pine forests cascading from the snowcapped mountains. On these mountains there are sporadic expanses of idyllic meadows which come to life in the summers, when the nomadic clans camp here with their livestock feeding on the lush grass.

Situated at a height of 8000 m, Baisaran, also known as 'mini-Switzerland', is one such meadow, popular among the tourists as a picnic spot and an ideal place for photoshoots. It also serves as a base camp for the trek to Tulian Lake. Located at a distance of about 6 km from the Pahalgam market, the meadow is accessible only on foot or a pony ride. On that fateful day, the place was bubbling with tourists from various parts of the country. Some were just soaking in the fresh air, feeling the pleasant chill under their wind cheaters and light pullovers, many others huddled around makeshift shacks sipping hot cups of tea and scooping up the ubiquitous tourist snack – Maggi noodles – served in paper bowls. The Kashmiri ponywallhas sat on the sidelines, smoking and chatting, patiently waiting to ferry the tourists back. Their ponies grazed about and occasionally neighed out of boredom. Everyone appeared to be happy – the extended families, the old and the young, some shooting videos on the zip line, the kids merrily zorbing or jumping on the trampolines and the love-struck honeymoon couples romantically loitering around without a care of the world.

Suddenly, four terrorists, armed with M4 carbines and Kalashnikovs, appeared from the forest overlooking the meadow. They were filled with murderous wrath as they moved from group to group, questioning the frightened men, *'Mazhab kya hai tumhara, Hindu ya Musalmaan? Kalma padh kar sunayo.'* [What is your religion, Hindu or Muslim? Can you recite the Kalma?] For the next twenty minutes, the serenity of the meadow was shattered by gunfire and the cries of the victims. Soon, twenty-six men – including a Nepalese citizen and a local pony operator – lay dead in a pool of blood, most shot through their heads at a point-blank range.

The unprecedented massacre of innocent vacationers not only left their families grieving but sent the whole nation into mourning. A photograph of a young bride kneeling helplessly beside her dead husband, with her hands resting on her knees, seared the soul of the nation. In the photograph, her bridal bangles and the vermillion in the parting of her hair are clearly visible. She was later identified as Himanshi, a schoolteacher, now widow of Vinay Narwal, a Navy lieutenant from Karnal, Haryana. The couple had married six days earlier and were honeymooning in Kashmir. The picture went viral in a short time, symbolizing the tragedy that had befallen the country, not merely the twenty-six affected families.

The responsibility of the massacre was taken by The Resistance Front (TRF), an offshoot of the notorious Lashkar-e-Taiba, a Pakistan-based jihadi outfit. Therefore, the complicity of Pakistani actors working in an ecosystem created by their government became evident. The strong Indian leadership was quick to act, taking a slew of political, economic and diplomatic measures to sever ties with Pakistan. The most significant step was to keep the Indus Water Treaty in abeyance.

The Partition of 1947 had facilitated the division of territory, armed forces, industries, assets and liabilities of the central treasury, including gold reserves and currency. The Indian Civil Service also divided its officers, staff, departmental records and even stationery and furniture. Under these circumstances, how do you distribute the water? The rivers in the Indus system originate from the Indian Himalayas or Tibetan glaciers and flow through the undivided Punjab to finally drain into the Arabian Sea. Who held the ownership of these waters? The Chenab, for example, originates from Baralacha La and enters Pakistan from Akhnoor to finally merge with the Indus. Does it mean that the Chenab has two mothers? If so, who has a lawful right over the daughter?

The sharing of waters became a contentious issue between the two countries and after prolonged negotiations, the Indus Water Treaty was brokered by the World Bank in 1960. According to the treaty, the control of the water of three eastern rivers – Beas, Ravi and Sutlej – was given to India; similarly, the control of three western rivers – Indus, Chenab and Jhelum – was given to Pakistan. Despite being an upper riparian country, the experts appreciated India's generosity, having conceded water in more than a just manner. Apart from the sharing of the waters, the treaty also laid down the protocols for dam projects, water storage, designs and data-sharing. The treaty also constituted a Permanent Indus Commission, having a commissioner from each country, to bilaterally solve any future disputes arising in the sharing of waters. Whenever tensions flared between the two countries, the sanctity of the treaty has been questioned. Pakistan's continuous support of cross-border terrorism once prompted the Indian prime minister to comment: 'Water and blood cannot flow together.' Despite grave provocations, the treaty stood the test of time, outliving three wars and periods of severe hostility. Whenever issues arose, they were amicably settled within the framework of the treaty.

The Baisaran massacre changed all the rules. A day after the suspension of the treaty, the sluices at Baghlihar and Salal Hydroelectricity Projects were closed. In the coming days, the water receded rapidly, turning the roar of the river to a whimper. At

Akhnoor, the water had reduced so much that the stones and pebbles emerged from the riverbed. It seemed that the invincibility of the river had finally been conquered. For the locals it became a wondrous spectacle, and they thronged Jia Pota Ghat in their thousands. Some rolled up the ends of their trousers and simply walked across the river. The crossing boats stood by, mute witnesses to this frenzy. Since the suspension of the treaty, India has made calculations about the stoppage and release of water.

On 7 May 2025, India launched 'Operation Sindoor' and smoked out terrorists from Muridke (the headquarters of Lashkar-e-Taiba), Bahawalpur (headquarters of Jaish-e-Mohammad) and seven other terrorist camps in Pakistan and POK. The precision strikes were meant to avenge the vermillion of Himanshi and others. On 9 May 2025, India, in blistering strikes, hit eleven installations of the Pakistan Air Force, which included the Noor Khan airbase in Rawalpindi and the Mushaf airbase in Sargodha. A day later, due to some seismic activity, it appeared that these were not innocuous strikes as rumours about nuclear radiation from the Kirana Hills started to float around.

The Kirana Hills or the Black Mountain, is an extensive rocky mountain range located between the Jhelum and Chenab rivers, the latter flowing by the southern edge of these hills. The range lies between the township of Rabwah (renamed as Chenab Nagar) and the metropolitan city of Sargodha. These hills have been linked with the nuclear ambitions of Pakistan. In 1970, the hills were acquired by the Ministry of Defense for the Pakistan Air Force which became an extension of the Mushaf airbase. This was followed by investigations by the Geological Survey of Pakistan for possible uranium reserves in these hills. In the late 1970s, the Pakistan Army Corps of Engineers acquired the range for nuclear tests and began its boring operations. The subcritical physical experiments on nuclear weapon designs were also carried out here, named as Kirana-1. Today, the hills are said to be riddled with a network of underground tunnels and fortified bunkers. It is said that these house essentials of Pakistan's nuclear arsenal.

The hits on Noor Khan and Mushaf airbases caused some seismic disturbance. Seemingly, it affected some subterranean assets, deep inside the Black Mountain. The speculation was further compounded when the presence of an American aircraft, B350 AMS – meant for nuclear emergency response – was reported over Pakistan's airspace. Reportedly, an Egyptian cargo plane was also hovering about, stocked with boron – a chemical used to suppress nuclear reactions.

Hopefully, there has not been any nuclear leakage. The International Atomic Energy Agency (IAEA) also ruled out any radiations. Let us pray it is true.

As far as the Chenab is concerned, let her flow and tell stories. Is it possible to halt or divert a river as mighty as the Chenab? Constructing dams and elaborate canal systems consume both time and money. Better sense should prevail in Pakistan so that granaries don't turn into deserts. If this happens, Sohni would not even need a pot to cross the river. Did Pakistan not turn the River of Lovers into a River of Enemies? Would they ever mend their ways and get out of their jihadi cloaks?

Experts have their views but let us hope that the Chenab finds her way. Bashir Badar wrote: *Hum bhi dariya hain, humein apna hunar maloom hai, jis taraf bhi chal padenge rasta ho jayega* [We are also a river, we know our skill, whichever way we go, a path will be created]. Let Mahiwal live across the river in a small hut. Let India and Pakistan continue to exist peaceably.

Acknowledgements

A major part of the research for this work was done through several books, Kashmir travelogues and official accounts, mostly by British officers and adventurists – Fredric Drew, Walter Lawrence, Otto Rothfield, C.E. Bates and G.T. Vigne. This taught me about the Chenab and the territories the river flowed through. I also read some parts of *Gulabnama* by Diwan Kripa Ram to understand the legacy of the Dogra Kingdom. *A Mission in Kashmir* by Andrew Whitehead is a wonderful account of the October 1948 tribal invasion leading to the illegal occupation of a part of Kashmir by Pakistan. To understand the military campaigns of Zorawar Singh, I read books by Sukhdev Singh Charak and Sat Prakash Suri. Much of the cultural and political history of the Chenab Valley was inspired by the writings of Aseer Kishtwari. Firdous Ahmed Baba's story was picked from Aditya Sinha's book *Death of Dreams: A Terrorist's Tale.* Similarly, V. Verma's book, *Pangi: A Tribal Habitat in Mid-Himalaya*, is an authentic account of the people of Pangi covering all aspects of their lives. I also drew from my own experiences of having travelled a lot around the Chenab during my career as a police officer. However, a number of vlogs and articles on travel writing refreshed my memory.

My special thanks to my family for their unwavering support and faith in this book. Also, I am grateful to my colleagues and friends for rendering help from their sources for this work – among others, I am thankful in particular to Bhim Sen, Sujit Kumar, Mubassir Latifi, Yasin Kitchloo, Romesh Kotwal, Surjeet Bhagat, Vivek Shekhar, Nihar Ranjan, Varun Jandial, Varinder Gupta, Bir Singh and others. Also, of Archives, Archaeology and Museums, the Government of J&K for access to some old, selected records. My thanks for Vishesh Mahajan for the photographs from Reasi and words of encouragement. In Srinagar, to Piku Uncle for the good old days of forest stories and fresh cherries. Also, to Nitin Wazir, for the first-hand account of Jammu Durbar. I am also thankful to Aprajit Jamwal and Arvind Langeh for the Akhnoor leg of the river's journey. To Rekha, Parikh, Yogita and Sarita for being among the first readers of the manuscript and for all the cheerleading. Also, to Devinder Jasrotia, for breathtaking photographs of the Chenab. I am immensely obliged to the professors at Jammu University for helping me in researching for this book, notably Dr Suman Jamwal, Prof. Sugandha Mahajan, Prof. Sandeep Pandita and Dr Harish Chander Dutt. In Himachal Pradesh, my sincere thanks to Nandita Gupta, SDM Pangi; Rajat Dogra and the Deputy Commissioner for answering my queries.

Let me profusely thank Ashish Chouhan, a blogger, columnist and chronicler of the history of Paddar. He provided whatever information I asked for at short notice. My sincere gratitude to Khalid Hussain saheb, a retired bureaucrat, winner of the Sahitya Academy Award and a prominent Punjabi writer, popular on both sides of the border. He regaled me with experiences and anecdotes from his long official stint in the Chenab Valley. I have used two of his published stories in this book. He also connected me with some of his literary friends in Pakistan, who provided me with useful information about the Chenab – the most significant being that in Pakistan, the river is revered as Pir Chenab.

At Writer's Side, I am extremely thankful to Narayani Basu and my agent, Kanishka Gupta, for believing in the work and finding me a top publisher. My sincere gratitude to Smita Mathur for wonderful editing and useful suggestions. At Juggernaut Books, my debt of gratitude to the copy editor Wesley D'Souza. Swati Chopra, editorial director (non-fiction), for being the guiding light of this book right from its acceptance to publication. Also, to Antra K., the cover designer of this book, for skilfully playing with the sky and the river. Finally, to all the readers, I hope you like some of these stories from unexplored lands.

Notes

1. The Lovers

1. P.K. Kaul, *Antiquities of the Chenāb Valley in Jammu: Inscriptions-copper Plates, Sanads, Grants, Firmāns & Letters in Brāhmi-Shārdā-Tākri-Persian & Devnāgri Scripts*, Eastern Book Linkers, 2001.
2. Ram Nath Sahni, *Lahoul: The Mystery Land in the Himalayas*, New Delhi, Indus Publishing Company, 1994.
3. Rama Shankar Tripathi. History of Ancient India. 1999. Motilal Banarsidass Publishers.
4. National Highway-3, or NH-3, is a national highway in India. It starts from Atari adjacent to the India–Pakistan border and near Amritsar, and terminates at Leh in Ladakh via Manali in Himachal Pradesh.
5. 'Jetsunma Tenzin Palmo's Biography', *Tenzin Palmo*, https://tenzinpalmo.com/biography/.
6. Ibid.
7. 'Dream of Atal Bihari Vajpayee's Friend Comes True after Opening of Atal Tunnel.' 2020. *The Economic Times*. 3 October 2020. https://economictimes.indiatimes.com/news/politics-and-nation/dream-of-atal-bihari-vajpayees-friend-comes-true-after-opening-of-atal-tunnel/articleshow/78465879.cms.
8. Gaurav Bisht, Naresh Thakur, 'Friendship That Bridged Tunnel of Hope at Rohtang', *Hindustan Times*, 30 September 2020, https://www.hindustantimes.com/chandigarh/friendship-that-bridged-tunnel-of-hope-at-rohtang/story-mR3n0vbAOfOw5vS05fO1JI.html.
9. @Paperclip_In, 8–15, *X*, 23 May 2022, https://x.com/Paperclip_In/status/1528708026324361216.
10. Tapas Kumar Ghosh. *A Profile of the Himalayan Lahaula*. Anthropological Survey of India. January 2002.

11. Rohan Chand Thakur, 'Colonel Khushal Chand: The Savior of Ladakh', *Outlook*, 4 February 2024, https://www.outlookindia.com/culture-society/colonel-khushal-chand-the-saviour-of-ladakh.
12. The Ladakh Scouts has a glorious history which dates back to the 1948 skirmishes with Pakistan. Soon after Independence, in order to save Ladakh from the Kabalis (tribal intruders) who came from across the border, the National Guards were formed out of the local Ladakhi warriors. In 1952, they formed the erstwhile 7th Bn J&K Militia. The 14th Bn J&K Militia was subsequently raised in 1959 in Srinagar. On 1 June 1963, Ladakh Scouts was raised by the merger of 7th and 14th Bns J&K Militia.
13. Ibid.
14. 'History of Tandi Village Lahaul-Spiti', *Himachal Pradesh General Studies*, 26 April 2020, hpgeneralstudies.com/history-of-tandi-village-lahaul-spiti/.

2. The Secret Valley

15. 'A Superachiever among Villages', *The Hindu Businessline*, 26 September 2014, https://www.thehindubusinessline.com/news/variety/a-superachiever-among-villages/article23031140.ece.
16. John Bray, 'A History of Moravian Church in India', *The Himalayan Mission*, Leh, Moravian Church, 1985, p. 33.
17. 'Shot Stories', *The Tribune*, 14 July 2019, https://www.tribuneindia.com/news/archive/spectrum/shot-stories-800527/.
18. 'Made A Statement On The Incidents Of Killings By The Militants In Chamba District ... on 3 August, 1998'. *indiankanoon.org*.
19. Archana Phull, 'Ultras Gun Down 35 in Himachal', *The Indian Express*, 4 August 1998, https://indianexpress.com/article/news-archive/ultras-gun-down-35-in-himachal/.
20. Praveen Swami, 'The Unquiet Peace', *Frontline*, 10 August 2023.
21. Avay Shukla, 'Rest Houses Chronicles – II', *Hill Post*, 4 September 2017, https://hillpost.in/2017/09/rest-house-chronicles-ii/109322/.
22. Prasar Bharti Archives, 'Pangwal Tribe | Tribes of India', *YouTube*, 5 November 2021, https://www.youtube.com/watch?v=gaeZnrQ4jWU.
23. V. Verma, *Pangi: A Tribal Habitat in Mid-Himalaya*, Indus Publishing Company, 1998.

24. Shefali Joshi, 'The Most Complete Guide to Pangi Valley', *Himalayan Travel*, 13 November 2023, https://discoverwithdheeraj.com/the-most-complete-guide-to-pangi-valley/.
25. V. Verma, *Pangi: A Tribal Habitat in Mid-Himalaya*, Indus Publishing Company, 1998.
26. Abhilash Rajendran, 'Nag Devta Temple in Killar Town, Himachal', *Hindu Blog*, April 2021, https://www.hindu-blog.com/2021/04/nag-devata-mandir-at-killar-town-in-himachal-pradesh.html.
27. V. Verma, *Pangi: A Tribal Habitat in Mid-Himalaya*, Indus Publishing Company, 1998.
28 Naresh K. Thakur, 'Remote Pangi Valley Bustles with Faunal Diversity', *Hindustan Times*, 16 May 2022, https://www.hindustantimes.com/india-news/remote-pangi-valley-bustles-with-faunal-diversity/story-qLNK0siLL8zd9hILCJE5cJ.html.

3. The Old Snow Lady

29. Paddar Machail Blog: Ashish Chouhan: A Brief History of Paddar.
30. V. Verma, *Pangi: A Tribal Habitat in Mid-Himalaya*, Indus Publishing Company, 1998.
31. Sat Prakash Suri, *General Zorawar Singh A Date with Destiny*, Akshay Prakashan, New Delhi, 2018.
32. Ibid.
33. Ibid.
34. Ibid.
35. Ibid.
36. Skyjems: The Mythology of Sapphire, 19 October 2020.
37. Richard Hughes, *Ruby and Sapphire*, RWH Publishing, Colorado, 1997.
38. Atul Sethi. 'The India Story: Royal Reinvention, Some Relics.' *The Times of India*. 23 April 2011. https://timesofindia.indiatimes.com/home/sunday-times/deep-focus/the-india-story-royal-reinvention-some-relics/articleshow/8068435.cms.
39. Ibid.
40. Richard Hughes, *Ruby and Sapphire*, RWH Publishing, Colorado, 1997.

41. V. Verma, *Pangi: A Tribal Habitat in Mid-Himalaya*, Indus Publishing Company, 1998.
42. Jyoti Parihar and Haqiqat Chauhan, 'The Legend of Himalayan Motherlode – Historical, Cultural and Economic Significance of Paddar Blue Sapphire', *Research Review: International Journal of Multidisciplinary*, 2021, Vol. 6., No. 12, pp. 50–6.
43. Valentine Ball (1885b), in Richard Hughes, *Ruby and Sapphire*, RWH Publishing, Colorado, 1997, p. 360.
44. Richard Hughes, *Ruby and Sapphire*, RWH Publishing, Colorado, 1997.
45. From the correspondence in the records of Archives, Archeology and Museums Department of J&K.
46. Ibid.
47. Ibid.
48. From the correspondence in the records of Archives, Archaeology and Museums Department of Jammu and Kashmir)
49. Shujaat Bukhari, '3 Sri Lankans Held for Sapphire Smuggling', *The Hindu*, 17 July 2011, https://www.thehindu.com/news/national/3-sri-lankans-held-for-sapphire-smuggling/article2233552.ece.
50. @elonmusk, *X*, 9 April 2022, 12.29 p.m., https://x.com/elonmusk/status/1512505545416224783?ref_src=twsrc%5Etfw.
51. 'Elon Musk: "Lithium Batteries Are the New Oil".' *Barron's*. 14 July 2022.
52. Khalid Bashir Gura, 'The Reasi Lithium', *Kashmir Life*, 22 February 2023, https://kashmirlife.net/the-reasi-lithium-vol-14-issue-47-310632/.

6. The Doda Files

53. Sandipan Sharma, 'A Bridge Too Far: Lust for Loot Denies Pakistanis Eid in Srinagar', *The Federal*, 30 October 2020, https://thefederal.com/operation-gulmarg/a-bridge-too-far-lust-for-loot-denies-pakistanis-eid-in-srinagar.
54. Ibid.
55. From the desk diary of Father George Shanks, illustrated in Andrew Whitehead, *A Mission in Kashmir*, Gulshan Books, 2014, p. 100.

56. The regional party Jammu and Kashmir National Conference was headed by Mohammad Sheikh Abdullah.
57. Ahmed Ali Fayyaz, 'Story of Kashmir's Little-Known 1947 Hero and Lesser Known Poet', *South Asia Monitor*, 10 November 2020, https://www.southasiamonitor.org/societyculture/story-kashmirs-little-known-1947-hero-and-lesser-known-poet.
58. Aditya Sinha, *Death of Dreams: A Terrorist's Tale*, HarperCollins India, 2000.
59. Pakistan's president, General Zia-ul-Haq, propagated the doctrine of bleeding India with 'thousand cuts' by using covert and low intensity warfare with terror and infiltration.
60. Praveen Swami, 'Disturbed Doda', *Frontline*, 18 August 2001, https://frontline.thehindu.com/the-nation/article30251542.ece.
61. Praveen Swami. 'Disturbed Doda'. *Frontline*. 18 August 2001.
62. M.L. Kak, 'Ultras Massacre 17 in Doda; Curfew in Kishtwar, Farooq Orders Probe', *The Tribune*, 5 August 2001, https://www.tribuneindia.com/2001/20010805/main1.htm.

7. The Call of the Muezzin

63. Press Trust of India, 'Protests Rock Paddar after Two Girls Go Missing', *The Hindu*, 13 July 2010, https://www.thehindu.com/news/national/other-states/Protests-rock-Paddar-after-two-girls-go-missing/article16195321.ece.
64. As narrated by Khalid Hussain in *Main Ek Zinda Aadmi Hun*, 2021.

8. The Land of Saints

65. 'An Amazing Spiritual Journey: Story of Great Reshi Saint Shaykh Zainuddin Reshi (R.A.), Kashmir Observer. 22 December, 2015.
66. Ibid.
67 'Muslim traditions thrive on "Urs" at Aishmuqam'. Daily Good Morning Kashmir. 17 April 2022.
68. Frederic Drew, *The Jammoo and Kashmir Territories*, E. Stanford, London, 1970, p. 84.
69. Yoginder Sikand, 'Different Kishtwar – One Which Showed the Ways in Religious Tolerance and Communal Harmony', *The Better*

India Specials, 21 August 2013, https://thebetterindia.com/7786/tbi-specials-a-different-kishtwar-one-of-communal-harmony/.

70. 'The Chenab Conflagration.' *Kashmir Life*. 18 August 2013. https://kashmirlife.net/the-chenab-conflagration-39654/#google_vignette.
71. Mohammad Afzal Guru was a convict in the Parliament attack of December 2011.
72. As told by a senior police officer involved in the initial investigation of the case.
73. Asif Iqbal Malik, 'HM Commander Denies Involvement in Delhi HC Blast', *Early Times*, 11 January 2012, https://www.earlytimes.in/newsdet.aspx?q=86907.

9. The Hill of Poppies

74. Praveen Swami, 'Twin Massacres in Jammu', *Frontline*, 27 April 2002, https://frontline.thehindu.com/other/article30244689.ece.
75. Praveen Swami, 'Blood on the Chenab', *Frontline*, 11 April 1998, https://frontline.thehindu.com/other/article30158965.ece.
76. Arun Sharma, 'A Story of Three Weddings and 25 Funerals', *The Indian Express*, 21 June 1998, https://indianexpress.com/article/news-archive/a-story-of-three-weddings-and-25-funerals/.
77. 'Vasuki Nag Temple of Bhaderwah – The "Land of Snakes", *JK Now*, 7 June 2020, https://www.jammukashmirnow.com//Encyc/2020/6/7/Vasuki-Nag-Temple-of-Bhaderwah-the-land-of-snakes-.html.
78. Blog: I am Bhaderwah, Mela Patt. *Bhaderwah*. https://www.bhaderwah.com/tourism/ptourism/mela_patt.html.

10. The Vertical District

79. Mohinder Kumar, 'Assar – A Story of Exploitation', *Daily Excelsior*, 21 June 2015, https://www.dailyexcelsior.com/assar-a-story-of-exploitation/.
80. Express News Service, 'J&K Man Stages Accident to Evade Loan Repayment, Found with Family in Haryana', *The Indian Express*, 9 January 2023, https://indianexpress.com/article/cities/mumbai/jk-man-stages-accident-to-evade-loan-repayment-found-with-family-in-haryana-8369352/.

81. Mukhtyar Ahmad, 'Militants Attack Army Transit Camp, 13 Killed', *Rediff News,* 18 November 2001, www.rediff.com/news/2001/nov/18kash.htm.
82. The Gazetteer of Kashmir, C.E. Bates.
83. 'Natrang Team Returns to Jammu after Performing in London', *Daily Excelsior*, 30 October 2016, https://www.dailyexcelsior.com/natrang-team-returns-jammu-performing-london/.

11. The Master and His Servant

84. Shaista Masood, 'What I Saw After I Watched a Massacre of Innocents in Kashmir', *The Wire*, 15 June 2018, thewire.in/rights/kashmir-pandits-exodus-shujaat-bukhari-militancy.
85. Rahul Pandita, *Our Moon Has Blood Clots: The Exodus of the Kashmiri Pandits*, Noida, Random House India, 2013.

12. Fork in the River

86. Express Web Desk, '"Taller than Eiffel Tower": All You Need to Know about World's Highest Railway Bridge in J&K', *The Indian Express*, 20 February 2024, https://indianexpress.com/article/what-is/worlds-highest-railway-bridge-jammu-kashmir-chenab-modi-9170256/.
87. Mukhtar Ahmad, '"The Village Resembled a Ghost Area with Beheaded Bodies Lying Scattered"', *Rediff News*, 20 April 1998, https://www.rediff.com/news/1998/apr/20jammu.htm.
88. Muzaffar Raina, 'Hindu Rebels in Jammu', *The Telegraph Online*, 26 May 2010.
89. '"We Never Knew He Was a Militant"', *Rediff News*, 19 September 2003, https://www.rediff.com/news/2003/sep/17spec1.htm.
90. 'LeT Terrorist Arrested in J&K was BJP's IT Cell Head, Party Denies He Was Member', *The Quint*, 4 July 2022, https://www.thequint.com/news/india/bjps-minority-morcha-leader-among-lashkar-e-taiba-terrorists-arrested-in-jammu-social-media-it-cell-talib-shah-hussain-jammu-kashmir-amit-shah.
91. From the interrogation report of Talib Hussein Shah.
92. From the interrogation report of Talib Hussein.
93. 'Former Reasi MLA Can Shave Off His Beard Now!', *OneIndia*, 9 July

2006, https://www.oneindia.com/2006/07/08/former-reasi-mla-can-shave-off-his-beard-now-1152469623.html.

94. Jigar Mohammad, 'Who Was Baba Jitto, the Most Authentic Voice of the Ordinary Dogras', *The Dispatch*, 23 January 2024, www.thedispatch.in/who-was-baba-jitto-the-most-authentic-voice-of-the-ordinary-dogras/.

95 Avinash Jha, 'Siv Khori – Legends and Facts about Home of God', *Tripoto*, 10 June 2015, https://www.tripoto.com/haryana/trips/shiv-khori-legends-and-facts-about-home-of-gods-58a21008a9a16.

96. 'Baba Banda Singh Bahadur – Life History & Shaheedi', *Sikhizm*, 24 June 2024, https://sikhizm.com/baba-banda-singh-bahadur/.

13. The Timber Trail

97. Swami Nikhilananda, *Vivekananda: A Biography*, Advaita Ashrama, 2010.

98. Tasavur Mushtaq, 'History in Floating Water!', *Kashmir Life*, 15 July 2013, https://kashmirlife.net/history-in-floating-water-36503/.

99 Kashmir Houseboats: A Short History – All you need to know about Kashmir's famous houseboats, Moustache Escapes, 3 November 2003.

100. Vinayak Razdan, 'Origin of Kashmiri House Boat and Some Other Origins', *Search Kashmir*, 17 October 2010, https://searchkashmir.org/origin-of-kashmiri-house-boat-and-some/.

101. Mohd Ashraf Wani and V.M. Ravi Kumar, 'Green History of Kashmir: Evolution of State Forestry under Dogra Rule', *International Journal of Research in Social Science*, 2018, Vol. 8, No.7, pp. 296–305.

102. Ashish Chouhan, 'Of Monk Nagsen and Nagseni', *Daily Excelsior*, 29 January 2023, https://www.dailyexcelsior.com/of-monk-nagsen-and-nagseni/.

14. The Light of the Eyes

103. KT News Service, 'Police Rules Out VDC Members' Involvement in Khanday's Killing', *Kashmir Times*, 26 June 2014.

104. Vinayak Razdan, 'Ambaran Buddhist Stupa, Akhnoor, Jammu', *Search Kashmir*, 14 December 2016, https://searchkashmir.org/ambaran-buddhist-stupa-akhnoor-jammu/.

105. 'Akhnoor the Ancient Capital of J&K', *Daily Excelsior*, 13 October 2024, https://www.dailyexcelsior.com/akhnoor-the-ancient-capital-of-jk/.
106. Henry Kamm, 'Pakistan Forces Take Ghost Town in Kashmir', *The New York Times*, 13 December 1971, https://www.nytimes.com/1971/12/13/archives/pakistani-forces-take-ghost-town-in-kashmir.html.
107. Book Excerpt: India's War Since Independence, 3 March 2016, Maj Gen Sukhwant Singh: 1971 War: The Battle of the Chicken's Neck.
108. Pratul Sharma, 'History of Failed Agreements: Why Shimla Is No Longer a "Summit" Destination', *The Week*, 12 August 2021, https://www.theweek.in/theweek/cover/2021/08/12/history-of-failed-agreements-why-shimla-is-no-longer-a-summit-estination.html.
109. Kalpana Sunder, 'The Battle Over Basmati Rice: Why India and Pakistan May Both Claim the Trademark', *South China Morning Post*, 17 July 2021, https://www.scmp.com/week-asia/politics/article/3141287/battle-over-basmati-rice-why-india-and-pakistan-may-both-claim.
110. Lalit Gupta, 'Remembering Malika Pukhraj', *Daily Excelsior*, 22 December 2013, https://www.dailyexcelsior.com/remembering-malika-pukhraj/.
111. Shreya Ila Anasuya, 'Her Swan Song: Revisiting the Memoirs of a Courtesan', *The Caravan*, 1 November 2019, https://caravanmagazine.in/literature/revisiting-memoirs-courtesan.

15. The New Passport

112. Wenlei Ma, 'Sydney: Sialkot – Pakistan, Home of More Than Half the World's Footballs', *News.com.au*, 6 August 2014, https://www.news.com.au/finance/business/manufacturing/sialkot-pakistan-home-of-more-than-half-the-worlds-footballs/news-story/eba72b81500c7ff80c8587225375f115.
113. Mariam Tahir, 'Tracing Faiz Ahmed Faiz's Roots Ahead of Faiz Festival', *Images*, 17 February 2023, https://images.dawn.com/news/1191535.

114. Aamna Aamir, *Analytical Study of Cutlery Study of Wazirabad*, Department of Geography, University of Gujrat, Pakistan, 2018, https://www.academia.edu/43436577/ANALYTICAL_STUDY_OF_CUTLERY_INDUSTRY_OF_WAZIRABAD_SUBMITTED_BY.
115. Aftaab Channa, 'Jamalo Sheedi's Ho Jamalo, Wah Wah Jamalo', *Sindh News*, 27 April 2022.
116. Arif Jamshaid, 'The Epic of Heer–Ranjha', *Academy of the Punjab in North America*, n.d., https://apnaorg.com/prose-content/english-articles/page-7/article-2/index.html.
117. Haroon Khalid, 'These Banyan Trees Are Proof of Pakistan's Roots in Inter-religious Peace and Harmony', *Scroll*, 20 October 2017, https://scroll.in/article/854720/pakistans-banyan-trees-are-proof-of-the-countrys-roots-in-inter-religious-peace-and-harmony.

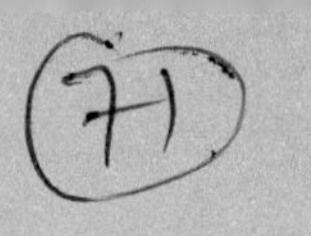